il/97

8/30
note: separated from spine

JAPAN

Spirit & Form

(FRONTISPIECE): Ise Jingu, the ancestral shrine of the imperial family, is located in an evergreen grove in Mie Prefecture on Japan's east coast. Comprising both an Inner Shrine and an Outer Shrine, Ise Jingu has become a popular site for pilgrimages. Dating from the third and late fifth centuries, torn down and rebuilt every twenty years, it remains an important symbol of celebration and ritual. As seen on the following page, a sea of pebbles and stones surrounds the small building occupying the adjacent empty lot in which the previous structure of the shrine was located.

SHUICHI KATO

JAPAN
Spirit & Form

with an Introduction by
ROGER GOEPPER

translated and adapted from the Japanese by
Junko Abe and Leza Lowitz

CHARLES E. TUTTLE COMPANY
Rutland, Vermont & Tokyo, Japan

Introduction translated from the German
by Edgar Honetschläger

The publisher gratefully acknowledges the generous
contributions of the following companies, individuals, and
associations toward the translation of this book:

∫HI∫EIDO

Yoshiharu Fukuhara, president and CEO of SHISEIDO
    Company, Ltd.
  GINMIKAI
  GINSHINKAI
  Japan Association for HEIB and Consumer Affairs/
    Professionals in Business
  KEPNER-TREGOE JAPAN, Inc.
of the Association for 100 Japanese Books

Published by the Charles E. Tuttle Company, Inc.
of Rutland, Vermont & Tokyo, Japan
with editorial offices at
2-6 Suido 1-chome, Bunkyo-ku, Tokyo 112

© 1994 by Charles E. Tuttle Publishing Co., Inc.
© 1992 by Motovun (Switzerland) Co-Publishing Company, Ltd., Lucerne
© 1987, 1988 for the picture material and original Japanese
text by Heibonsha Limited Publishers, Tokyo

LCC Card No. 94-60344
ISBN 0-8048-1969-6

First English-language edition, 1994

Printed in Italy

Contents

INTRODUCTION

Japan and the West:
a Productive Dialogue

**IN THE BEGINNING,
THERE WAS A SHAPE**

The Shape of Jomon; The
Meaning of Patterns and Shapes;
Two Isolated Cultures;
From Jomon to Yayoi

**A UNIVERSE IN THE
PALM OF THE HAND**

The Irregularities of the Tea-
ceremony Bowl; An Aesthetic
Revolution; A Five-point Grammar
of Japanese Culture

**THE WOMEN OF
*UKIYO-E***

Civilization and Conceptions
of the Body;
The Elements of *Ukiyo-e;*
The Women of *Ukiyo-e*

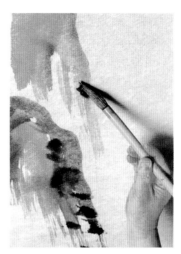

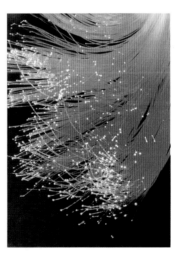

Japan and the West:
A Productive Dialogue

OPPOSITE PAGE: An aerial photograph of Kyoto, the old imperial capital, exposes the still-existing grid pattern of the streets. Traditional-style temples are surrounded by high-rise buildings.

Although such views are gradually changing, mistaken and widespread presumptions about Japan and the Japanese continue to exist in the West; a woman dressed in a formal kimono is automatically assumed to be a geisha, while *sumi-e* brush painting is thought to be a mystical art form. In the face of such suppositions, one fact has long been overlooked: throughout their history, after adopting and adapting foreign cultural achievements, the Japanese have always been able to transform them with creative potency and make out of them something new and notable.

It has been said that a fundamental aspect of the Japanese character is the ability to quickly grasp the essence of things and then to transform that essence into something that is able to stand on its own. This interesting trait might be the basis of a general open-mindedness found among the Japanese, who traditionally have not been able to comprehend singular devotion to any one thing at the exclusion of all else, even in the case of religion. For the Japanese of today, it is natural to feel comfortable with various kinds of beliefs and to use them according to need. Generally, a follower of Buddhism, depending on his character, may feel attracted to any one of the many and very diverse schools. In addition to being Buddhists, many Japanese are also Shinto-ists, which means they believe in the ancient Japanese religion of nature worship with its mountain gods, tree gods, and a sun goddess from whom the Japanese imperial family allegedly descended. Because of this early familial connection, Shintoism developed into a state religion, one often possessed of nationalistic undertones. To stress its importance to the average Japanese, some of the most important junctures in life, such as marriage, continue to be performed ceremoniously by Shinto priests.

Moreover, the Japanese are also quite possibly bound to Confucianism, as it concerns rituals of politeness and behavior that guarantee societal and family matters function smoothly. In this context, Western subscribers to the "Japanese way" and to Japanese culture, particularly to Zen Buddhism, very often look at the actual reality rather myopically. In the United States a version of Zen Buddhism consisting of meditation, a simple lifestyle, and immediateness in thought has aroused a great deal of interest and has been taken up as a fad by many young people in recent years.

Undoubtedly, Zen Buddhism has had an impact on Japanese culture since the Middle Ages, and its form of discipline has been carried into the spontaneity of ink drawing and calligraphy as well as into the aesthetic rituals of the tea ceremony. However, the fact that the strict mental discipline of Zen demands years of training and exercise to reach the point where spontaneity becomes possible has been generally overlooked by young Western practitioners. The rigorous subordination of the student to an ethical norm that can sometimes lead to relinquishing one's personality seems scarcely bearable. For such students, a discovery or rediscovery of Japanese civilization would be absolutely appropriate. This book and the discussion it engenders can serve as a valuable catalyst.

The first Western discovery of Japan occurred in 1543 when a Portuguese adventurer named Pinto, who was traveling with Chinese pirates who took him on board after his ship ran aground in Macao, landed on Tanegashima island, just south of the larger island of Kyushu. He pretended to be an official envoy of the Portuguese, and the Japanese governor of the island took an immediate interest in his firearms. After

returning home, Pinto wrote a book about his experiences, the first book about the island empire.

When, in 1549, Jesuit missionaries followed the famed Francis Xavier to Japan, certain daimyo rulers tried to gain advantages for their principalities by dealing with the Portuguese and converting to Christianity. Soon, however, the shogunate discovered what it deemed the dangerous invasion of alien ideas and in 1587 the first ban on the establishment of missions was imposed. However, Christian cells continued to flourish underground until after 1600, at which time a strict ban on Christianity was pronounced, immediately followed by a period of bloody religious persecution. When the government imposed the policy of Sakoku (national seclusion) in 1639, all of the foreigners were driven out of Japan with only the Portuguese and Dutch merchants allowed to remain in a state of virtual imprisonment on the tiny artificial island of Dejima in Nagasaki Bay.

Sakoku was to have a profound impact on Japanese art, architecture, and modes of thought. With regard to art, a new direction of painting that leaned toward a Western style had come into existence in connection with the missions, but it soon died out. It was called the "painting of the south barbarians" (nanban-e) and was an exotic adjunct to the art movements of the time.

The developing and lasting influence of Western ideas and, along with them, Western art recommenced when the import ban on foreign books was lifted in 1720. The Dutch sciences (rangaku) of practical-oriented natural studies such as medicine, anatomy, astronomy, physics, and botany began to flourish. Systematic methodologies had been as yet unknown in East Asia, but soon educated Japanese, especially samurai, began translating from Dutch texts. Meanwhile, Japanese artists were being inspired by the naturalistic etchings of the Europeans which were gradually leading them to new perceptions of objects and space. They were also inspired to attempt painting with oil colors and to experiment in a manner influenced by these European works of art.

It was two Germans who offered an amazingly objective idea of Japan in the early days of national seclusion. Engelbert Kaempfer of Lemgo in the Duchy of Lippe landed in Nagasaki in 1690, accompanying a Dutch mission. He was a keen observer of Japan at the time and can be counted as the original scientific discoverer of Japan. Philipp Franz von Siebold, who had also come along with the Dutch, was expelled from the country as a spy after staying in Japan for six years. His book on Japan and his collection of Japanese objects that were shown in several museums deepened the Western public's perception of Japan and led to a more realistic understanding.

When people spoke of the mutual influence of Japanese and Western cultures, opinion fluctuated between "empathy" and "fruitful misunderstandings." Both characterizations held a certain grain of truth, as did the term "dialogue."

What caused difficulties in the "dialogue" was the fact that the fundamental positions of these two cultures were different, and even diametrically opposed, to a certain degree. The West tended to look at the world by focusing on the human being, whereas the East tended to focus on the human being in relation to nature. In the Western view, the human being—whether individually or in a group—stood in opposition to nature and tried to subject nature to its own needs.

Therefore, the aim of Western artists from the Middle Ages on, since emancipation from the dominance of Christianity, was to give an objective depiction of the world, nature, and objects. An attempt at realistic three-dimensionality in the depiction of objects reflected that attitude toward nature.

In contrast, people in East Asia understood themselves to be an integral part of

OPPOSITE PAGE (DETAIL): This byobu *(Japanese folding screen) dates from the sixteenth or seventeenth century. Musicians are shown in European costumes.*

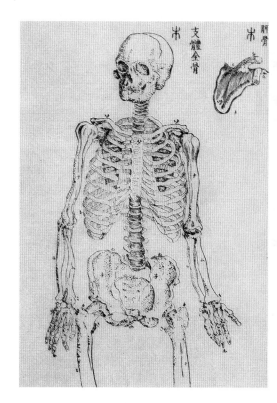

ABOVE: Painters from the Akita school, such as Odano Naotake (1749–80), copied illustrations from Dutch medical texts and made important contributions to the development of the modern natural sciences in Japan.

ABOVE: *The oil painting* The Cooper (about 1790), *by Shiba Kokan, reveals that in the eighteenth century Japanese artists were beginning to consider the problems of light and shadow and that the technique of using linear perspective was also being adopted.*

nature: both man and nature are made up of the same kind of energy; therefore, man cannot view the creations of nature as being in opposition to himself. This view was embedded in an intuitive, not analytical, way of seeing the world, a fact that became significantly obvious not only in the work of visual artists but also in that of the literary world. Depiction of landscapes very often included a flowing perspective that was not fixed on a single point of view. Instead, the viewer was invited to step into the picture and to look at it from the inside out for the very first time.

That man could be the measure of all beings, as propounded in the West, was a disconcerting idea for Asian artists. Whereas the Greek and Roman classical sculptors expressed their ideal of beauty in depictions of the nude human body, a Japanese master of the thirteenth century covered the body of the goddess of fortune Kichijoten with magnificent robes to the extent that the body vanished entirely, leaving only the

"I envy the Japanese for the enormous clarity that pervades their work. It is as simple as breathing, and they draw a figure with just a few lines."
—Vincent van Gogh

face and hands visible. In the same century, on a scroll showing idealized portraits titled *The Thirty-Six Immortals of Poetry,* a Japanese court painter depicted a poet in such a way that her figure became totally drowned in the overlapping robes spread out around her. Her face was stylized to the degree that it became a mask, while the magnificently emphasized, decorative clothing became the aesthetic means of artistic expression. Looking at this work, one can hardly think of a greater contrast to the portrayal of female allure than Nicolas Poussin's *Resting Venus with Amor,* whose uninhibited nudity seems perfectly natural.

In general, the Japanese artist had difficulties with the depiction of the nude body. He did not have the technical means to transfer delicate three-dimensional nuances of nude bodies into two dimensions, even in the unabashedly erotic *shunga* (spring pictures) by Kitagawa Utamaro. From early on, depiction of the human figure had as

ABOVE LEFT: Shiba Kokan (1747–1818) (under the pseudonym Harushige Suzuki) masterfully copied colored woodcuts by the well-known Harunobu Suzuki. He succeeded in combining the Western technique of using linear perspective with the style used in traditional Japanese portraits.

its chosen topic the clothed human being. Clothing symbolized the social rank of the person within the society, and to societies such as those of the Chinese or Japanese that had been shaped by Confucian ethics, the nude body would have appeared vulgar since it would have stood apart from social context.

If we now move to the invasion of Western ideas and techniques that has occurred in Japan since the middle of the nineteenth century, the country most worthy of mention as a source of inspiration to Japanese artists and thinkers is France. It was a Frenchman who erected the first arc lamp in Tokyo in 1885 and, by so doing, might

RIGHT: *A scroll from a painted series of the thirteenth century,* The Thirty-Six Immortals of Poetry, *shows the poet Ko no kimi surrounded by her extravagantly drawn robes. The decoratively arranged cloth appears to support the body within, while her face remains impersonal, as still as a mask.*

BELOW: *The painting* Resting Venus with Amor *(1630, Gemaeldegalerie Dresden) by Nicolas Poussin (1594–1665) radiates an open sensuousness. The viewer can sense the physical appeal of the model's youthful skin.*

have provided the first tentative impulse toward the development of the Japanese electronics industry. In the wars of the twentieth century, it should be noted that the extraordinarily successful Japanese military power was modeled on the French system, and the development of aviation was also based on models of French design. The French influence reached a variety of fields in Japan, as is readily apparent.

However, in the fields of jurisprudence and legislation, German influences predominated. This pattern became apparent when the first Japanese constitution was

LEFT: Kongo-rikishi, a guardian god carved in the thirteenth century by Unkei and Kankei, stands more than eight meters tall. The piece is considered one of the most magnificent examples of realistic sculpture from the Kamakura period. Note the exaggeration of the musculature to the extent that it seems almost ornamental. Todai-ji temple, Nara.

ABOVE: When the woodblock-print master Kitagawa Utamaro (1753–1806) created this erotic shunga *(spring picture), he translated the round forms of the female body into fine lines and without employing any shadowing techniques, in contrast to Poussin.*

drafted in 1899. The civil code of 1896 and the commercial statutes of 1899 were also based on German models.

After 1870 Emperor Meiji encouraged the industrialization of the country in keeping with contemporary ideas of an organized central government that could maintain control over economic development. The army was modernized and an elementary school education was made compulsory for all social classes. In all of these areas, the Japanese government ensured that foreign advisors were available to provide assistance and, further yet, to provide support to Japanese scholars who were sent abroad to study.

After World War II, the state's political program was one that brought about low defense expenditures, causing an increase in investment possibilities and eventually an enormous upturn in the economy. Parallel to this development was a rearrangement of Japan's social structure. In 1870 seventy to eighty percent of the population was engaged in agriculture. After the war, farmers represented the second highest level in the severely stratified class system. By 1970, however, only twenty percent remained in this sector. Today, those who have left the farmland for the cities are certainly more open to new developments in terms of technology.

When one considers the process the Japanese have undertaken in accepting Western circumstances into their lifestyles, the simple facts of metropolitan life should not be underestimated. Everyday rhythms of life in large metropolises have increasingly affected Japanese housing styles. Early on, Western structures were not completely adopted, but particular elements were integrated into the traditional context. New technological comforts determine the interior of modern metropolitan apartments (*apāto*). However, even though the living room may reflect elements of Western taste, such as upholstered seating and chests of drawers, other rooms remain furnished with tatami mats and people still sit on the floor. Many people still sleep on the floor in traditional futon bedding that can be folded and stored in closets. Western-style bedframes are available, however. In the entryway of most homes, a low step and space for removing and storing shoes can still be found.

Because the Japanese have to live in confined spaces, the extended family is a rarity, while the feeling toward the culture of the individual is one of ambivalence. The tokonoma alcove, borrowed from the traditional teahouse where it was meant to hold a *sumi-e* scroll or a sample of calligraphy, is commonly seen in even the smallest of apartments and now often holds the family television set. Japanese television

BELOW: The teahouse Ko-an was moved from its original location in the Nishi Hongan-ji temple in Kyoto in 1908 to the Daitoku-ji temple. The simplicity of its design, in the style of the late Tokugawa period, suits the aesthetics of the tea ceremony of the Oribe school.

ABOVE RIGHT: The interior roof supports and the architect's consideration of the refined primitive aesthetics of Zen Buddhism are revealed in the Pavilion of Waves and Moonlight (Geppa-ro) located on the grounds of the imperial prince's palace near Kyoto.

OPPOSITE PAGE: From the exterior the Geppa-ro teahouse appears extremely simple, being harmoniously integrated into the environment. The park seems to be the result of natural growth, but was actually designed to achieve this effect. The name of the teahouse was taken from a poem by Bo Juyi, a poet of the Tang dynasty.

stations themselves often show programs based on American models and are seen by some as contributing to the decline in close personal ties.

Furthermore, whereas traditional Japanese housing distinguishes itself through an agreeable emptiness and clarity, modern apartments in the cities are often ruled by surprising disorder. This pattern can be seen from one angle as a symptom of the still not successfully concluded integration of Japanese and Western cultures. It is also a reflection of the growing consumerism and acquisitiveness that illustrates the Japanese penchant for collecting goods, among them, Western imports.

More than in the area of fine art, the adoption of Western approaches and elements in architecture caused fundamental changes in the Japanese perception of the environment. The design and construction of traditional living spaces and public buildings were based on wooden frames covered with light walls, frames that did not function as foundations. The inner rooms were separated from each other by thin sliding doors. Living in such homes, one keenly felt the elements of nature.

These sliding doors, often opening onto the garden, helped create a designed landscape that was supposed to appear to have grown naturally. It was possible to design such gardens to the extent that the natural exterior space appeared to continue

LEFT, and BELOW (*DETAIL*)*: The Kaichi Gakko school, built by Tateishi Kiyoshige in 1876 in Matsumoto, is an example of the eclecticism of Japanese architects of the Meiji period. An entrance with a curved roof and rich decorative carvings, inspired by seventeenth- and eighteenth-century castle architecture, was added to the Western-inspired main construction. The door is reminiscent of Chinese models, while the octagonal cupola was inspired by the Buddhist pagoda.*

on into the interior of the structure. Residents of such traditional-style homes were constantly exposed to the natural fluctuations of the weather and the seasons. With walls and niches, builders strived to retain such unadulterated effects.

From the middle of the nineteenth century on, English architects such as Thomas J. Waters, who planned the successful reconstruction of the Ginza area after the fires of

OPPOSITE PAGE: In the painting Maiko *(1893), by Kuroda Seiki, the artist managed to successfully combine the Impressionist's spontaneous oil-painting technique with the sectionalized composition style of the* ukiyo-e *painters as a result of his sojourn in France.*

LEFT: Samuel Bing published the journal Le Japon Artistique *in Paris from 1888, contributing to the sudden interest in Japan that occurred at the turn of the century.*

1872, and especially Josiah Conder, who designed and built about seventy buildings into which he incorporated elements from eclectic Western styles, caused a complete shift in Japanese views toward urban architecture. Japanese architects began to transform those impulses into pseudo-Western amalgamations with varying degrees of success.

From 1915 on, according to the theory of nonaesthetic architecture *(kenchiku higeijutsu ron),* a new approach toward architecture could be seen in connection with steel and ferroconcrete constructions. Between 1920 and 1930, many young Japanese architects went abroad, primarily to study at the Bauhaus and with Le Corbusier. The actual modern phase of building did not begin in Japan until later on, with construction booms in the large metropolitan areas. At the same time, architects such as Kenzo Tange and Kiyoshi Seike initiated a revival of traditional housing styles. Exterior concluding walls were reduced in size, and attempts were made to restore the traditional relationship between inner and outer space. From the sixties on, extremely futuristic visions of city planning, such as those conceived by Kiyonori Kikutake, came into existence. This was followed by a Postmodernist tendency in which architectural styles and techniques from different eras were manipulated to innovative effect.

Japan's modern metropolises, especially the old imperial capital of Kyoto, present themselves as extraordinarily appealing and exciting conglomerations, blending very modern skyscrapers of often fascinating design with neighborhoods of traditional

ABOVE: The entrance to the gallery L'Art Nouveau in the Rue Chauchat in Paris was decorated with flower patterns. These patterns later became a central motif for the entire movement, named after this gallery.

ABOVE: Ichikawa Danjuro V *by Shusho Katsukawa.*

wooden houses. The ancient temples and palaces with their beautiful gardens are peaceful islands embedded in an active cityscape. To walk among them is to enter another world.

Many Japanese artists studied in Europe, especially in France, where they were directly confronted with the contemporary art movements of the time, e.g., Impressionism. This experience became a decisive element in the incorporation of Western painting styles into Japanese art that occurred in the second half of the nineteenth century. Of no less importance was the founding of academies and artists' associations in Japan. In 1868 the private school of Kawakami Togai, where both ink painting and oil painting were taught, was founded. The Hakubakai (White Horse Society) group devoted itself to the painting of nudes and landscapes, and after the official Meiji Art Exhibition, painters who mainly had been educated abroad began to teach art students in Japan.

Japanese artists, even today, continue to adopt current European and American styles of art in both their two- and three-dimensional work. In some cases, only the subject matter reveals the Japanese origin of certain works of art, but there also were and are highly talented artists whose work is based on traditionally Japanese artistic principles and who are able to compete and to maintain their positions as Japanese artists in the international art scene.

However, a subtle form of Western influence can still be traced in those Japanese paintings *(nihon-ga)* that deliberately refer to cultural traditions. Even here one cannot overlook the fact that the Western point of view has completely overtaken previous techniques used for depicting space and three-dimensionality.

Museums tried to compensate for the lack of Western art collections by following the Japanese practice of striving for the highest quality possible when exhibitions of Western works were shown in Japan. The traveling exhibitions arriving from Western museums included artworks of a very high standard that consequently brought in large numbers of visitors, as seen when the Mona Lisa was on exhibit. That contemporary Japanese collectors have been willing to pay enormous sums for paintings by van Gogh might be explained by the need to compensate for this lack. On the other hand, the situation mirrors the current Japanese attitude that only the very best is good enough.

Conversely, in the West, visual artists and writers have long been attracted by the exotic visual aesthetic of Japan. However, whereas in the case of Japan's adoption of Western art and culture one can speak of empathy and adjustment, the influence of Japanese art forms on the West occasionally stands under the heading "fruitful misunderstanding," with one exception, as we will see below.

By the seventeenth and eighteenth centuries, Japanese design motifs were being used by the silk manufacturers of Lyon, France. In Chantilly and in Saint-Cloud, kakiemon and nabeshima porcelains were being copied. Madame Pompadour and Marie Antoinette appreciated and collected Japanese-style lacquered furniture, even though this phenomenon can best be understood as an aftereffect of the earlier fashion for collecting chinoiserie.

The Japonisme that reached wider segments of society than did the chinoiserie trend of the eighteenth century (almost entirely limited to the aristocracy) began after the 1867 world's fair in Paris, where a booth was set up and Japan was represented by a high-ranking delegation, including the brother of the shogun. From then on, art dealers in Paris started to sell Japanese woodcuts such as those collected passionately by Edouard Manet, Edgar Degas, Henry Toulouse-Lautrec, and Vincent van Gogh. (When van Gogh died in 1890, his doctor discovered a box next to his bed containing fourteen Japanese woodblock prints.) The influence of this art movement is commonly seen in the work of the Postimpressionists and also in the work of the American painter James McNeill Whistler and in that of the Englishman Aubrey Beardsley, as well as in the work of the Belgian Alfred Stevens, the Austrian Gustav Klimt, and the German artists Otto Eckmann and Emil Orlik.

Nevertheless, writers and artists perceived Japanese woodcuts from a slightly different perspective than that of historical reality. Woodcuts are not as representative of those highly refined East Asian forms of art as was thought at the time. Rather, they were a type of *manga* (comic strip), similar to our picture and starlet postcards. Even

BELOW LEFT: A large bowl by the English ceramicist Bernard Leach shows how strongly Western arts and crafts were influenced by Japanese techniques. Leach painted an abstract landscape in the Japanese style onto the irregular glaze.

Madame Chrysanthème, the book by Pierre Loti that introduced the ideal Japanese woman to European society, was known to have inspired van Gogh. The fashion and fads associated with Japonisme finally climaxed in the story of Madame Butterfly, an opera based on a romantic distortion of reality.

Japanese participation in the world's fairs of London, Paris, and Vienna had an impact on different arts and crafts in the West. After 1851, the British architect A. Godwin, a friend of James McNeill Whistler, began to use straight lines and simple surfaces in his designs for furniture and interiors. Art Nouveau arts and crafts were inspired after 1890 by colored woodcuts and the curved lines and floral motifs taken from Japanese textiles and paper patterns. Most recently, the English ceramic artist Bernard Leach was influenced by the tactile properties of Japanese tea-ceremony implements, leading him to manipulate and to combine the effects of their subtle coatings and colors with the random effects available with the use of special glazes obtained during the firing process. Relatively modern American architects, notably

ABOVE: This Art Nouveau vase with blossoms modeled after the bud of the columbine was created in glass by Emile Gallé. Floral motifs were very popular in Art Nouveau and Jugendstil.

Frank Lloyd Wright, also tried and managed to incorporate principles of Japanese architecture based on the ideas of simplicity, balance, and form into their designs. And then, too, the principle of the open-to-the-exterior Japanese style of housing fit the climatic circumstances of the American West Coast.

A special form of fruitful Western misunderstanding must be considered: the artists of the Informel movement and the Action Painters of the fifties often made reference in their work to Japanese calligraphy. However, there is only an external and superficial connection between the two art trends; Japanese brush writing, one of the highest and most sophisticated forms of art, is subject to strict formalistic and technical rules that can be mastered only after years of daily training. Spontaneity becomes possible and is allowed only after the calligrapher has thoroughly internalized the rules. Even then, the characters are still readable and their literal meaning is easily deciphered.

In contrast we must consider the calligraphic lines drawn in the works of such Western artists as André Masson, Fritz Winter, and Marc Tobey, who dealt with the meditational state of mind found in the teachings of Zen Buddhism. One could not interpret the lines as recognizably readable symbols but rather as expressions of heightened, individual states of mind. Being directly expressed, the works therefore do not submit to any rules other than those composing the self-expression and creative potential of the individual. This is a singularly Western point of view.

Since both Japanese and Western civilizations are extremely developed culturally, give and take in the form of high-level dialogue has been possible. To this day, both sides have profited by selecting from each other that which suits their own needs, thereby ensuring that rapid progress and ever more advanced future developments will continue to be achieved.

—Roger Goepper

"This has nothing to do with calligraphy. For me, these black signs are the possibility of revealing everything at once."

—Pierre Soulages

RIGHT: *The calligrapher Iwasaki paints spontaneously onto paper. The lines reveal the character and state of the artist at the moment.*

ABOVE: With a wide brush, the Chinese Zen priest Xutang Zhiyu has drawn two characters onto the empty surface of the paper. The strict formal regulations for writing the characters and the immediacy of the workmanship form a fascinating synthesis.

LEFT: Composition in Blue *(Busch-Reisinger Museum, Cambridge, Massachusetts) by the German artist Fritz Winter (1905–76) might remind us of our first glimpse of Asian calligraphy and might even have been inspired by it.*

During the Paleolithic period (ca 2,000,000–10,000 B.C.), the inhabitants of the Japanese archipelago lived inland. With the arrival of the Neolithic period, also known as the Jomon period (ca 10,000–300 B.C.), they moved to the seashore, where they remained in isolation from the outside world for almost ten thousand years. During this period they produced earthenware in which to cook and store food and also left behind shell mounds *(kaizuka)*. The earthenware they produced is what we now know as Jomon (straw-rope pattern) pottery.

It is best to begin with the Jomon period

BELOW: A deep vessel excavated in Ueno-hara, Yamanashi Prefecture. Scrollwork on the four large handles adds to the unity of the form. Yamanashi Prefectural Archaeological Museum.

In the Beginning, There Was a Shape

OPPOSITE PAGE: Patterns found on Jomon earthenware. From the top: excavated in Nukui, Tokyo, Board of Education of the city of Koganei; excavated at Shakado, Yamanashi Prefecture, Board of Education of Yamanashi Prefecture; excavated in Katsurano, Yamanashi Prefecture, Board of Education of the city of Misaka; excavated in Narahara, Tokyo, Hachioji Museum of Local History.

in describing the history of Japanese art because of the astonishing originality in the shape and pattern of the pottery from that era. Among examples of Jomon pottery, one can find a deep bowl covered with a complex, three-dimensional design of what seems to be flames shooting up from the mouth of the vessel. The question as to whether this ornamentation is indeed of flames (or if it has any symbolic meaning at all) can be set aside for the moment. What is remarkable is the fact that these powerful, dynamic shapes never reappear in the world of formative Japanese art. Indeed, such shapes are not to be found in earthenware in any other part of the world. Other Neolithic-period cultures have been recognized on the old continent, in the New World, and in the South Pacific, yet few developed to such a high level of originality and variety as can be found in the work of the artists of the Jomon period.

If one regards the history of art as the history of shapes, then the history of Japanese art has its origins in this earthenware. The development of Jomon earthenware spread throughout Japan but became concentrated in the eastern part of the island of Honshu. A tremendous variety of shapes can be found according to geographical location and the historical period in which a certain piece was produced. Of course, earthenware

has its own utilitarian purposes that, to a certain extent, limit the possible varieties of shape. Still, containers, for example those used in cooking, could appear in any number of shapes as long as they fulfilled their function. In other words, a shape can extend well beyond the necessary confines of a designated purpose. If ornamentation appears on the surface of a utilitarian vessel, that ornamentation is not necessarily connected to the purpose of the container. However, if a ceremonial vessel has symbolic ornamentation, such ornamentation can be seen as contributing to the aims of the ceremony. Even then, the same symbol can be handled in any number of ways. The use of snakes as a decorative symbol could be meaningful as a mythological configuration, although artistic representations of a snake can vary considerably. Therefore, to a certain extent, use or purpose or taste could determine the general characteristics of surface ornamentation.

Given these variables, what are the strongest factors determining particular shapes once utilitarian function has been fulfilled? These factors are limited to the creator's—whether collective or individual—passion for the shapes themselves and the desire to establish an aesthetic order independent of the object's intended purpose. If one is allowed to call it a creative impulse, then Jomon earthenware is indeed a powerful testimony to this impulse.

When one examines Jomon earthenware in greater detail, it is evident that ornamentation is not necessarily restricted to the flame shapes mentioned above. In fact, many complex levels of design appear, including wave formations, shell shapes molded in a linear fashion, and a variety of swirl shapes repeated in rows. Among the many complex or simple flame-shaped ornamentations, there is a great variety of size. Some appear well proportioned to the body of the vessel, while others are so disproportionate that they overwhelm it entirely.

It is possible, therefore, to surmise that once this type of ornamentation began to appear around the open mouths of the vessels, the creator's attention focused largely on that particular area, without consideration of the structure as a whole. In some cases, the total balance of the object was apparently disregarded in the effort to create expressive and elaborate ornamentation.

Conversely, straw-rope patterns, swirl shapes, and many other abstract geometrical designs appear in exquisitely delicate arrangements on the surface of certain pieces

of Jomon earthenware in patterns that can only be described as the result of a highly sophisticated aesthetic sense. Neither potter's wheels, glazes, or high-temperature kilns were available at that time, yet, even under such primitive circumstances, control of limited space is evident in the sense of proportion, the ability to create shifts in design, and the skillful pattern repetition exhibited on the curved surfaces of this type of Jomon-period earthenware. Such mastery attests to a highly developed aesthetic sense and a complete understanding of the geometry of spatial perception by the people of the Jomon period.

Let us assume that attention to a particular portion of a vessel for its own sake demonstrated one aspect of Jomon culture. This tendency, coupled with the highly developed aesthetic sense and mastery of space we have already noted, is inherent in many later masterpieces of Japanese art. For instance, the *Genji Monogatari Emaki* (Picture Scroll of *The Tale of Genji)* is considered a masterpiece for the way its subtle partitioning of abstract space creates a unique harmony with the portions of the scroll into which miniaturized details have been brushed. These same elements can also be found in the *Sekiya Miotsukushi-zu Byobu* (*Screen of Sekiya Miotsukushi* [see the chapter beginning on page 116]). Thus, there is some basis for the

speculation that the levels of culture that produced Jomon earthenware, *Genji Monogatari Emaki,* and *Sekiyamiotsukushi-zu Byobu* were not entirely dissimilar.

However, in retrospect, the meaning and significance of the Jomon period do not only concern the shape of its pottery. Jomon culture had very few outside influences and may actually hold some answers to the question of what may or may not have happened during the long isolation of the Neolithic period. Another such example occurs in the New World, specifically in Central American culture, which was also isolated from the outside world for almost ten thousand years. Naturally, major differences exist between the achievements of the Jomon and Central American peoples; however, there are some astonishing similarities between the two that should not be overlooked.

Jomon pottery can be classified into five different periods throughout which various transformations in shapes occurred. Typical specimens from the Early period (5000–3500 B.C.) are sharply angled at the base and wide at the mouth. One explanation for this peculiar shape maintains that the vessels were meant to be buried. Some are cone-shaped, while others bulge slightly from the opening to the base. Still others have openings that have been pressed wider, molded into wave shapes, or marked with relatively complex pressed patterns and streaks made by shells (for example, articles excavated at Sannohe-gun, Aomori Prefecture). The tendency to create ornamentation around the vessel opening began to be seen during this period.

During the first half of the Middle period (3500–2000 B.C.), bases were flattened and openings were enlarged, although some vessels rounded outward and downward under narrow and constricted necks. The middle of the Late period (2000–1000 B.C.) signaled the emergence of the extremely complex flame-shaped ornamentation discussed above.

From the latter half of the Late period to the latter half of the Final period (1000–300 B.C.), ornamentation appeared in more simple and balanced forms. Some late Final-period crocks with shallow line patterns etched onto their surfaces exhibited a shift toward Yayoi-period (300 B.C.–A.D.300) earthenware (e.g., the wide-mouthed crock excavated at Kamiiso-gun, Hokkaido, and the narrow-necked jar excavated at Sannohe-gun, Aomori Prefecture).

In short, changes found in the shapes of Jomon-period earthenware reveal that similar creative movements occurred at a par-

OPPOSITE PAGE: Lipped earthenware bowls excavated in Chiba Prefecture. Did the people of the Jomon period use the attached spouts for pouring out soups? Board of Education of Matsudo City.

ABOVE: A piece of Jomon earthenware with curved shoulders and perforations around its mouth found in Dokihara in Gunma Prefecture.

LEFT: A deep bowl with a wave-shaped mouth, 27 cm in height, excavated in Chiba Prefecture. Musashino Museum of Local History in Tokyo.

ABOVE: Another deep bowl, 25.9 cm in height, found in Hanatoriyama, Yamanashi Prefecture. Archaeological Museum at Kokugakuin University, Shibuya, Tokyo.

ticular time despite different geographical locations. One such movement was toward an increasing variety of shapes that started from a simple cone, led to a style with bulging middle sections, and then to a vase shape with the opening supported by the vessel's neck. Another movement was made with the growing complexity in ornamentation around the mouth of the vessels that reached its peak in the Middle period and reverted back to simplicity in the Late period. This change occurred over a very long span of time, and it may be due to such lengthy spans of time that an art form could experience the changes necessary for it to emerge, to develop and decline, and to head toward decadence.

However, what remains unclear is whether or not the complex ornamentation around the opening of some specimens of Jomon-period pottery was intended simply as ornamentation, or whether it was intended to impart a certain symbolism. For example, a shape presumably representing a snake (e.g., a Middle-period deep bowl with snake-shaped handles excavated in Hachioji, Tokyo) might have had a specific meaning related to animism. On the other hand, what is seen as flame-shaped may simply have been labeled this by artistically inspired modern viewers. We have no way of knowing whether the molded shapes actually signified flames to people in the Middle Jomon

period. Such ornamentation took time to create, was fragile, and could possibly have obstructed the supposed purpose of the container since it was sometimes vastly disproportionate to the container itself. It is, therefore, easy to believe that such elaborate ornamentation was applied to the vessels with other intentions than just decoration. Today, however, we are almost completely lacking in the ability to decipher or interpret such designs, and that mystery alone could possibly explain why the robust, creative, sculptural expressions in clay have such mass appeal to people of the present age.

THE MEANING OF PATTERNS AND SHAPES

As the term Jomon earthenware indicates, the representative straw-rope pattern made by rolling a rope on the earthenware's surface is what identified the objects as Jomon. A variety of patterns could be created according to the method used in twisting the rope. Materials other than rope were sometimes used; carved sticks were rolled over the clay, or shells were pressed into it. Patterns created by these techniques typically cover the wide surfaces of the earthenware of this period. A method of making indentations by pressing cords made of thinly rolled clay was also used. With this method, the

ABOVE, BELOW (DETAIL): The body of this peculiarly shaped earthenware, 57.3 cm in height, is composed of many layers. Abstract and rhythmical patterns vary gradually from layer to layer. Found at Tonai in Nagano Prefecture.

shape and depth of the indentations could be freely controlled. The representative pattern created by this method was the scroll pattern, which can be seen quite often decorating the body or the open rim of the earthenware. In addition, the scroll pattern often appears in combination with other patterns, including concentric circle-shaped indentations of various sizes.

A generally accepted theory that explains the meaning of the scroll pattern so often found on Jomon earthenware has not yet been established. However, since Jomon people had a tendency to congregate on the beach, rowed canoes, gathered shellfish, and fished, it is only natural to seek the origin of the scroll pattern in water currents since, in fact, some of the scrolls do resemble patterns made by flowing water. However, pressed-shell patterns are also seen. Thus, the origin of the scroll pattern can conceivably be attributed to the shape of some species of shell. The conch shell was a natural object exhibiting the spiral shape and was often found near the habitats of the Jomon people. In some cases, scroll ornamentation can also be viewed as examples of sea serpents (such as on the aforementioned Middle-period bowl excavated in Hachioji, Tokyo). Nevertheless, it is not realistically possible to determine whether the scroll pattern actually represented water currents, shells, or

snakes. It might be more plausible to consider the possibility that the patterns did not represent one single element but rather two or three separate elements.

The *dogu* figurine is a small human figure made of clay and fired at low heat. These figurines appeared early on during the Jomon period, eventually developing into definably human figures complete with facial features and limbs, only then to disappear during the following Yayoi period. Some *dogu* figurines were highly abstract and exhibited strong deformation in shape. The purpose of the *dogu* is unknown; however, it is clear that the figures had some relationship to the female sex. Gender is not always clear in many of the figures, although when gender is apparent, it is always female. In fact, a *dogu* figurine from the Middle period representing a pregnant woman was excavated in Chino, Nagano Prefecture, and *dogu* with enlarged breasts and hips from the Late period were excavated from a *kaizuka* in Inashiki-gun, Ibaraki Prefecture. Still, there are many such figures that do not exhibit any particularly female attributes, so the theory that holds that they are representations of an earth goddess cannot therefore be universally applied. Some believe that they were either amulets or fetishes, while another theory holds that they were used during birth in incantation for a smooth delivery. There is

ABOVE, BELOW (DETAIL): Probably used as a burial urn, this deep bowl was found in Iwate Prefecture. Collection of the Tsunagi elementary and junior high schools.

FOLLOWING PAGE: Flame-shaped designs are featured on this piece of Jomon earthenware excavated in Niigata Prefecture. Tokamachi City Museum, Niigata Prefecture.

some support for the theory that these figures are toys, but, again, these views do not account for the characteristics of all the artifacts that have been found. In short, the extreme variety of shape found in these figures has long obfuscated their true purpose.

Some of the *dogu* figures have concave, dishlike faces with narrow slanted eyes. Three-eyed or three-fingered *dogu* have also appeared (Middle period, excavated in Yashiro-gun, Yamanashi Prefecture). The chest of one *dogu* is flat; its breasts are missing. Another has large eyes made of two concentric circles, similar to the eyes of an owl (Late period, excavated from a *kaizuka* in Sono-o, Chiba Prefecture). Yet another has a hollow, short body, thick arms, and a face consisting entirely of two enormous eyes with horizontal lines slicing through the middle of each eye (Late period, with one other such example excavated in Odate-shi, Akita Prefecture). Another has the distinctive feature of eyes and nostrils carved in round holes on a heart-shaped concave plane; the upper arms extend almost horizontally. Mere traces of lower arms and hands are visible on a body that is sharply scooped out on both sides. The waist is narrow and the lines traced along both sides of the body extend to both legs, which are split apart in a decisive manner. Three scroll patterns are found, respectively, on both arms and on the center of the body, which is assumed to be the figure's chest. Two different scroll patterns, connected with other patterns drawn in fine lines, appear on the left and right

sides of both knees. The whole configuration is in perfect symmetry, its details skillfully condensed (Late period, excavated in Azuma-gun, Gunma Prefecture). The level of abstraction found in this particular piece is far more advanced than that of the owl-eyed *dogu* or the protruding-eyed *dogu*. Indeed, an amazing diversity in levels of abstraction can be seen among the excavated *dogu*, including one figure whose shape emphasizes the features of female puberty.

Found oceans away, the Mexican Olmec stone figures are far superior in descriptive expression to the *dogu*, while some Greek stone figures exhibit a much more thorough abstraction including one such female image, dating from between 2500 to 2200 B.C., now in the collection of ancient Greek and Roman objects at the Louvre. Nevertheless, Jomon-period *dogu* also successfully attained a unique sophistication of shapes as can be seen in the numerous methods of physical abstraction. An examination of the *dogu* of this period makes it clear that there were a few outstanding artists among the people of the Neolithic period in Japan.

TWO ISOLATED CULTURES

People who migrated from the Asian continent to the Japanese archipelago remained in isolation until the continental culture arrived sometime during the second century B.C. Conversely, Asians who arrived on the American continent lived in equal isolation

BELOW: *The designer Luigi Colani was fascinated by a formative piece of Jomon pottery. Shape communicates directly to people's hearts, disregarding the cultural differences between East and West.*

BOTTOM LEFT: *An example of Jomon earthenware, 20 cm in height, found in Kanagawa Prefecture has a handle and is thought be have been used as a lamp due to the soot and traces of a wick found within. Sugikubo Archaeological Site Investigation Group.*

BOTTOM RIGHT: *A very shallow bowl, 15 cm in height, found in Aomori Prefecture. Aomori Prefectural Museum of Local History.*

OPPOSITE PAGE LEFT: Jomon artists exhibited a great capacity for abstract expression and excelled in depiction of cohabitants of the natural environment. This earthen article in the shape of a sea creature (31.2 cm in height) was found at the archaeological site of Mimi 4 in Hokkaido. Board of Education of Chitose City, Hokkaido Prefecture.

for an equal length of time. Their contact with the Asian continent was severed by the emergence of the Bering Strait, and this contact was not restored until the Spaniards' discovery and devastation of the New World.

These two Asian cultures established villages and initiated a primitive form of agriculture during approximately the same period (ca 7000 B.C.) on both the western and eastern sides of the Pacific Ocean. Jomon people began making earthenware early on, while aborigines on the eastern side of the Pacific created their first clay figures around 2000

stead on levers, logs, and ropes, even when moving huge rocks. In general, the Central American aborigines did not have the technology to convert linear movement into revolving movement or vice versa. Their sole source of energy was human power, and there is no evidence that they used animals as a means of transport or conveyance or for cultivation. Horseback riding was not known in America until the Spaniards arrived and was unknown until the Kofun period in Japan, the period of ancient burial mounds (A.D. 300–710). The technology required to

ABOVE: The owl-shaped handles on this deep bowl, 55 cm in height, are attached to the rim. Union of Museums of Remains from the Shakado Archaeological Site.

B.C. But this was not their only accomplishment.

In the areas of technology, both invented agriculture and processed stone and wood to create tools and weapons, although metal was not used for purposes other than ornamentation (in Neolithic culture, for example). In Central America, agricultural technologies became highly sophisticated although the people did not have wheels, relying in-

utilize nonanimal natural power (water or wind) had not yet been developed on either side of the ocean; thus, water mills and windmills did not exist. Central American Mayan civilization left behind an alphabet that included numerals. The use of an alphabet to record and communicate information was not known to exist on the Japanese archipelago until after the Jomon period ended.

When continental culture began to heavily

BELOW: The shape of the handles on this deep bowl, approximately 55 cm in height, found in Saitama Prefecture appears to be taken from the head and tail of an animal resembling a flying squirrel. Board of Education of Fujimi City.

BELOW: One theory suggests that this vase, 58 cm in height, found in Yamanashi Prefecture, represents a pregnant woman giving birth. Board of Education of the town of Sudama.

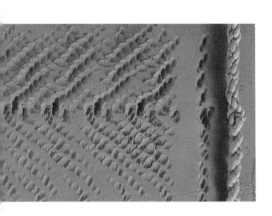

influence Neolithic-period Japan, ironware was already in production in China (reputedly since about 400 B.C.) and domesticated animals, including horses, were being fully utilized, as were highly advanced agricultural systems, including rice growing. An early technology in civil engineering had been adopted, and documents were being produced in abundance that used characters already bearing a resemblance to those used in China today. National unification came about through the dictates of a strong central government (the Han dynasty) and the people had a rational world view (Confucianism). As is well known, Japan began to absorb and to adopt the continental culture of China from the Yayoi period on. Planned learning, as exemplified by the actions of *kento-shi* and *kenzui-shi*, Japanese envoys to the Tang and Sui dynasties, continued to be practiced throughout the Heian period (794–1185). Across the Pacific, the first outsiders encountered by the Aztecs, who prospered in Mexico from the thirteenth to the early sixteenth century, were the Spaniards who arrived from across the Atlantic, rode horses,

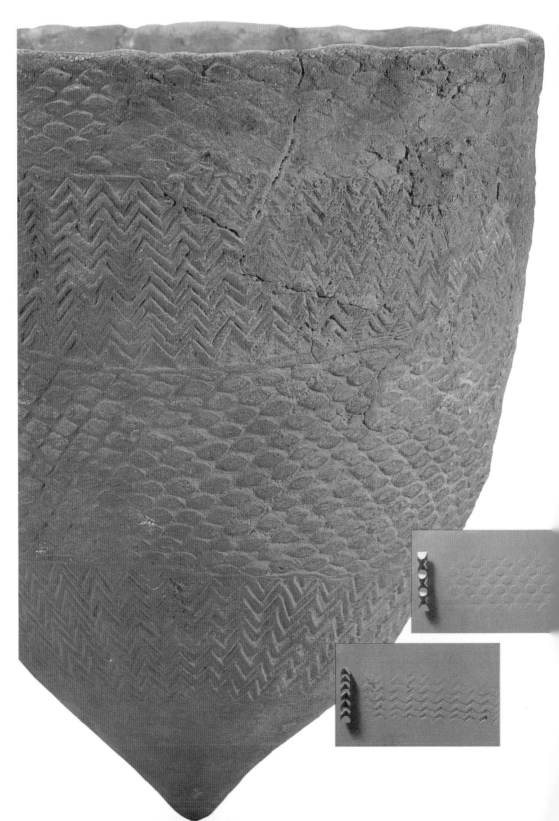

carried iron swords and firearms, and held an exclusive ideology. The ancient yet vulnerable society of the Aztecs was consequently conquered and colonized, and their long-established and intricate culture was subsequently ruined. However, such a drastic change at certain stages of development in technological history, particularly in the development of military technology, does not always signify a resultant stagnation in general technological progress. The characteristics of isolated cultures often do not represent technological stagnation, but rather,

the growth of sophistication in traditional technology.

However, if we label a jump from one technological stage in early cultures to the next—in other words, not the mere improvement of a technology within a set framework, but rather an innovation in the basic technological perception defining the framework itself—as technological revolution, then we can say that such change did not occur either in the Japanese archipelago or in Central America. Such a revolution is not likely to occur in an isolated culture without an

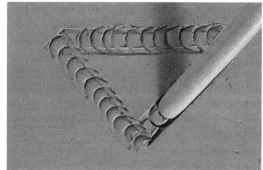

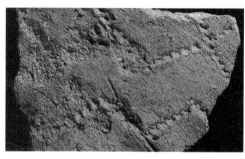

ABOVE: The scalloped edges of ribbed bivalves were sometimes pressed into the wet clay to make patterns that mimicked the shapes found in nature.

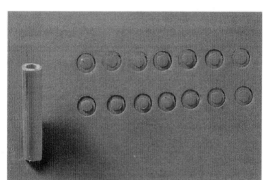

BELOW: Other patterns were made by pressing the backs of shells into wet clay. The pointed tips of conch shells were also used.

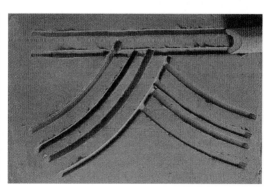

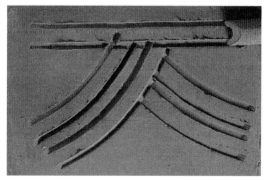

ABOVE: A piece of bamboo was used as a stamp to create repetitive patterns on the surface of some vessels. A split piece was used to trace designs of parallel lines. Actual samples are shown at the left.

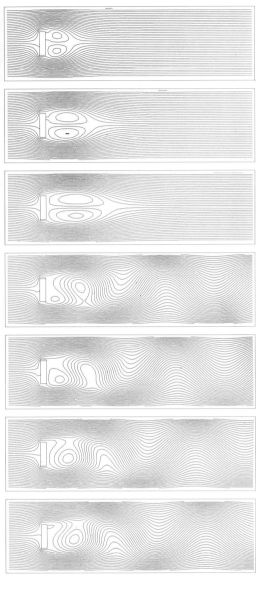

outside stimulus. Exceptions, of course, can be found in agricultural revolution, the settlement of villages, and the cultivation of edible plants. What did not occur during the periods of isolation experienced by both civilizations was a shift from stoneware to metalware, nor did a concept facilitating the conversion of linear movement to circular motion appear (and thus the wheel was not invented). Further, animal energy was not utilized. In short, it becomes easy to surmise that technological revolution in terms of material, machinery, and energy does not readily occur in an isolated culture.

The reason such technological innovations do not occur within a culture that has had no contact with an outside, heterogeneous culture is that perhaps without such an encounter, a traditional culture and its framework cannot be placed in perspective. A heterogeneous culture can be defined as one that is based on different frameworks and one with different ways of thinking. When an isolated culture comes into contact with a heterogeneous culture, it may totally reject it, refusing to learn anything from it. Nevertheless, the encounter at least informs the isolated culture that a value system or technology different from the given system does indeed exist. Without that consciousness, it is difficult to question the general framework, common sense, customs, and traditional perceptions of one's own culture. The people of the Han dynasty in China were constantly threatened by aliens from north of the border and at the same time were exposed to the cultures of the Western nations through trade. Citizens of ancient Egypt and Greece maintained a tradition of relatively autonomous culture, but were also influenced by the many cultures of the Mediterranean coast. Such cultures, constantly subjected to outside influences, naturally were able to progress at different speeds.

Secluded Central American cultures invented complex social structures such as, at the very least, the division among kings, military personnel, priests, producers of goods and services, and the hierarchical structures that bound them together. They also had a highly developed mythology that supported the complex social structure and was based on a system deifying the sun, rain, corn, snakes, and jaguars. Also, as has been mentioned, they invented an alphabet (commonly thought Mayan or Oaxacan in origin) that shows a high level of skill in mathematics and a superb knowledge of astronomy, including an extremely accurate calendar, an achievement comparable to that of ancient

Egyptian civilization. The fact that an isolated Neolithic culture could create a kingdom, mythology, and mathematics, even though it did not invent metalware, is remarkable. And this was not the end of the story, for the culture was also able to create its own unique shapes.

Natives of Central America constructed many pyramid/temples in Veracruz, in the Mexican Ravine situated over two thousand meters above sea level, in the state of Oaxaca close to the southern border of present-day Mexico, and in the jungles of the Yucatan Peninsula. These four places are the center of what is known as pre-Columbian American civilization. For three thousand years, until around A.D. 1500, the people of each of these areas developed independently to a considerable degree and yet influenced one another. Many cultures reached the height of civilization during the period between A.D. 300 and 900, in what is known as the Classic period of Mexican archaeology.

The pyramid/temples were sometimes built in isolation, but those built in groups

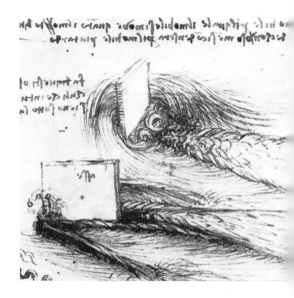

ABOVE: Leonardo da Vinci's scientifically inspired drawings of water (1507).

were usually arranged around a plaza with an avenue extending away from the temple and with pyramids arranged on both sides of the avenue (notably, Teotihuacán). Typically, the arrangement was symmetrical, but some irregularities can be seen. The pyramids were built by piling steeply slanted stone stairs onto a square or rectangular base, with the temple placed on the platform of the apex. Today, most of those temples are lost, and in many instances, only the pedestal remains in the ruins. There are some examples (e.g., Palenque) where one-story temples of stone

ABOVE: When the velocity of water current passing around a stabile object is slow, twin whirlpools are created behind the obstacle. When the velocity increases, they will gradually be transformed into what is known as Karman swirls, which can be seen as S-shaped. Presumably, the people of the Jomon period used the shapes seen in water currents to create new patterns. (Reading of water currents from the Hydraulic Engineering Laboratory of Tokai University, Tokyo).

have been restored and rebuilt. Raised ornamentation can be found on the outer walls of those temples. In Mayan temples, the inside ceilings were raised and exhibited pointed stonemasonry tops now called Mayan arches. Irregularities in design are sometimes seen, including niches where rows of narrow roofs were attached to a vertical surface (e.g., the roofs at El Tajin). In rare instances, the bottom of the pyramid was not made of stairs but composed of oval shapes bearing four curved ridge lines surfaced with smooth masonry. Two sets of stairs were usually installed at the front and back of the pyramids at differing slanted angles (as seen in the pyramids at Uxmal).

Groups of large temples of the period were almost always accompanied by attached buildings whose numbers and types varied widely. In a historical note, the name "convent" was given to some of the structures by the Spaniards, who were reminded of the religious convents in Spain. The name has nothing to do with the original use of the buildings, which is, in fact, unknown.

On the western side of the Pacific, the inhabitants of the Japanese archipelago did not necessarily create such definite and abundant shapes as those found on the buildings of Uxmal dating from their period of isolation. However, in consideration of this and in defense of the Jomon-period culture, any attempt to compare Jomon civilization with Central American civilizations is out of the question. The situation merely helps to illustrate not how far Jomon culture *would* have developed, but how far it *could* have developed had it been isolated from outside influences for a long enough period of time, something that was simply not possible on the Japanese archipelago since it lies in such close proximity to the Asian continent. The people of the Jomon period did produce

shapes that can be said to be unique. The shape of Jomon earthenware itself can be seen as original and independent and cannot be regarded as merely a variation of continental earthenware. Closed Neolithic society in Japan, while it did not attain absolute technological innovation, was still able to create increasingly sophisticated expressions and artistically unique shapes.

Since it has now been shown how lack of originality in technology and originality in artistic expression are characteristic of isolated cultures, how the two aspects are related within a given isolated culture can also be discussed. Artists create new shapes not because they renew their themes, materials, or tools, but because they renew their approach to observation. Phidias set the standard for classic Greek sculpture, not *despite* the fact that he worked on the same mythological gods with the same materials (marble) and the same tools (chisels) as other sculptors of the fifth century B.C., but *because* of it. The same goes for Michelangelo. Florence in the sixteenth century was open to nature and to the cultures of ancient Greece and Rome, but was closed to non-European cultures. Since Michelangelo did not have knowledge of Unkei (a Japanese sculptor of Buddhist images in the early Kamakura period, 1185–1333), he could not create a carved wood Nio (Deva). Instead, he carved the marble David in a manner different from Donatello's, or in his own unique style. Artists of the Central Mexican heights repeatedly carved snakes with wings (Quetzalcoatl) on stone walls. The Jomon people in the eastern area of Japan concentrated on firing earthenware adorned with ornamentation around the vessel's mouths for several thousand years. The Jomon artists created unique shapes, not because they attempted to change traditional techniques, but rather because they

ABOVE: The surface of this deep vessel, 50 cm in height, is filled with swirls. The flowing manner in which the pattern develops suggests that the artist's image was quite definite. Found in Katsurano in Yamanashi Prefecture. Board of Education of Misaka-cho, Katsurano.

BELOW LEFT (DETAIL): The structure of the patterns shows smaller swirls springing from larger swirls. From a bowl found in Nukui, Tokyo, and currently in possession of the Board of Education of Koganei City.

BELOW RIGHT: Ripples spread outward from the reverse S-shaped pattern of this deep vessel found at Chojagahara, Niigata Prefecture. Itoigawa City Local History Museum.

did not attempt to change the existing framework at all.

What happens when outside influences enter? When the potter's wheels and high-temperature calcination methods were imported, Japanese pottery completely lost its former quality of uniqueness. It was not until about a thousand years later that Japanese pottery reclaimed something of its own distinct qualities. The traditional culture of Mexico was destroyed by outsiders, and when indigenous peoples began to paint the Virgin Mary instead of carving Quetzalcoatl on stone, the originality of their artistic culture vanished. They did not recover their originality through oil painting for the next four hundred years, until resistance to the successors of the original invaders occurred during the Mexican Revolution. However, regarding Japan, we need to consider Yayoi earthenware and its culture prior to the introduction of potter's wheels and high-temperature kilns, for it was during this period that continental influence began to change the direction of Japanese artistic taste and culture.

FROM JOMON TO YAYOI

Japanese earthenware did not shift from the Jomon-period style to the Yayoi-period style overnight. The style of the Yayoi period originally emerged in northern Kyushu, the area closest to the southernmost corner of the Korean Peninsula, and from there spread to Kinai, the provinces surrounding ancient Nara and Kyoto. Even when Yayoi-period earthenware became dominant in western Japan, Jomon-period earthenware and *dogu* figurines were still being produced from the Kanto Plain (Tokyo area) to the Tohoku area (northern part of the main island of Honshu), particularly in northern Tohoku and on the island of Hokkaido. This was because Yayoi earthenware accompanied the incoming wave of continental influences that arrived via the Korean Peninsula between the latter half of the third century B.C. and the first half of the second century B.C. Also, the tradition of Jomon-period earthenware was probably stronger in eastern Japan than in western Japan since a new style is more easily accepted on the physical, cultural, and historical peripheries of the old.

RIGHT: Many of the mysteries of the pyramids of Uxmal, Mexico, remain unsolved to this day. The meticulous detail of the stone carvings can be seen on the walls of the structure to the left.

Two aspects of imported continental culture had a decisive influence on Japanese culture. The first was the acquired technique of rice growing and the subsequent use of rice as a staple food. The second was the introduction of metalware, particularly as it was used in the manufacture of bronze swords and shields, *dotaku* bells, and mirrors. The changing designs in Yayoi-period earthenware accompanied these imported innovations and were perhaps also inspired by Korean earthenware, some of which was without surface patterns.

It is now an established theory that a form of early agriculture existed in the Jomon period, as traces of its existence have been found. The tendency toward the settlement of villages appeared and the cultivation of rice was known. However, agriculture as a main means of securing food had not yet been developed. In other words, the Japanese archipelago did not experience a long period of agricultural development and proliferation, such as is found with the history of the cultivation of taro in the South Pacific or of deccan hemp, millet, and wheat in northeast Asia. The agricultural age in Japan made a sudden jump over that stage of its development under the influence of the far more advanced continent and plunged directly into the cultivation of rice with all of its difficult techniques. It goes without saying that such anthropological leaps would never have occurred without outside influences that had already undergone the usual, gradual, developmental stages. The same can be said for metalware. Pieces of metalware brought over from the Korean Peninsula included bronzeware and some ironware, which meant that Neolithic Japan suddenly came into contact with the culture of ironware. Thus, Japanese history essentially skipped the Bronze Age experienced in other cultures in the development of agricultural tools, devices, and weapons—or rather, the Japanese Bronze Age was exceptionally short.

It is well known that the proliferation of rice growing throughout Asia had a great deal of social and cultural significance although its main characteristic was that it was labor-intensive. Rice growing required not only settlement of villages (*mura*) but also the cooperative labor of the villagers, thus leading to the formation of a community. It also required facilities that could control irrigation of the paddies. The appearance of villages built with surrounding channels that were found dating from the Yayoi period probably signifies that the establishment of the community was connected to the technology of irrigation. The boundary between inside and outside was physically apparent in these villages, which can also be seen as a reflection of the emphasis placed on boundaries both social and physical between members of the community and outsiders. In the Yayoi period, the community was obviously becoming central to agricultural rites and festivals and was responsible for overseeing marriages and burials; therefore, it was only a matter of time before the community would become the dominant social unit. It was the community that made contact with outside cultures, for example, with that of metalware cultures. Likewise, it was the community that began to determine acceptance or rejection of contact or conditional contact with outside cultures. It was also the community

as a whole, rather than individual artisans, that made earthenware. All social and cultural activity was done in pursuit of the goals of the community and accomplished with the community's then current technology.

Metalware experienced changes in shape and use when it began to be manufactured in Japan. Bronze swords on the continent were intentionally narrow since they were intended to be used as sharp weapons, whereas in Japan swords were transformed into wide, long shapes that were probably used as symbols of power, rather than as weaponry. On the Korean Peninsula, the *dotaku* bells were smaller in size and were used as musical instruments. However, Yayoi-style *dotaku* were larger and wider and bore complex

OPPOSITE PAGE, FAR LEFT: Repetitive gargoyle-like carvings of the Central American rain god Chac are shown. Chac brought rain but also caused storms and floods.

OPPOSITE PAGE, TOP: A section of the wall of the "convent" building has beautiful stone carvings placed over latticework to create a delicate effect.

OPPOSITE PAGE, CENTER: More than six hundred dogu *have been excavated at Shakado, Yamanashi Prefecture. Many of the* dogu *exhibit female characteristics and are thought to have been used as objects of worship or in rituals for productivity and fertility. Union of Museums for Shakado Artifacts.*

OPPOSITE PAGE, BOTTOM: In ancient Central America, scroll-pattern motifs symbolized water and represented the Mayan gods of rivers, lakes, and rain. The pattern also was closely associated with snakes, another symbol for water. A few of the scroll-pattern motifs from the pyramid/temple site of Uxmal are shown.

ABOVE LEFT (DETAIL): Orderly patterns found on a Jomon vessel are oddly reminiscent of Mayan stone carvings.

ABOVE RIGHT (DETAIL): Small stones and clay were used to completely fill empty spaces on these vessels excavated in Yamanashi Prefecture. This feature was common to both Jomon and Uxmal works. Union of Museums for Shakado Artifacts.

BELOW: Along with ironware, bronze weapons eventually became objects of ritual. A bronze blade, 20 cm long, found in Hyogo Prefecture, National Museum of History and Folklore, Tokyo; a bronze sword, 54.3 cm long, found in Nagasaki Prefecture, Nagasaki Prefectural Fine Art Museum; and a bronze halberd, 28.9 cm long, found in Hyogo Prefecture, Board of Education, City of Kobe.

ornamentation. Also, they had lost their original function as musical instruments. Some excavated samples bear reliefs depicting scenes of hunting or animals and insects related to daily agricultural life. It is likely that the *dotaku* were kept in the possession of the community and were used in agricultural rituals. Bronze mirrors, which are assumed to have been used as makeup devices on the continent, seem also to have become instruments for incantation. Mirrors were used by female shrine attendants, but later became objects of worship at the shrines. The Three Sacred Treasures of the Imperial Family, the presumed symbols of the legitimacy of the Japanese imperial family (a belief belonging to a later period, as the imperial family did not exist during the Yayoi period), consist of a sword, a mirror, and a precious amulet, a selection of objects which raises the possibility that the treasures were so chosen as a result of the tradition of designating imports from the continent as objects of incantation and ritual. In short, one of the characteristics of Yayoi-period culture is an early version of the Japanization of imports, rather than an imitation of them. It was exactly in this manner that Japan later Japanized Buddhism and Confucianism.

Yayoi-period earthenware exhibits three types, each corresponding to a different use. Jars *(tsubo)* were used to store food, pots *(kame)* were used for cooking, and small tables for a single person *(takatsuki)* were used to serve food. The earthenware from this period is typically reddish-brown in color, although some is black, and was fired at low heat. This earthenware is much stronger than Jomon earthenware, and differs from it in its absence of wave-shaped openings, its smoother surfaces, and the overall balance of its design. Ornamentation is simple, consisting mainly of abstract patterns constructed with many shallow and straight lines. In particular, many pieces are patterned with straight lines that circle around the necks and bodies of the vases. Some vases are constructed in a style that appears to reflect the transition from Jomon period to Yayoi period, with Jomon-period patterns used alongside Yayoi-period patterns, although it is not always easy to differentiate between the two in individual vessels. However, in general, the styles of the Jomon- and Yayoi-period vases and vessels are in sharp contrast to each other and exhibit diverse cultural influences and backgrounds. The former is extremely ornamental, unique in shape, vigorous, and dynamic. The latter appears calm, balanced, and plain. However, in spite of

their lack of originality in shape and design, Yayoi-period ceramics often exhibit a beautifully simple sturdiness.

In retrospect, it appears that the abstract, controlled aesthetics of Yayoi-period earthenware, rather than the powerful Jomon-period earthenware, set the basic underlying tone of the subsequent history of Japanese creative impulses. The calm restraint of the pottery and the agricultural innovations of the rice-growing *mura* community could conceivably be regarded as the main determinants of the consequent culture of the people of the Japanese archipelago.

A form of political unification had been initiated on the main islands of Japan as early as the third century. A writing system was soon devised, but no real literature had been produced. Sophisticated technology in the artistic fields of sculpture, painting, architecture, and city planning was also in its earliest stages.

Such was the state of the arts in Japan when the first international religion arrived, completely equipped with a well-developed doctrine and organized temples, abundant

Shintoism and Buddhism: An Encounter

ABOVE: *Buddhist statue in bronze, probably from Horyu-ji in Nara. National Museum of Tokyo.*

literature, majestic rituals, advanced medicinal practices, sophisticated images of the Buddha, and highly accomplished architectural techniques.

Under the overwhelming influence of Buddhism and with the introduction of Chinese calligraphic characters, Japanese culture began to maintain a steady level of creativity. In order to fully understand the history of Japanese culture, we need to visualize the cultural conditions of Japan during the influx of early continental influences. It should first be noted that the advent of Buddhism did not eradicate the existing patterns of faith in Japan, but rather allowed Buddhist and non-Buddhist beliefs to coexist. The eclectic practices of both Buddhists and non-Buddhists continued to prevail. It is worth noting that non-Buddhist practices survived longer among the population of farming villages, particularly in secluded mountains and on remote islands, than among intellectuals in urban areas. (In this regard, the non-Buddhist customs found in modern Okinawa are significant.) In trying to understand the phenomenon of eclecticism, we can suppose that it derives from the combination of two factors: a foreign system of religious worship and a native view of the world. By observing one of the factors and studying the results of this observation, we should be able to clearly understand the other factor. In this we have the basic ethnological approach

to the reconstruction of Japanese culture prior to the arrival of Buddhism and the subsequent phenomenon of cultural and artistic eclecticism that continues to prevail.

When looking back at the history of Japanese culture prior to the sixth century, we may find that conceptualization of a consistent and simple model of Japanese culture is very difficult to achieve, mainly because of the complex mixture of cultures with probable origins on the northern continent, on the southern continent, and in the South Seas. As will be explained in detail later, some early Japanese gods were said to have descended from heaven (northern regions), while others visited from beyond the sea (southern regions). Post-death destinations and descriptions of the afterlife therefore varied from place to place.

The Chinese character for "god" eventually became the Japanese word *kami*. However, apart from the definitive meaning of the Chinese characters that form it, the character for *kami* had roughly two sets of meanings (as many of the characters do). The first included a variety of natural objects such as the sun, the moon, mountains, trees, water, fire, rocks, and other objects such as the column of a building or a few species of animals. The second set included the human soul, the spirit of the dead, and ancestral spirits. In short, from their inception, the early Japanese gods were either natural or ancestral.

However, the natural gods of Japan were of three types. The first existed in animism, where natural objects such as mountains, rivers, grass, and trees were imbued with spirits. In animistic beliefs a mountain itself could be a god. A second type was where a natural object served as a dwelling for a god who might temporarily occupy the object. Trees are one of the most typical examples of this kind of dwelling; the tree is sacred but is not itself a god. (This is quite probably the origin of the well-known and popular notion of the "sacred bough" or "sacred column.")

The third case was that of visiting gods. The persona of a god in the act of visiting a community during a certain period of the year was often assumed and related actions were performed by a costumed member of the community. The few remaining remnants of this custom suggest that the performer's appearance was purposely strange and grotesque, perhaps even quite frightening. The performances apparently were based on primitive worship of an ancestral god.

Ancestral gods in a variety of forms are

widely seen in northeast Asia. An ancestral spirit of a single tribe was known as an *ujigami* (clan deity). The *ujigami* were thought to visit the community on special occasions, where they were welcomed with offerings, mainly of food. Such beliefs and practices were later combined with Buddhist practices in a yearly event called *Obon*, or the Festival of Lanterns, that is still observed throughout modern-day Japan in both urban and rural locations. Family members come from near and far to clean the family gravesite in preparation for the return of the dead.

PREVIOUS PAGE and ABOVE: On the night of March 12 during the festival of Omizutori held at Todai-ji temple in Nara Prefecture, novice monks draw water from a sacred well and offer it to an eleven-faced image of Kannon. This ceremony is said to symbolize the arrival of spring.

These customs are traditionally observed from July 13 to 15 every year. The ancestral spirit is welcomed to a spirit altar set up in front of the *butsudan,* a Buddhist altar most families still tend.

Where did the gods, particularly the ancestral spirits, come from? To raise the question is to ask where the ancestral spirit resided, and it is difficult to separate this question from another more obvious one: Where does the human soul go and where does it stay after death? According to the *Kojiki* (Record of Ancient Matters, Japan's oldest extant chronicle recording events from the mythical age of the gods up to the time of Empress Suiko [r 593–628]), the destination

of the dead is the land of Yomi, an underground world of darkness and impurity.

On the main island of Okinawa, the spirits of the dead go beyond the ocean to a home thought to resemble Shangri-la. Today, one of the most famous Okinawan festivals is Izaiho, which is held every twelve years on Kudaka Island just off the southern coast. In this festival, the ancestral gods are received from their home beyond the ocean. It has been described as existing either on or beneath the sea and in the latter case is associated with a Dragon Palace.

On the southern island of Miyako, the dead do not arrive from beyond the sea but from a dark underground world. Judging from the various customs that continue to be practiced despite the fact that they are spread over a wide geographical area, the destination of the dead is not at all consistent, except in cases where Buddhism, Confucianism, or Taoism exert a strong influence. However, what remains clear is that ancestral worship was prevalent in extensive areas of Japan and that the arrival of Buddhism did not eradicate a practice begun many years previously. As we have noted, the early Japanese held natural phenomena such as water, the sun, stones, and even silence itself in reverence. Soon, they began to identify particular sacred areas and to purify themselves in those locations. This practice was later called Shinto (way of the gods).

The function of the Shinto gods, whether animistic or ancestral, was either to provide benefits, which could arrive in the form of good harvest and rain, or to protect against damage, which could be in the form of disasters such as drought. The community expressed its desire for protection during their festivals. Such ritualistic festivals, however, did not always reveal the gods' will. To learn the will of the gods, a special ceremony was orchestrated in which communication with the gods could occur. Such action usually consisted of two steps. The first rid the actor of impurities, mainly through the use of fire or ablution with water. Oceans, rivers, and waterfalls thus were regarded as sacred and became objects of worship. Purification also required consuming sacred food that had been prepared over a sacred fire. Shinto priests at Izumo Taisha Shrine in Shimane Prefecture continue to build sacred fires by rubbing special pieces of wood against each other and continue to eat sacred food prepared over the sacred fire.

It is likely that these early sacred places

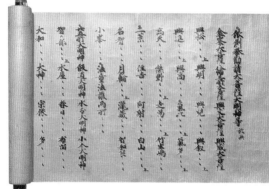

ABOVE: *This paper scroll is a directory of the names of all the Japanese gods. The names are read aloud every night during the Omizutori ceremony, which lasts from March 1 to March 14.*

LEFT: *Five* hinoki *(cypress) boards, each about five meters in length, are arranged in the southern corner of the Nigatsu-do hall. Novice monks strike their heads, both elbows, and both knees against the boards during the ritualistic ceremony known as* gotai tochi *(throwing five parts of the body onto the ground). The sounds they make in repentance for their own sins and those of all humanity echo throughout the hall.*

ABOVE: *Novice monks during a chanting ritual held in the Nigatsu-do hall.*

were exceptionally beautiful, set apart from the landscape by natural stone boundaries or by piles of rocks that created natural demarcations. It was in these places that worship was conducted in utter silence and with the absence of ritual. This purest form of nature worship still exists in areas within the Ise Jingu shrine located in Mie Prefecture, whose atmosphere is believed to be imbued with the spirits of the gods. In the second step toward the attempt at communication with the gods, the purified individual resided in the gods' dwelling where the gods appeared to the dreamer in his sleep and communicated their will. The gods might offer warnings or prophecies, decree orders, make promises, and sometimes enter into pacts.

On other occasions, communication with the gods occurred through a medium. The medium, or shaman, made certain initial preparations and then moved into a trance-like state. The gods spoke to the mediums or shamans during the trance. Shamanism was an important element in pre-Buddhist faith in Japan and continues to remain so to this day in some of the more traditionally oriented areas of the country, particularly in Okinawa and the Ryukyu Islands.

Perceptions of another world exist in Japanese animism, ancestor worship, and shamanism, but there was no clear boundary between this world and the next. Gods were

known to sail from the other world on vessels, while ancestral spirits were said to descend from mountains. Further, *ujigami* did not transcend the community, but existed only to the extent in which they could exert some concrete influence. In the earliest days of these religious beliefs, there were no standard doctrines nor was there any organization of shrines. Shinto was later to develop its own forms of art and architecture, rituals and clergy, but its origins were in the indigenous worship of natural phenomenon.

THE ADVENT OF BUDDHISM IN JAPAN

Buddhism is said to have arrived in Japan in the middle of the Kofun period (A.D. 300–710), but this relationship between Japan and Korea was quite close by the time Bud-

dhism was transmitted in its first stages. It was introduced to the court of Japan in the middle of the sixth century (the second stage), and in the early seventh century, Prince Umayado, who later took the name Prince Shotoku (574–622), decisively promoted Buddhism as a national religion (the third stage). Prince Shotoku was a scholar and statesman who personified the sophistication of the Japanese culture of his time. He was born into a court which for twenty-one years had received Buddhist images from Korea.

Prior to Prince Shotoku's activites promoting Buddhism in Japan, Buddhism had traveled along the merchants' Silk Road from India, arrived in northern China during the Han dynasty (202 B.C.–A.D. 220), then reached Korea by the fourth century. Japan had maintained the colony of Kaya on the southern tip of the peninsula since the middle of the fourth century and had a close relationship with the other peoples living on the peninsula; thus, it was natural for Buddhism to

have gradually become known in fourth-century Japan (the first stage).

However, it was not until the middle of the sixth century, when the king of Paekche (Korea) sent a gift of an image of Buddha and Buddhist scriptures to Japan, that this international relationship became apparent (the second stage). The event was recorded as the official introduction of Buddhism into Japan in the *Nihonshoki* (Chronicles of Japan, completed in A.D. 720) and in other early, historical texts.

The sixth century included the period of the Three Warring Kingdoms on the Korean Peninsula. Koguryo was the kingdom in the northern part of the peninsula. The southwestern section was known as Paekche, while the easternmost part was occupied by the kingdom of Silla, with the Japanese colony of Kaya (near present-day Pusan) in between. These three kingdoms were embroiled in complex wars, and Paekche, threatened by Koguryo from the north and Silla from the east, must have had to cooperate with Japan for the Japanese colony of Kaya to be maintained. Therefore, the introduction of Buddhism to Japan would have strengthened the intercontinental relationship with Paekche. At the same time, as the Japanese failed to prevent Silla's advance into Kaya, they attempted to take advantage of the conflict among the three kingdoms and to use the powers of Koguryo and Paekche to control Silla. In view of the political maneuvering it is easy to understand why there would have been considerable motivation on the part of both Japan and Paekche to seek an approach to each other.

The introduction of Buddhism thus involved not only a religious aspect, but one of diplomacy as well. Both were also linked to the domestic struggle for power occurring in Japan at the time. The initial attitude of the Japanese ruling class toward Buddhism was divided. The Soga clan (and the Otomo clan), who had a close relationship to Paekche and wanted to be even closer in terms of diplomatic policies, supported Buddhism. On the other hand, the Mononobe clan (and the Nakatomi clan), which insisted on establishing diplomatic relations with Silla, appeared to oppose Buddhism. One side built temples and the other ruined them. One side carved images of Buddha and the other burnt them. The struggles between the two sides reflected a difference in attitudes not only toward Buddhism but also toward a willingness to accept imported, foreign culture. It is not very

difficult to imagine that the power struggle between the Soga and Mononobe clans was at the root of these violent events. Such was the second stage in the introduction of Buddhism into Japan.

The third stage began when the power struggle concluded with the assassination of the head of the Mononobe clan by the Soga clan, which was followed by a continuous monopoly of power through the line of Empress Suiko (554–628). Her nephew, Prince Shotoku (574–622), was succeeded by Prince Soga no Umako (ca 626), a concentration of power that was not unique to Japan.

In China in the year 589, national unification was accomplished by the Sui dynasty, which was followed by the grand Tang dynasty (618–907). Japan and the warring Korean kingdoms are known to have taken tributes to the Sui and Tang dynasties. China had already adopted Buddhism, and the three Korean kingdoms and Japan were in the process of doing the same. There were extreme disparities both culturally and technologically between China and the four domains, and Japan probably had no choice but to adopt Buddhism and continental culture in its attempts at national unification and reformation. By doing so, Japan thus maintained its place in the international community of East Asia, which centered around China.

Upon ascent to power through civil war and a coup d'état, Prince Shotoku sent a

ABOVE (DETAIL) and OPPOSITE PAGE: The bronze Vairocana Buddha of Todai-ji temple in Nara (also known as the Nara Daibutsu) is nearly fifteen meters tall. Casting of this Nara-period statue was supervised by Kuninaka no Muraji Kimimaro and others, and the consecration was held in 752. This image of the Buddha has experienced several disasters, and only a few small sections of the lotus-flower throne remain from the original Nara-period casting. Most of the image in place today was created during the Kamakura period (1185–1333), while the figure's head was restored during the more recent Edo period (1603–1868).

delegation to the court of the Sui dynasty in A.D. 600, then instituted twelve ranks of public judiciary officials (603). The delegation to the Sui must have served to create foreign policy, while also researching a model for the reformation of society. Institution of an official ranking system served to prevent the clan system from being dispersed and helped maintain a concentration of power in the courts. Introduction of a calendar became a symbol for the introduction of continental culture. The Constitution of Seventeen Articles (604) initiated by Prince Shotoku included Buddhism as one of the principles of national unification and as the new and official ideology of the new power (Article 2). In retrospect, this declaration was a decisive one, taking into account the history of Japanese philosophy that followed the adoption and instrumentalization of foreign, intellectually sophisticated ideologies begun during the reign of Prince Shotoku. This instrumentalization of an intellectually sophisticated foreign philosophy has been a consistent element of Japanese philosophical history ever since.

There were three types of concentration of power. The first was monopoly of power by the king himself (Paekche), the second was monopoly of power by a vassal (Koguryo), and the third was concentration of power in a member of the royal family who had the right to succeed to the throne (Silla). The power structure in Japan at the time was of the third type, in which power was concentrated in and around an individual (Prince Shotoku). Thus, when that individual died, the struggle for power began again.

In Japan, following the death of Prince Shotoku, the Soga clan attempted to achieve the second type of concentration of power by dislodging and eliminating Prince Shotoku's influence. They arrested his son, killed his family, and forced the other family members to commit suicide. They burnt Ikaruga Palace in 643, and in 670 burnt the site of the Wakakusa-dera temple. Prince Shotoku's legacy was so firmly established by then that the clergy and aristocracy saw to it that the temple was immediately rebuilt; it was renamed Horyu-ji. The Soga clan was finally defeated, however, by the united front led by Nakatomi no Kamatari (later Fujiwara no Kamatari) and Prince Naka no Oe (later Emperor Tenji), who instituted the Taika Reform of 645. This move, which established the third type of power structure, reinstated the line of Emperor Kotoku, who was

followed by Empress Saimei, then by Emperor Tenji.

From the beginning of the seventh century, construction of Buddhist temples became prevalent. At the same time, images and paintings of Buddha became popular. The *Nihonshoki* records that as early as the end of the Suiko era (624), there were forty-six Buddhist temples and 1,385 Buddhist monks. From that point on, the mainstream of Japanese art history was overwhelmingly dominated by Buddhist arts.

What had happened in the vast areas of Asia also happened in Japan. Buddhism absorbed native gods and was simultaneously transformed by contact with an indigenous system of worship and values. Finally, Japanese gods themselves were also transformed by Buddhism, as gods who once were objects of worship prior to the arrival of Buddhism did not have their own myths, doctrines, shrines, or images. Under the influence of Buddhism, consistent myths and doctrines were created, the architecture of Shinto shrines was developed, and images of gods were produced. In short, the Japanization of Buddhism was accompanied by the transformation of native beliefs to those of a more Buddhistic nature.

The first large-scale Buddhist temple was Asuka-dera, established by Soga no Umako in Asuka, Nara Prefecture, begun in 592 and completed in 596. According to the *Nihonshoki, busshari* (Buddha's ashes) and Buddhist monks arrived four years prior to that year from Paekche, along with carpenters and painters. It must have been the artisans and craftsmen from Paekche who actually engaged in the construction of the temple, later lost in a fire (1196). The only details of construction available today are what we can gather from recent excavations (1956–57). The plan of the temple compound structures *(garan)* was completely symmetrical, with three golden pavilions surrounding a central pagoda. Corridors encircled the pavilions and an inner gate was installed at the front of the pagoda. Such a symmetrical arrangement is said to have descended from the Koguryo style.

The large-scale temples constructed after Asuka-dera were Shitenno-ji of Tennoji Ward in Osaka and Horyu-ji in Ikaruga, Nara Prefecture. Shitenno-ji was repeatedly burnt down and rebuilt; thus, none of the original features remain today. Only the arrangement of the compound structures is known to be truly original. There was only one golden pavilion at Shitenno-ji. An inner gate, a pa-

BELOW: This five-string musical instrument decorated with mother-of-pearl and carved out of sandalwood is one of the items stored at the Shoso-in treasure house of Todai-ji. This is one example of the excellent, handcrafted articles brought to Japan along with Buddhism.

goda, the golden pavilion, and a lecture hall were placed in a straight line from south to north. The golden pavilion and the pagoda were surrounded by corridors said to be constructed in the styles of Gunshurihai-ji of Paekche and Koryu-ji of Silla.

Horyu-ji temple is the oldest extant temple in Japan and contains some of the oldest wooden buildings in the world. The original Horyu-ji temple, Wakakusa-dera, appears to have been built shortly after the death of Prince Shotoku in 622, where the East Hall is presently located, but it was completely demolished in a fire set by the Soga clan in 670. An excavation conducted in 1939 revealed that the arrangement of the buildings was the same as that of Shitenno-ji. In other words, despite the fact that there are no remaining architectural structures dated ear-

surrounded by an inner gate and corridors, although when viewed from the front, it does not appear symmetrical. The original plans of Asuka-dera, Shitenno-ji, and the original Horyu-ji temples were made in imitation of continental styles. Therefore, would the arrangement of the rebuilt Horyu-ji from the end of the seventh century denote a kind of Japanization? If so, it signals a shift from symmetry to asymmetry and suggests the emergence of a characteristic peculiar to Japanese aesthetics. This variance in thought revealed itself more clearly as time passed.

IMAGES OF THE BUDDHA

Many images of the Buddha can be found in Horyu-ji temple. Representative pieces

OPPOSITE PAGE and RIGHT: At the celebration for the completion of a major restoration of Todai-ji in 1980, the original dance costumes from the Nara period were revived. The colors and designs came from all over Asia.

lier than the Taika Reform, it is apparent that architectural designs of those days were made in the style of either Asuka-dera or the Shitenno-ji. The existing Horyu-ji was rebuilt at the end of the seventh century during the Hakuho period (the unofficial name of the period associated with Emperor Temmu [672–686]). The arrangement of the temple buildings differs from the original Horyu-ji and does not belong to the Shitenno-ji style. A pagoda and a golden pavilion were arranged on a line east to west in the space

from the Asuka period (593–710) include images of the Buddha as well as the bronze Shaka Trinity (623) at Horyu-ji temple. When we add the 275.7-centimeter-tall Great Buddha of Asuka-dera (606) and the Miroku Bosatsu of Koryu-ji in Kyoto (representing a bodhisattva sitting in quiet contemplation and carved from a single trunk of Japanese red pine), we can very well imagine the general pattern of Buddhist images constructed or carved during the first half of the seventh century.

The central figure of the Shaka Trinity sits with its right palm facing upward and with the index and third fingers of its left hand extended and straightened. The neck is long and straight, the eyes narrow, the nose triangular, and the lips rather thick, fixed in an august smile. The drapery that hangs over the top tier of the pedestal is quite large compared to the height of the images. The folds in the drapery are highly abstract designs extending outward in the shape of an almost symmetrical trapezoid.

The original Miroku Bosatsu (The Benevolent One) posed in meditation did not exist in China, but one such image currently in place at the National Museum in Seoul (ca 600) bears a strong resemblance. Such Buddhist images were made in Japan quite often during the latter half of the seventh century, the most representative being the Miroku at Chugu-ji; therefore, it is possible that the Miroku at Koryu-ji was imported from Korea since it dates from such an earlier period.

Many of the Asuka-period Buddhist images from the first half of the seventh century were found to be either imported from the continent or created in Japan by naturalized or visiting continental artists. The images are mostly in the Han-dynasty style which was used throughout the first half of the sixth century. If we assume such figures were produced in Japan in the latter half of the seventh century, it becomes apparent that there was a gap of about half a century between the creative progress of the Korean Peninsula and that of Japan. Although Japan did not invent any new sculptural styles, within their given limitations, the Buddhist images produced in Japan were of a particularly high standard both technically and aesthetically.

The Buddhist images from the fifth and sixth centuries are exceptional in their spiritual expression and can be ranked with Western Christian sculptures of the twelfth and thirteenth centuries. The Horyu-ji Kenno Homotsu (Treasures received by Horyu-ji)

ABOVE: *A pair of male and female gods from the end of the ninth century. These woodcarvings represent the more rugged austerity of Japanese gods. Matsuo Taisha shrine, Kyoto.*

ABOVE: *This woodcarving of the Shinto goddess Nakatsu-hime dates from the end of the ninth century. Was it the ancient belief in trees as the habitat of Shinto gods that caused the artists to use one piece of wood to carve these Buddhistic images? Yakushi-ji, Nara.*

ABOVE: *This Shinto god was depicted as a Buddhist monk at the end of the ninth century. The Hachiman-gu shrine was built within the grounds of Yakushi-ji te in Nara around the year 890, and this statue, the oldest known statue of a god, became the guardian deity of the shrine's main hall.*

OPPOSITE PAGE: *The site of this fifty-five-meter-tall Buddha, carved in the stone surface of a cliff in Bamiyan, Afghanistan, is believed to be sacred Buddhist ground. The figure was brutally defaced by invaders, who often destroyed or damaged such images.*

include quite a few small, gold-plated images of Buddha assumed to be from the Asuka period. The faces of the images express a rather ordinary calm and dignified quality.

In the latter half of the seventh century, specifically during the Hakuho period, further influences from the Han dynasty began

were created. The wooden Miroku Bosatsu at Chugu-ji in Ikaruga, Nara Prefecture, was the most remarkable of these. A double chignon of hair adorns the head. The upper torso is completely unadorned, while the legs are covered by a robe. The image is not extreme in manner of design; there is no stiffness. It has a supple and balanced upper

RIGHT: A Guze Kannon carved in wood during the seventh century. Horyu-ji temple, Nara.

CENTER: A Kudara Kannon carved in wood during the middle of the seventh century. Horyu-ji temple, Nara.

ABOVE: An image of Shaka dating from the latter half of the second century. The realistic depiction of bones and skin expresses the ascetic practice Shaka chose to endure.

to emerge. Later, the Sui- and Tang-dynasty styles (from the beginning of the seventh century) were added. Naturally, most Buddhist images dating from the eighth century Nara period (710–794) continued to follow the Sui and Tang styles, although by the time of the Asuka period, images of Buddha had begun to completely change in terms of style. Elements of both the old and the new styles can be seen in sculptures created during the transitional period.

Statues of Buddhas and bodhisattvas posed in meditation appeared on the Korean Peninsula in the sixth century. In the latter half of the seventh century, some (mainly of gilt bronze) were brought to where many others

torso, a calm and fine expression on its beautiful face, and quiet eyes. Tranquillity seems to emanate from the position of the right hand. The face of the seated figure of the Yakushi Buddha at Horin-ji is different in many ways from the one of the Bosatsu at Chugu-ji. It is, in fact, rather closer to that of the Shaka at Horyu-ji. The figure has a long face with a triangular nose and a firm mouth set in a relatively classical style. The robe is simple, the face is lively, and the torso and both hands are gracefully sculpted. The Kudara Kannon (Kudara is the Japanese name for Paekche) at Horyu-ji has yet different facial features and body and has been composed in another style entirely. This

statue of painted wood is assumed to have been made in Japan. It probably was called the Kudara Kannon because people in Japan had never before seen a similar statue. The face with its small eyes and nose is unique, while its thin and elongated torso is particularly unusual. One theory suggests that it had its origin in the extremely tall and thin *wakizamurai* (secondary warrior) found in a cave in Bakuseizan, China, in the first half of the sixth century.

Some outstanding Bosatsu images from the Nara period include the Yakushi Trinity (bronze, 729) found at the Yakushi-ji temple in Nara and particularly one of its *wakizamurai*, the Gakko Bosatsu (bod-hisattva of the moon). Its sumptuous form does not distort the balance of the human body but represents an ideal. The upper torso is nearly naked but for a necklace. Nothing covers the body except a thin robe sliding down from both shoulders. The covering from the waist down is also thin, exposing the fullness and firmness of the thighs. The posture of this bodhisattva is not straight (as had been the case in other statues until this period); the hips are twisted to the left and the right knee is slightly bent. Quiet movement is implied by the way the weight of the figure has been placed on the left leg. In contrast to statues from the seventh century, this image can be admired from all sides

since the emphasis on symmetry and an anterior focus has been eliminated. The body is voluptuous, with graceful curves suggestive of sensual pleasure. The crown it wears is relatively small, while the face is round, with narrow eyes and a straight nose. The intrinsic harmony of the two contesting elements—the dignified expression combined with the voluptuous body—creates an exquisite piece of sculpture.

The physical characteristics of the Gakko Bosatsu are derived from the style of the Tang dynasty. The image can best be described as representing an ideal human figure in statuary, rather than as a statue bearing idealized human features. This style represents a world of form with a completely

Hachibushu (the Eight Followers of Kannon, Buddhist deities with human- or animal-shaped heads), and the Judaideshi (the Ten Grand Disciples), all of which exhibit facial expressions both subtle and sharp. In fact, one of the characteristics of Nara-period sculpture is the achievement of a certain realism. The clay Shitenno of Todai-ji temple in Nara are placed in the four corners of the Kaidan-in (the hall for ordination of monks), clad in armor and standing upright on the bodies of monsters. Some of the statues appear to be roaring, while others stare straight ahead with tense, closed lips. In particular, the expression on the face of the Komokuten (one of Four Heavenly Kings, faithful servants and guardians of Buddhist law),

different direction from that of the style of the Han dynasty, where transcending images of Buddhist statues were approached through artistic alteration of human figures. It seems that early Japanese artistic sensitivity was best expressed in this new style; thus, the Buddhist images of eighth-century Japan are not only the culmination of the history of Japanese sculpture, but are also among some of the unparalleled masterpieces of Japanese art.

Among the Buddhist statues of this period, there are figures other than the Nyorai Buddhas (who have attained the highest level of buddhahood) or the Bosatsu (who remain destined to wait for buddhahood). There are those of the Shitenno (the Four Devas), the

emphasizes his strong will and determination. He seems capable of seeing through any falsehood and is said to be on the verge of recording the truth as demonstrated by the rolled paper in his left hand and the thick brush in his right.

The famous dry-lacquer Ashura, a mythological Hindu demon king and one of the Hachibushu of Kofuku-ji temple currently stored in the Nara Museum, has an exposed, thin, upper torso. The king stands with both legs closed, hands meeting at the chest. Two extra arms extend from each shoulder, forming an almost geometrical symmetry. Two extra faces are attached to both sides of the head in a symmetrical manner. The subtly melancholic expression of the main face has

a somewhat feminine demeanor and is that of a youth who appears to be under duress, caught in a particularly trying and emotional moment.

The most powerful in terms of expression of violent emotion among the clay figures of Horyu-ji temple are several screaming samurai surrounding the depiction of Nirvana on the north side of the pagoda. Their upper torsos are naked, their heads appear shaven. Some look up to the sky, some have their hands on the ground, some make fists, and some twist their hair. Their wide-open mouths express despair. They are arranged in a line in front of a reclining Buddha, behind which there is a crowned figure with a sorrowful but comparatively calm expression. These clay figures were intended to express perfectly and absolutely the feelings of those who were close to Shaka at the moment of his death. They are considered masterpieces of Japanese sculpture. At the same time, because they do not convey anything more than sorrow, they are visual proof of the limits that Japan had reached in terms of its understanding of Buddhism.

THE SYNTHESIS OF BUDDHISM AND SHINTOISM

The Constitution of Seventeen Articles promulgated by Prince Shotoku mentioned neither tutelary gods nor ancestral gods and attempted to promote Buddhism as a principle of national unification. Buddhism was promoted as having mass appeal beyond the restrictions of time and beyond the boundaries imposed by identification with a certain group. However, once Buddhism was accepted officially, the first undertaking was the construction of *uji-dera*, temples created for each respective blood-related community and their ancestors, not intended solely for individuals or the collective populace. In other words, the purpose of an *uji-dera* was to promote the prosperity of the clan. Japanese Buddhism thus begins and continues as an eclectic mix of Buddhism and Shintoism.

Later in the Nara period, a branch of the Usa Hachiman Shrine was begun on the grounds of Todai-ji temple in connection with the creation of the Great Buddha. At the very beginning of the ninth century the Buddhist priest Saicho founded the temple of Enraku-ji on Mount Hiei near Kyoto and introduced the Tendai sect of Buddhism, while the priest Kukai (Kobo Daishi) returned from China and founded Kongobu-ji on Mount Koya in Wakayama Prefecture (819), the first monastic training center for the Shingon sect. Both paid the highest respects to the native gods residing in those mountains (namely, Hie Sanno Gongen and Jishu Koya Myojin).

The teachings of the Tendai and Shingon sects exerted an overwhelming influence during the Heian period (794–1185) and furthered the synthesis of Shintoism and Buddhism. The adoption of Shintoism into Buddhism was based on the premise of *honji suijaku* in that the manifestation of the prime Buddhist being was said to be incarnated in the form of various Japanese gods. Simply put, in the early days Japanese gods were described as manifestations of the Buddha. Later, specific Nyorai and Bosatsu were made to correspond to specific gods.

OPPOSITE PAGE, TOP: The Hokke-do hall in Todai-ji temple, Nara, houses this clay Gakko Bosatsu.

OPPOSITE PAGE, LEFT CENTER: The dry-lacquer Fuku Kensaku Kannon is three meters in height. Hokke-do hall, Todai-ji.

OPPOSITE PAGE, BOTTOM: The clay Gekko Bosatsu is part of the permanent collection at Hokke-do hall in Todai-ji. The Gakko and Gekko Bosatsu are said to have been moved from one of the other halls located on the temple grounds.

OPPOSITE PAGE, CENTER: The altar of the Fuku Kensaku Kannon inside Hokke-do hall at Todai-ji.

ABOVE: The Kasuga Shika Mandala is a bronze statue of a deer carrying a mandala on its back. The deer (shika) who graze at Kasuga Taisha Shrine in Nara have been regarded as divine since ancient times.

ABOVE: The Kashimadachi Shinei-zu is an early painted mandala, dating from the Muromachi period (1333–1568).

Buddhist art in the Heian period began at the time the Shingon sect was introduced by Kukai. One characteristic of the Buddhist images of this time was the restricted use of available materials. Bronze and clay came to be used less and less. Dry lacquer, although it still existed, also began to be rarely seen. Wood alone came to be used for almost all Buddhist statues. Many explanatory theories hold that bronze became scarce after so much of it was used in the casting of the Great Buddha of Todai-ji in Nara, while clay became unpopular because it is extremely fragile and lacks durability. However, dry-lacquer images were light and sturdy and their surfaces were easier to carve than wood. There must have been quite compelling reasons for forgoing dry lacquer in favor of wood. What could they have been?

Both Kukai and Saicho made use of local mountainside worship sites to begin the establishment of Buddhist temples. As explained earlier, Shinto gods often dwelled in trees. To the degree that a synthesis of Shintoism and Buddhism already existed, the belief that certain trees were also sacred representations of gods must have been accepted. Therefore, the custom of making Buddhist statues out of the dwellings of gods might have been initiated at that time and come to be widely practiced. The expectation that Shinto materials rendered in Buddhist style would strengthen the omnipotence of the gods and the Buddha is in keeping with the fundamental concepts accompanying the synthesis of Shintoism and Buddhism.

The style of Buddhist images of the first half of the Heian period differs from that of the Nara-period or the Fujiwara-era (late ninth century to 1185) Buddhist images. If we look at the early Heian-period Nyorai and Bosatsu statues, we can see that while their bodies are bulky, most of their distinctive characteristics are concentrated on their heads. For example, the Yakushi Nyorai and the Kokuzo Bosatsu seated figure (painted wood, ninth century) found in Jingo-ji temple in the northwest sector of Kyoto are typical cases. The Nyorai has wavy hair, while the Bosatsu wears a high crown. Both have finely chiseled faces and impressive, massive heads. Their hairlines are low across their narrow foreheads and the eyebrows are large arcs across the bridge of the nose. The long eyes are not wide open but are narrow and piercing; the viewer feels their fixed gaze. Lips are carved clearly with a deeply curving upper lip that creates a sensual effect. The seated Miroku Bosatsu at Todai-ji (carved

from one piece of wood in the ninth century) has features that are even more emphatic than the features on the figures at Jingo-ji. The whole of the head juts forward and the face wears a vigorous, powerful gaze.

These were the only instances in which Japanese Buddhist sculptures in the images of Nyorai and Bosatsu exhibited such graphic physicality. These Buddhist images are not there to meditate or to listen to appeals but to confront monks. Although they may not actually pass judgment, they order, make demands, correct wrongdoing, and see through lies. The fervor of their restlessness naturally permeates the space. The basis of their demands is Buddhistic training, a phased approach to the cosmic order centering on the Dainichi Nyorai (or rather, originating from Dainichi, the Great Sun Buddha) and has nothing to do with internal tranquillity or benevolence to others. If the facial expressions of Buddhist statues were meant to reflect attitudes such as tranquillity and the like, the statues would not have been created with such calm eyes.

Buddhist statues in the Heian period had distinctive characteristics not only in style but also in shape. First, the worship of the Kannon, personification of eternal compassion, was popular throughout the Heian period, and the number of figures of the Senju Kannon (Thousand-arm Kannon) was greater than those of the Juichimen Kannon (Eleven-faced Kannon), which were prevalent throughout the Nara period. The "thousand arms" was not meant literally, but each arm of the figure held an object with which a person could be saved; there were as many different and concrete ways of salvation as there were arms. This practice appears similar to the manner in which the early Japanese gods had separate roles and functions in each of their respective areas. The Senju Kannon was popular during the Heian period because it was the image most reminiscent of the earlier forms seen in native, ritualistic worship. The practice of worshiping Kannon can therefore be seen as a form of religious eclecticism, a combination of Buddhism and Shintoism.

A second distinctive characteristic is that images belonging to a group of Myo-o (Kings

LEFT: *The complex, large mandala is known as the* Kumano Nachi Sankei Mandala *and dates from the end of the Muromachi period.*

of Light or Wisdom) were created in large number from the first half of the Heian period. In particular, the Fudo Myo-o (Acalantha, the Immovable One) became one of the most popular Buddhist images at that time. Myo-o were Indian gods who were adopted into Buddhism although they do not have much meaning when taken out of the context of Indian religions. A widely depicted figure in both sculpture and painting, Fudo Myo-o was the bearer of light and wisdom whose powers could be called forth through prayer. As a result, he became a popular household icon. Naturally, since they were rarely seen in China, images of the Fudo Myo-o were scarcely seen in Japan during the seventh and eighth centuries, the period in which Japan was imitating continental Buddhism. The reason for their appearance in the ninth century is thought to be that the history of the Shingon sect brought back from China by Kukai and the Lotus sutra of the Tendai sect were not deeply rooted in Japanese history. Thus, there was a strong inclination toward preserving the original Indian format even though there was no apparent connection to Japanese styles of worship.

There was a duality in Buddhist attitudes toward salvation and sin (sin being earthly desires). The notion that one could attain salvation in spite of having sinned depended on the benevolence of Buddha (represented by Kannon). On the other hand, one also could be saved by overcoming one's sins. This could be accomplished through the help of Fudo Myo-o. It is easy to understand that Kannon and Fudo Myo-o thus represented the two aspects of Buddhism providing adequate means of salvation. The influence of Kannon is one that works from top to bottom; this transition is well described in the many illustrated episodes of the Kannon appearing and mingling unrecognized in the human world. Fudo Myo-o has only one eye (his left eye is always closed) and a childlike face. He was not originally a superior being, but climbed from a lower status than humanity to a higher one. In short, Fudo Myo-o assists the common person's upward drive from bottom to top. The ascent is a process of ridding oneself of earthly desires (earthly desires being spiritual darkness, as emancipation is spiritual enlightenment). The Fudo Myo-o cuts off earthly desires with the sword in his right hand and the rope in his left hand. The fierce struggles he engages in are symbolized by his expression of indignation; a tooth on the left bites his lower lip, while

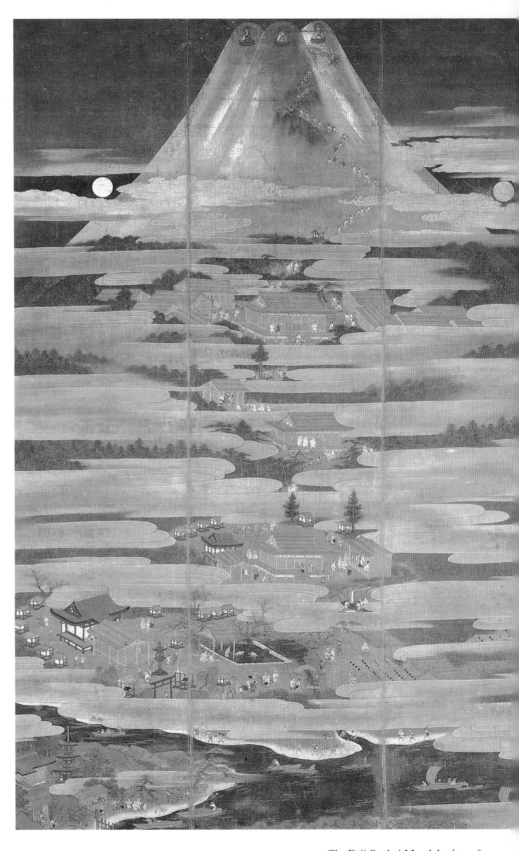

ABOVE: *The* Fuji Sankei Mandala *dates from the Muromachi period. This Sengen Jinja shrine is known for its worship of Mount Fuji. Fujisan Hongu, Sengen Jinja shrine, Fujinomiya City, Shizuoka Prefecture.*

one on the right bites into his upper lip. His powers were so extraordinary that no earthly evil could outdo him. The ultimate expression of his ferocity is the destructive force of the flames always blazing from his back and from behind his head.

The worship of fire for its purifying qualities is a tradition that existed long before Buddhism. It is difficult to determine whether Heian aristocrats worshiped Fudo Myo-o himself or the fire that erupts behind him. Further, with the addition of water into Buddhist rituals, the Shinto practice of purifying sins and other impurities, including a variety of evil spells, would be complete. The Shintoistic customs of standing in a waterfall followed by a fire-making ceremony, practices that are still seen today in contemporary Shinto shrines, apparently began and existed in accordance with the teachings of Fudo Myo-o.

The mandala is another unique art form that was imported along with esoteric Buddhism, in which the central Buddha is Dainichi Nyorai. The two aspects of the Dainichi mandala are the realms of Taizo (dynamic enlightenment) and Kongo (wisdom), which are represented in mandalas. Both realms of understanding place the Dainichi at their center and depict the Nyorai, Bosatsu, Myo-o, and Tembu (heavenly beings) Buddhistic deities as incarnations of Dainichi. Taizo mandalas consist of a central square surrounded by many smaller squares that gradually increase in size. The boundaries of the mandalas are filled with many Buddhist images and their related objects. In the middle square there is an eight-petaled lotus, and in its center Dainichi is seated with a different Buddha placed in each one of the eight petals.

The Kongo mandala is divided into nine squares with a large circle in the top center square where the seated image of Dainichi is placed. Each of the remaining eight squares also has a large circle drawn in it. Straight lines divide the circles evenly into nine sections and a small circle appears in each of the nine sections and on the four corners outside the large circle. Thus, the total number of small circles in each of the eight squares is thirteen, and one or four Buddhas are arranged in each of the small circles. These form highly abstract, geometrical arrangements.

The mandala represents a mystical metaphysics that encompasses all existence in the universe and reduces it to a uniform and abstract order based on a fundamental principle of extreme enlightenment. The mandala's allusion to inclusiveness, abstractness, and the fundamental principle of enlightenment sharply contrasts with a system of worship oriented toward practical profit and accepting of many gods. Here there was no allowance for an eclectic mix of Shintoism and Buddhism, thus there appeared to be no possibility of the mandala itself becoming popularized beyond esoteric Buddhist temples.

However, when the philosophy of Dainichi (incarnated as the various Buddhas) was embraced, it was thought that the Buddha could be replaced by gods. This was the *suijaku* (incarnation) theory proposed by esoteric Buddhism. After the *suijaku* theory became popular at the end of the Heian period, the *suijaku-ga* mandala appeared in numerous works during the Kamakura (1185–1333) and Muromachi (1333–1568) periods. Some of them depicted arrangements of *honji* (original Indian) Buddhas (the Sanno Honji mandala at the Nezu Art Museum in Tokyo is one), while others depicted *honji* Buddhas along with *suijaku* gods in the mountains (the Kumano Honji mandala at Shogo-in in Kyoto). One is of a Shinto shrine that had a picture of Buddha hanging under its eaves (the Sannogu mandala at the Yamato Bunka-kan [Yamato Culture Center] in Nara), while another depicted a *honji* Buddha floating over a mountain forest behind a Shinto shrine (the Kasuga mandala at Kasuga Shrine in Nara). Common to all of these mandalas is the total absence of partitions. They simply depict specific shrines, paying particular attention to the concrete images of Buddhas, gods, or divine beings, and disregard the relationships among objects. There was no interest in a specific world order represented in the mandalas, but a deep interest in concrete and individual objects was shown. Moreover, orientation toward the fundamental principles of thought was not displayed in these works. The visual world dominated. Apparently, it was not the all-inclusiveness of abstract metaphysics but the beautification of concrete perceptual distinctions that was of interest here. The term "mandala" probably remained because the development of the *honji suijaku* theory began with the Shingon sect of Buddhism. It is also probable that the nature of the contents of the mandala changed because the world of the original Shingon mandala was fundamentally different from the world of Shintoism and a certain amount of loyalty to Shinto beliefs continued to exist.

ABOVE: *The portrait of Koya Myojin dates from the Kamakura period. The characters above the image suggest that Myojin is a* suijaku *(incarnation of a god) of Dainichi Nyorai. Kongobu-ji Buddhist temple complex, Wakayama Prefecture.*

In China, the worship of the Buddha of Boundless Light, called Amida in Japan, first became popular toward the end of the sixth century during the Sui dynasty (581–618). In Japan, however, the worship of Amida did not become widespread until much later, during the latter half of the eighth century.

One of the beliefs of the Jodo sect of Amida worshipers was that the only way one could be reborn in Jodo paradise was through the power of Amida. The Jodo sect held that paradise could be reached through chanting *nenbutsu (Namu Amida Butsu,* I

From This World to the Pure Land

ABOVE: Yasunori Eri, a master Buddhist sculptor living in Kyoto, is shown working on a prototype of a clay sculpture of the contemporary Zen master Mumon Yamada.

OPPOSITE PAGE: A statue of Basu-sennin, 156 cm in height, from the thirteenth century. Sanjusangen-do, Kyoto.

take my refuge in the Amida Buddha) invocations of the Buddha. The practice also entailed chanting Amida's name, praying to Amida, and seeing the image of Amida with the mind's eye. It was thought that in order to be met by Amida at death, believers must perform both invocations and meditation.

These doctrines of the Jodo sect, having descended from the previously established Tendai sect, began to exert an overwhelming influence on Heian Buddhism in the tenth century, when the spiritual leaders Ryogen (912–85) and his student Genshin (942–1017) came to prominence. When Ryogen authored the *Gokuraku Jodo Kubon Ojogi* he placed equal emphasis on Buddhist invocations of Amida and on other forms of training. The writings of Genshin, however, placed greater emphasis on Buddhist invocations than on other forms of training, and his *Ojoyoshu (The Essentials of Pure Land Rebirth,* 985), is said to have exerted a stronger influence on Heian aristocratic culture than any other work of the period. In the *Ojoyoshu,* Genshin describes scenes of the Jodo sect's version of paradise and hell in vivid detail. The world, *edo* (impure land), is described as a world of sensual desire from which the believer must escape in order to pursue Jodo or risk falling into hell.

The pictorial expressions of the Jodo sect created during the Fujiwara era (late ninth century–1185) gave birth to paintings of the Pure Land of Amida. However, the greatest artistic influence of the time is said to have come from the tapestry known as the *Amida Jodohen,* or the *Taima Mandala,* that was brought to Japan at the end of the eighth century and is now at the Taima-dera temple in Nara Prefecture. Very few depictions of the descent of Amida remain to this day even in China, although it appears that they were being made for centuries. One of the earliest examples of such mandalas dates from the mid-eleventh century and is found at the Ho-odo (Amida hall) at Byodo-in temple in Kyoto.

The most highly formative expression of Jodo meditation was the Amida statue. Heian aristocrats, who were greatly influenced by the *Ojoyoshu* of Genshin, frequently created images of Amida that were then placed in meditation halls. The most representative of such aristocrats were Fujiwara no Michinaga and his son Yorimichi in the eleventh century. Michinaga established the temple Hojoji in 1019. Its Amida hall (Muryoju-in) houses nine Amida figures. (It is also interesting to note that Michinaga himself was later to die in that very hall.)

Yorimichi erected another Amida hall at the Byodo-in temple (1053) and placed there an image of a seated Amida created by Jocho (ca 1057). The extant Ho-odo, built facing a pond, is a two-story wooden structure with a central hall flanked by symmetrical wings. The delicate balance of its front view is composed of fine pillars, a narrow second floor, and large roofs with gracious, buoyant curves. Inside the central hall, ornamental patterns are drawn on the ceiling and pillars leading downward to images of Amida welcoming his believers. An exquisite canopy hangs above the main figure of the Amida, who is seated squarely on the central dais. The entire arrangement is an intense expression of Yorimichi's vision of an otherworldly paradise.

In short, the architecture, sculpture, and paintings created by the Jodo sect of Fujiwara-period aristocratic society up to the eleventh century centered on splendid imagery of Amida and the Pure Land. The teachings of the Jodo sect were brought from China to the inner circle of the Tendai sect at Mount Hiei and developed from there. As these teachings further permeated Heian-period aristocratic society, the Jodo sect became increasingly aestheticized and took on

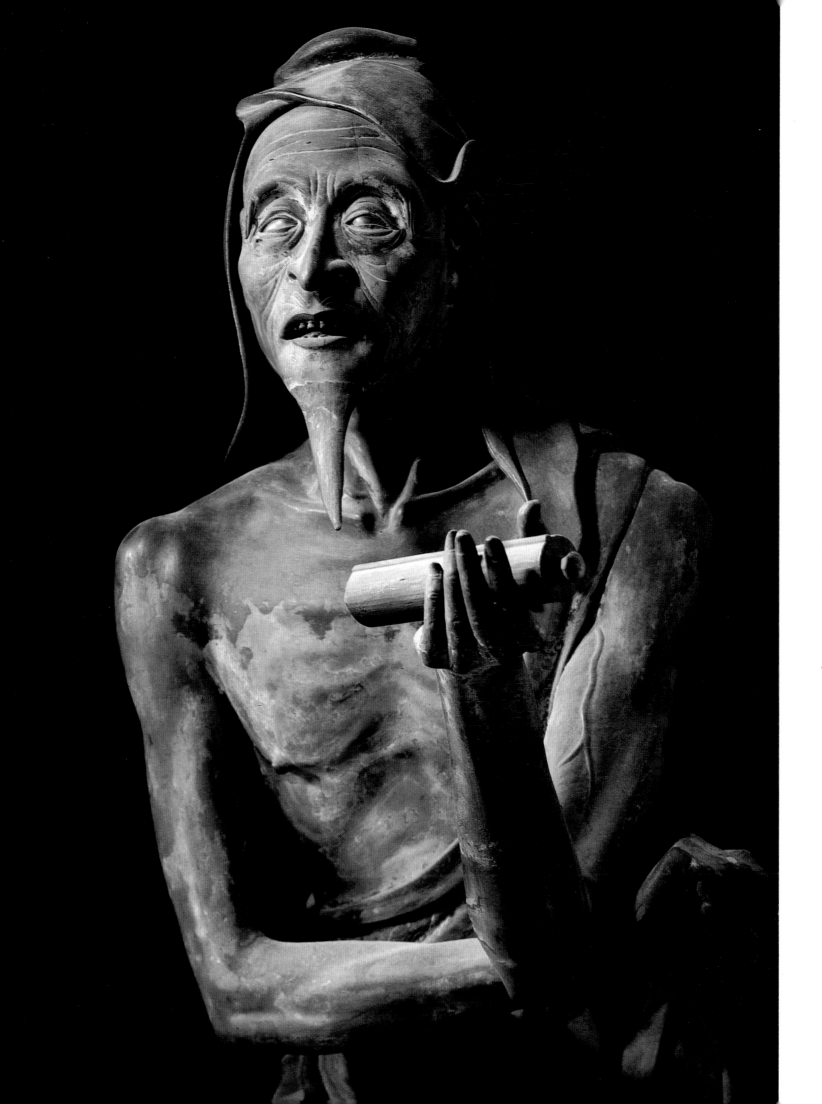

more of a Japanese sense, essentially becoming Japanized.

It is interesting to contrast the images of the Jodo sect with those of the Tantric Buddhism of the early Heian period (794–1185). For example, the Yakushi Nyorai statues, dating from the end of the ninth century and in place at the Golden Hall of the Jingo-ji temple in Kyoto, have substantial mass, their muscular bodies bulging from their roughly carved clothing. The eyes of the Nyorai are piercing and their lips are full and sensual. In contrast, the seated Amida of the Byodo-in in Kyoto, dating from the mid-eleventh century, has a calm face and gentle eyes. Its body is covered by the delicate folds of its thin robe that is treated not as something to represent the lines of the body but as an entity in itself. As such, it is fashioned in a delicate and beautiful manner and displays little of the sensuality seen in the Jingo-ji Nyorai. The spirituality of the images of the Asuka period in Nara, the realism of the Tempyo era (729–749), the transcendence of sensuality in the Heian period, and the idealization of everyday life found in images of the Fujiwara era reflect the changes in Japanese imagery from the end of the seventh century on.

It should be noted that great political and economic upheaval occurred toward the end of the Heian period from the late eleventh century into the twelfth century. From the latter half of the twelfth century, central power struggles often escalated into armed conflicts. In Kyoto, law and order had deteriorated to such an extent that it was dangerous to go out at night without a weapon. Compounded by outbreaks of major fires and the onset of famine in the region, the collapse of the Heian regime became simply a matter of time.

The final collapse of the Heian court in 1185 was epitomized by the Buddhist term *mappo no yo* (the latter days of the law). After the death of the Buddha, there were three periods: *shoho, zoho,* and *mappo.* The *shoho* period is marked by *kyo* (teachings), *gyo* (asceticism), and *sho* (nirvana). The *zoho* period is composed of teachings and asceticism, but nirvana cannot be attained. In the chaotic stage of *mappo,* the teachings of Buddha are all that remain. It is a time of complete chaos and, as such, little can be

expected. Still, life must go on, and one must resort to every available means to survive. Some of those, such as stealing and killing, were clear transgressions of Buddhistic commandments. We can well imagine that the fear of hell could only have been more pronounced in such an environment. Thus, the art of the Jodo sect from the latter half of the twelfth to the thirteenth century emphasized this anxiety and fear of hell on the one hand and the strong wish for the advent of Amida on the other.

Three important scrolls were produced at the end of the twelfth century, namely the *Jigoku-zoshi Emaki, Yamai no soshi Emaki,* and *Gaki-zoshi Emaki.* In the mid-thirteenth century, the fifteen-piece set *Rokudo-e* made at the Shojuraiko-ji temple in Shiga Prefecture described the Human Road and the Hell Road. The paintings of the Human Road, or *Yamai no soshi,* depicted the sorrows and hideousness of humanity in great detail. The Hell Road, or *Jigoku-zoshi,* showed monsters and bizarre manifestations engaged in every conceivable atrocity. However, the human being who has fallen to hell is clearly portrayed as the victim. Interestingly enough,

the images in both roads are almost the same in terms of their depiction of human agony and hideousness. It appears that both were drawn to serve as a pictorial "lesson." Those who viewed the frightening scrolls would probably become even more afraid of hell and would thus worship Amida more fervently.

Regardless of their didactic purposes, the painters who drew scenes from hell or something close to hell had three characteristics in common: first, they did not share the values of Heian aristocrats, who pursued a luxurious and sensuous existence; second, they were keen observers of the reality of society in and out of the court, even in its extremes of suffering; and, third, they were quite technically adept at drawing what they so keenly observed.

Therefore, depictions of hell, *jigoku-e,* did not appear merely because the reality of the time was hellish. In fact, while the Fujiwara clan was in power, *edo* was not to be painted; its existence was to be expressly ignored. What in fact probably happened was that depictions of *edo* began to appear as people increasingly lost hope that those in power

ABOVE LEFT: *This work is believed to have been painted by Kano Motonobu as part of volume five of the* Seiryo-ji Engi *(1515). Seiryo-ji temple, Kyoto.*

ABOVE RIGHT: *A Shaka Nyorai standing statue, 160 cm in height, ca 985. Seiryo-ji, Kyoto.*

FOLLOWING PAGES: *Statues of the Sentai Senju Kannon Bosatsu, 165–168.5 cm in height, dating from the Kamakura period. Sanjusangen-do, Kyoto.*

ter half of the twelfth century to the thirteenth century, when *mappo* views were most prevalent, include the *Yamagoe Amida* (Passing over the hill Amida) and the *Haya Raigo Amida* (Early descent of Amida). In the former, an enormous Amida emerges at close range as a luminous figure half-visible from behind mountains, as if he were a rising moon. In some instances, several saints are arranged on the sides of the mountains. The *Yamagoe Amida* dating from the thirteenth century and found at the Zenrin-ji temple in Kyoto is a typical example of this style of depiction.

The most representative of the latter style, that of *Haya Raigo,* is the *Amida Nijugo Bosatsu Raigo-zu* (Twenty-five bosatsu and descending Amida) from the thirteenth century. Here, Amida and a party of saints are supported by a white cloud. Having already come over the ridges, they sweep down from the top left of the picture toward a man at the bottom right who has his hands clasped in prayer. Amida is shown standing, and although he might not actually be dramatically cutting through the skies as heavy winds do, the velocity of his movement is expressed in the angle of his descent and in the shape of the cloud trailing behind him as he swiftly approaches the man. Such a death scene can be seen elsewhere and was often painted during the thirteenth century along with versions of the *Yamagoe Amida.* Since none of these works remain in China, these may be regarded as Japanized versions of Chinese *Raigo-zu.* In short, the *Raigo-zu* created in Japan became more dynamic and dramatic than their Chinese predecessors owing to the social and political changes occurring in Japan at the time.

Another style of painting that has no precedent in China and no remaining examples today is that of *Niga Byakudo-zu* (Two rivers and a white road). A river of raging waves and a river of fire are placed between this world (bottom of the picture) and the paradise of Jodo (top). One can reach the other side by following the white road symbolizing the ascetic practices of the Jodo sect. Such paintings were most likely produced as a means of indoctrination into the sect.

In short, we can surmise that the imagery of the *mappo* period of strife strengthened people's interest in Jodo and in turn promoted the Jodo sect. The first result was that the tenets of the sect themselves were promoted. Secondly, contact with the general public changed the Jodo sect itself. Genku (1133–1212), a Tendai sect monk who lived at Mount Hiei, chanted from the treatise

ABOVE: A statue of Fujin, the god of wind, is paired with the statue of Raijin, the god of thunder (OPPOSITE PAGE, LEFT).

could bring stability to the world. Thus, if hell—which was invisible up to that point—became visible, then the perception of paradise or Jodo must also necessarily change. As a result, the paradise of the Jodo sect was no longer thought of as an extension of this world. Rather, it became something diametrically opposed to it, and since jumping from one world to the other is difficult if not impossible without the help of Amida, the appearance of Amida came to be fervently desired.

In the typical eleventh-century depiction of Amida descending to this world, the viewer can observe a quiet emergence in which he is seated squarely faced by Buddhist saints. By contrast, the typical *Raigo-zu* of the lat-

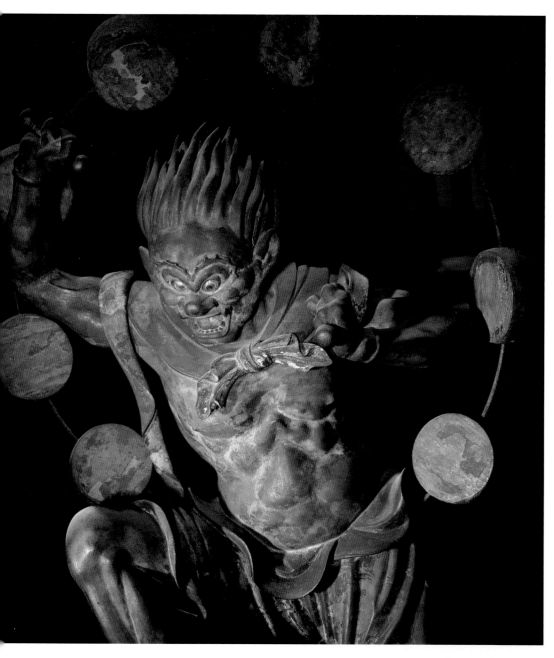

Senchaku Hongan Nenbutsu (The Selection of the Nenbutsu of the Original Vow) and ultimately left the mountain to live within the city of Kyoto. His name was changed to Honen Shonin, and attaining Jodo paradise after death became his ultimate purpose in life.

THE REDISCOVERY OF THE FAR SHORE

If one follows the argument of the *Senchaku Hongan Nenbutsu* of 1198, it appears that Amida made certain choices in determining the components of his religious world view. However, the original vow and the choices made by Amida as set forth in

this document must have been a reflection of the fundamental desires of the author himself. With this understanding, we must ask ourselves what it was that Honen chose.

First, he chose the Jodo sect's version of a western paradise as his ultimate goal from among the many Mahayana Buddhist Jodo versions. This meant, in effect, that he was choosing a paradise located in the west out of many other versions of paradise. In addition, to choose a particular sect essentially meant to choose a fundamental Buddhist sutra. Therefore, he chose the three sutras of Amida over many other sutras, particularly over the Hokke sutra.

Second, the chant he chose out of many other forms was the holy invocation *shomyo nenbutsu*, embodying the belief that by concentrating on chanting alone and thereby paying homage to the Amida Buddha, one could achieve salvation. This chant was based on the principle of "casting off difficulties and choosing easiness," an aspect that is further reflected in the third choice, which was that of inviting the common people to join the sect, thereby enabling them to attain paradise as converted believers.

The tenets of Genshin's Jodo sect permeated aristocratic society, which came to Mount Hiei to worship. Honen, however,

ABOVE: *A statue of Priest Chogen, 82 cm in height, from the thirteenth century. Todai-ji temple, Nara.*

LEFT: *A eleven-faced Kannon, 177 cm in height, from the Heian period. Kogen-ji temple, Shiga.*

left Mount Hiei precisely because he wished to be with the common people. This desire was also behind the selection of the easy chant. His reason for making this particular selection did not end there.

Choosing to reach the common people instead of the aristocracy of Mount Hiei meant that Honen essentially chose individual internal faith over the collective group and its traditions. The Tendai sect and aristocratic society were extremely closed to the outside world and were organized according to their own internal class structure. Therefore, when Honen said that he would enable the common people to pass to heaven equally, it was his intention for this equality to be among individuals, rather than among groups. The common people are a group of individuals who are equal when they pass away and are not, in any real sense, an organized group. So while tradition belongs to groups, faith can belong to an individual. This third choice, the individualization of faith, made the possibility of salvation available to the common man.

Such choices were not made in a chrono-

logical or logical order. Rather, they appear to have been made concurrently and simultaneously. Honen's "choices" came down to individual internal subjectivism, a subjectivism that can be generalized to the relationship of the believer to an absolute transcendent Amida. That relationship marked a decisive change in Japanese Buddhism. Thus, it can be said that the subsequent version of Buddhism emerging during the Kamakura period (1185–1333) that followed was created by Honen when he became conscious of his choices and the position he was put in by having made them.

His way of thinking was as far from the eclecticism of Shintoism and Buddhism as possible. It was also by far the most overtly critical statement against tradition made at the time. Indeed, his position was in sharp contrast to the perceptions revealed in artistic expressions and images then being made. Meditation gave rise to statues of members of the Jodo sect and of Amida, but *shomyo* (chanting Amida's name) was purely vocal, lacking tangible form. As there was no direct expression for *senshu nenbutsu* (invocation), the six kanji characters used in the phrase *Namu Amida Butsu* came to be the principal image of worship; the name of Amida began to appear rather than his image. There also were some eight- or ten-character versions, but in all cases, the characters were symmetrically arranged in a straight line with a lotus-flower pedestal painted below them.

Images and paintings of Buddha did not completely disappear; the *Raigo-zu* described earlier were painted frequently in Honen and Shinran's time. Disciples of Honen and Shinran (founder of the Jodo Shinshu sect of Buddhism, 1173–1262) repeatedly created statues of the founders and *e-den* (pictured legends) depicting their lives and missionary work. One of the images of the founders is the seated figure of Zendo (613–681) done in wood mosaic with jade eyes (at Raigo-ji in Nara, dating from the early thirteenth century). Zendo is shown chanting the *nenbutsu* with his left knee raised and his hands clasped in prayer. The founder's strong

LEFT and ABOVE (DETAIL): The Kusoshi Emaki *picture scroll from the middle Kamakura period. The* Kuso, *or nine phases, represent the process by which the human body decomposes.*

will and personality are apparent in his accentuated bone structure and sharp expression.

Images of both Honen and Shinran were also made in the form of seated wooden figures. For example, a seated figure of Priest Honen (thirteenth century, Taima-dera temple in Nara Prefecture) is shown with slightly closed eyes and with his hands gripping prayer beads. The figure of Priest Shinran in a sitting position (thirteenth century, Saisho-ji, Niigata Prefecture) is stylistically similar. Neither figure has as strong an individualistic expression as the earlier figure of Zendo.

Some paintings nonetheless depict the founders with quite individualistic expressions. The most outstanding example is the portrait kept at Nishi Hongan-ji temple in Kyoto called *Kagami no miei* (Mirror portrait), painted in *sumi* on paper by Sen Amidabutsu, the son of Fujiwara no Nobuzane. Here, the figure is standing, looking to the right at an angle, holding prayer beads in both hands. The robe covers the figure from the tip of its head to its toes. Folds on the sleeves flow down from the shoulders, with the rims on the bottom of the robe drawn in simple, thick ink lines of deep and light shades. The robe vividly reveals the posture and well-built body within it. In contrast, the face is drawn in fine lines that vibrantly capture the fleeting expression of firm, inner conviction. Details such as thick eyebrows, tense lips, and sunken cheekbones emphasize the effect. In short, this masterpiece is representative of Kamakura realism at its height.

The *e-den* depictions of the great founders

include *Honen Shonin E-den* (volume 48 of *Honen Shonin Gyojo Ezu,* Chion-in temple, Kyoto) from the fourteenth century and the *Shinran Shonin E-den* (Nishi Hongan-ji temple, Kyoto). The creation of the former, in particular, involved many painters and is said to have been completed in the mid-fourteenth century only after scenes were added over several decades. Aside from its considerable artistic merit, it is highly valuable as a historical reference that describes the contemporary culture of the era.

The quality of painting is particularly high in the *Ippen Shonin E-den* (volume 12 of the *Ippen Hijiri-e,* ca 1299, Kanko-ji temple, Kyoto) that begins with Priest Ippen's birth, describes his ascetic practices in Shikoku and Kyushu, follows his trails of missionary work throughout the island of Honshu, and ends with his death in Hyogo Prefecture. It offers a vivid depiction of men and women who traveled and lived in nature—in the mountains, trees, fields and rice paddies, rivers, and at sea. It also shows the structure of Shinto shrines and Buddhist temples, as well as describing various classes of people, including aristocrats, samurai warriors, Buddhist monks, hunters, fishermen, and traveling entertainers. Healers and members of the merchant and lower classes were also pictured.

The perspective is one of looking down from above at an angle. The relationship between humans and the surrounding environment is portrayed clearly. The observa-

ABOVE: *The* Amida Shoju Raigo-zu *from the latter half of the twelfth century. Juhachikan-in, Wakayama Prefecture. Page 83*

tions are keen, the touch of the brush exquisite and precise, and the overall descriptive effect of these sketches of groups of people is quite superior, whether taken as landscape paintings or as records of the architecture and culture of the times.

These works are different from the *Shigizan Emaki* scroll painting created earlier in the late twelfth century, insofar as individuals are not depicted with exaggerated facial features or postures. The colors used here are deeper, and the descriptions of nature in the background are much more graphic. They are also stylistically different from the portrayal of women in the *Genji Monogatari Emaki* (Scroll painting of *The Tale of Genji*) in that they are far less ornamental and employ a dynamic, powerful use of line. The extensive background scenery, along with the variety in the classes of people shown, not only makes *Ippen Shonin E-den* a significant accomplishment, but also marks the creation of a unique style that began at the end of the Heian period and continued into the Kamakura period.

When speaking of the various sects of Buddhism that arose during the Kamakura calligraphy done by Zen monks. These works, called *bokuseki,* are configurations of basic words related to satori. Since neither chanting Amida's name nor attainment of satori has a corresponding pictorial representation, if any visual expression is to be made, there is no choice but to resort to the representation of Chinese characters.

散二心チヒルカヘシ
瞋二河ノ譬喩ヲトキ
顔ノ信心守護セシム

period, it can be said that the Jodo Shinshu sect (New Jodo sect) emerged from within, while Zen sects founded by Eisai (1141–1215), known as the Rinzai sect, and that founded by Dogen (1200–53), known as the Sodo sect, actually originated outside. However, Zen satori is a completely individual salvation, as preached in the work entitled *Shobo Genzo* by Dogen, teaching that going beyond life and death is an absolute salvation transcending both history and society. We can see that the Jodo Shinshu sect and early Zen sects shared certain fundamental characteristics in terms of individualization and internalization of faith and transcendence. Thus, the art created by both of these sects shares common features.

One is that the use of Amida's name in the Jodo Shinshu sect appears in many works of

Many of the *bokuseki* are viewed as unconventional both in China and in Japan. Chinese custom does not hold *bokuseki* in as high regard as does Japanese tradition, which pays great respect to them, as we will see later in the chapter beginning on page 94.

Another common feature is that Zen temples originally did not house Buddhist images or paintings, but rather held portraits of founders or distinguished monks that stylistically correspond to the founders' images created by artists who were also members of the Jodo Shinshu sect. Such paintings include the *Rankei Doryu Zo* (Kencho-ji temple, Kamakura) from the Kamakura period, and the *Ikkyu Osho Zo* (National Museum of Tokyo) from the Muromachi period, supposedly painted by Bokusai. The former is painted on silk in a single ink tone and

ABOVE LEFT: *The* Niga Byakudo-zu *depicts desperate travelers receiving light as they make progess in their journey, spurred on by their belief in Amida.*

ABOVE RIGHT: *A portrait of Priest Zendo from the early Muromachi period. The figures seen emerging from the priest's mouth represent the six kanji characters for writing the Buddhist chant* Namu Amida Butsu.

depicts a typical monk seated in a priest's chair with a stick held in his right hand, looking ahead from a slight left angle. The latter shows only the bust turned slightly to the left and looking straight ahead from an angle. Both of the paintings fully capture the subjects' subtle, fleeting expressions; a striking individuality is reflected in their faces.

Among the sculptures of the Kamakura period, the figure of Butsu Zenshi (Hokoku-ji, Aichi Prefecture) seated squarely on a priest's chair is outstanding. His strong body, the staff held in his right hand, his firm lips, and his piercing eyes reveal a work of unparalleled power. Although there were these common features, great differences in artistic expression began to emerge between the Jodo Shinshu and Zen Buddhist sects. One such difference can be attributed to the fact that the Jodo Shinshu sect contributed little to the development of architectural styles, whereas Zen Buddhism introduced a new architectural style to the previously conceived structure of Buddhist temples. Among the elements it introduced were the symmetrical arrangement of buildings including the gate and Buddhist sanctum on the central axis, the addition of dirt floor of the abbot's square chambers, and the appearance of the steep roofs.

Another difference was the absence of a Zen counterpart to the *e-den* made by the founders of the Shinshu sect. The reason was that the traveling monks verbally spread their beliefs among common people, who continued the trend.

Contact between the members of the Zen sect and the common people was extremely limited. The tenets of the Zen sect promoted "self-salvation" in contrast to the tenets of the Jodo Shinshu sect, which espoused "salvation by faith in Amida's power." Further, Zen emphasized "rigorous ascetic practices" rather than the "easy practice" found in Jodo Shinshu. Major Zen temples were sometimes supported by the ruling samurai class, but were not very successful in garnering the support of the common people.

KAMAKURA REALISM

Zen Buddhism contributed many elements to the art of the Kamakura period, although some of the arts were influenced more than others. At about the same time, a style of sculpture known as the new Kamakura realism emerged, although many of the sculptors working in the new style were associated with the old Buddhism. For example, many

existing masterpieces of Unkei (ca 1223), a representative Buddhist sculptor of the early Kamakura period, are housed at the Todai-ji and Kofuku-ji temples which are located in Nara and which were founded in the Nara and Heian periods. Why is this so?

Naturally, the leaders of the new Buddhism of the Kamakura period could not establish large temple-based organizations because they were variously denied the priesthood (as in the case of Shinran), condemned to exile (as was Nichiren, 1222–82), or in self-imposed exile in a remote area (as was Dogen). Thus, one of the main reasons this group of sculptors remained associated with the old Buddhism was that shortly after Minamoto no Yoritomo established the Kamakura shogunate, he undertook to rebuild structures that had been destroyed or had fallen into disrepair in the wars at the end of the Heian period. The reconstruction of old Buddhist temples provided a venue for the activities of the innovative Buddhist sculptors of the southern capital of Nara: Kokei, Unkei, and Kaikei (ca 1183-1236).

Art cannot be called innovative unless in some sense it repudiates the artistic styles of the preceding period. Further, a new form is not considered truly artistic unless it has some relationship with the classical arts of the preceding period as well. Generally speaking, innovation in style rejects the prevalent style and exhibits an affinity with the styles of earlier generations. In this respect, the sculpture of the Kamakura period was innovative; the new Buddhist sculptors showed a strong tendency to revive the Tempyo style of the years between 729 and 749. Thus, the new Kamakura realism can be seen as "innovative revivalism."

Most Buddhist statues of the Kamakura period were made of wood, although some are of metal in keeping with the tradition of the Heian period. Woodcarving techniques saw great advances at the time, including the use of mosaic. Throughout the Heian period, the Kamakura sculptors must have been able to take advantage of such techniques in order to utilize wood as freely as if it were dry lacquer or clay. They must have reasoned that if the subtle expressions and curves in the figures of Buddhist images from the seventh and eighth centuries could be reproduced in wood, they would be much more sturdy and durable than their predecessors.

Such technical sophistication underwent further development from the end of the Heian period to the early Kamakura period. This advance is apparent in the sharper edges of the carved folds of the garments, in the fine detail of the fingers, and in the newly introduced element of eyes made of polished jade. Jade eyes emitted a variety of expressions and were extremely effective in simulating piercing gazes and stares. Thus, Japanese woodcarving techniques of the period were of the highest level in their handling of detail. Some examples include the gorgeous flowing lines of the robe of the

In reviving Tempyo-era Buddhist sculpture, the new sculptors sought to reproduce the three-dimensionality and idealization of the human form. In doing so, emphasis shifted from a frontal view to a more three-dimensional view, and from thin, stationary forms to ones that were more voluptuous and more flexible. There was also a move away from using concealing robes toward

Miroku Bosatsu by Kaikei (1192, Daigo-ji temple, Kyoto), the fine detailing of the hands of Unkei's Miroku (1208, Kofuku-ji), and the expression of the eyes of Bishamonten by Tankei (thirteenth century). Such finely rendered physical details cannot easily be separated from the development of woodcarving technology as a whole. In short, they provide ample evidence of the expert technique for which Kamakura realism is now known.

displaying a delicate body line with more imaginatively rendered drapery.

Examining these works clearly shows that idealization of the human body differed according to the kind of Buddhist statue being created. For example, in images of Nyorai and Bosatsu, the goal of idealization was a calm, exquisite face and a full, flexible, and well-proportioned body. Examples of this type include the Yakushi Trinity at Yakushi-ji, in particular the guardians Nikko and

ABOVE (DETAIL) and OPPOSITE PAGE, LEFT: Calligraphic mandala of the six characters of Amida's name dating from the Kamakura period. Ryujo-ji temple, Nara. Each character depicts one of the six worlds of Amida. The character for butsu *(the Buddha) is shown in the detail.*

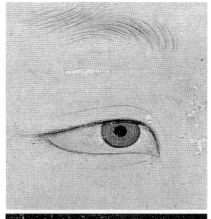

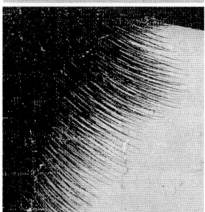

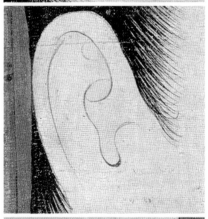

Gakko Bosatsu, and the guardians of the Amida Trinity by Unkei (ca 1189) at Joraku-ji temple in Kanagawa Prefecture. The hips are slightly twisted with the weight of the figure resting on one leg while the other leg is slightly bent. Three-dimensional mass is expressed in the splendid musculature, from the chest to the abdomen to the bulging thighs. This posture is flexible and full of variety; however, the position of the head facing directly forward assures the statue of a certain lack of dynamic movement. Thus, these figures are rendered in forms that are

raised. Their upper torsos are exposed, and the robes covering their lower torsos flow at an angle parallel to that of one leg posed in a stance of advancing but frozen motion.

The folds of the Devas' robes are not carved in fine detail, yet the enormous statues appear to be standing in a whirlwind with their movements captured by their flying robes. These standing statues, although modeled after the human figure, are transformed into super-beings that emit a feeling of power greater than that of human beings.

We can see that the major representative

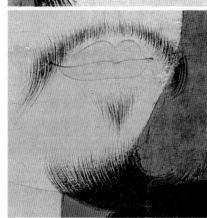

fundamentally still, elegant, and imbued with a sense of eternal calm. Despite the fact that they might resemble human figures in terms of bodily proportion and components, they express a certain transcendence of being, an existence totally free of sensual perceptions (embodied in the world of lust) and the vicissitudes of human emotion (embodied in the world of avarice).

However, the creator's purpose in depicting the muscular Deva Kings (Unkei and Kaikei, 1203) positioned at the Nandai-mon gate of Todai-ji temple was fundamentally to express their ferocious power. Here, the idealized body is one of perfectly defined muscles. These figures assume a menacing pose with large, glaring eyes and firm lips. Their legs are braced, their thick arms are

works of the new Kamakura sculpture, whether they be in the form of statues of Bosatsu or of Devas, had their origins in the human form. The sculptures of Bosatsu appear benevolent while the Devas appear menacing, because benevolence and menace have long been accepted as part of their nature.

From a philosophical point of view, human nature, will, and emotion are not momentarily or individually determined, but universal and absolute. Whatever individual differences exist in the expression of these natures is unavoidably removed by idealization. Bosatsu and Deva statues do have different faces, but it is because each sculptor had an individual image in mind during the process of creation. Subtle differences appear in the folds in the robes of the different

ABOVE: *Portrait of Ikkyu Osho by his disciple Bokusai from the latter half of the fifteenth century. National Museum of Tokyo.*

LEFT: *Self-portrait by Vincent van Gogh (1888) at the Fogg Museum of Harvard University. Van Gogh shaved his head and beard to portray himself as a Japanese Zen monk. Here, van Gogh's eyes bear a resemblance to Ikkyu's, as both paintings reflect an intense pursuit of discipline.*

OPPOSITE PAGE: *These portraits of Taira no Shigemori (right) and Minamoto no Yoritomo (left) are said to have been painted by Fujiwara no Takanobu in the latter half of the twelfth century. Jingo-ji temple, Kyoto. (Details appear on the left.)*

Bosatsu or in the fingers of the different Deva statues, but more apparent expressions of individuality can often be seen in sculptures and paintings that were also portraits.

Three changes that occurred during the Kamakura period of artistic realism are noteworthy. First, sculptures that were portraits of a particular person were made more frequently than during the previous periods. Second, models for such works began to become more diversified with the creation of images other than those of distinguished monks sitting facing squarely ahead. Third, changes in style promoted the depiction of fleeting expressions (diachronic peculiarity) in addition to expressions of individualism (simultaneous peculiarity).

In considering the first obvious change, it should be remembered that portraiture began in Japan long before the Kamakura period. If the expression of the individuality of models is realism, then the style of this period, when many portrait sculptures were made, can be called realism.

The second aspect of Kamakura realism concerned the depiction of common people rather than the depiction of the aristocratic class. The statues of Kuya (903–72) at Rokuharamitsu-ji in Kyoto and of Basu-sennin at Sanjusangen-do in Kyoto, often cited as being the most representative of the characteristics of this period, are neither idealized distinguished monks nor images of founders. Rather, Kuya is clad in rags and holds a cane topped by the antlers of a deer in his left hand. His right hand hits the cymbals on his

chest as he chants the *nenbutsu*. His eyes are closed lightly and a row of small characters representative of the phrase *Namu Amida Butsu* emerges from his mouth. His face is set in a trancelike stare. He is thin, his collarbone is clearly visible, and his posture reflects the weariness that results from a long journey. In short, the combination of the tired body and trancelike emotional state represents an archetypal itinerant saint portrayed in a superbly realistic manner.

The figure of Basu-sennin shows her clad in tattered robes. She is emaciated, her skin rendered in sagging lines. She is an old woman, yet her eyes are strangely piercing. Whether she is a true *sennin* (hermit wizard) is not entirely clear, but what is clear is the fact that she exists outside the class of urban aristocrats or the rural agricultural community as did the itinerant monks. Such individuals, who must have been in increasingly close contact with everyday people throughout the Heian period and later, had not been painted or sculpted prior to the late Heian or early Kamakura periods. Thus, we see again that Kamakura sculpture extended its scope of models to the common people. If the tendency to extend artistic focus beyond the ruling class and to describe the larger reality of society is realism, then this too is an aspect of Kamakura realism.

The third characteristic of the portrait sculpture of the Kamakura period lies in its pursuit of fleeting facial expressions in addition to other aspects signifying individuality. This tendency can be seen clearly in a comparison of the statues of the Buddhist priests Ganjin (687–763) and Chogen (1121–1206) found at the Shunjo-do hall of Todai-ji temple. Ganjin sits squarely with his eyes closed, his hands posed in a symbolic gesture. The finely detailed facial bones and strong, sturdy body seem to capture the characteristics of the model himself with the stillness of the meditating posture giving the figure an added dignity. Details such as the fine lines on the skin appear to have been abstracted and reduced. His ears are quite

OPPOSITE PAGE: Construction on the Notre Dame de Paris was finished in the early thirteenth century. Temples such as the Sanjusangen-do (pictured on pages 74–75) were being constructed during the same period in Japan.

BELOW: The Annunciation by Simone Martini (1333). Uffizi Gallery, Florence.

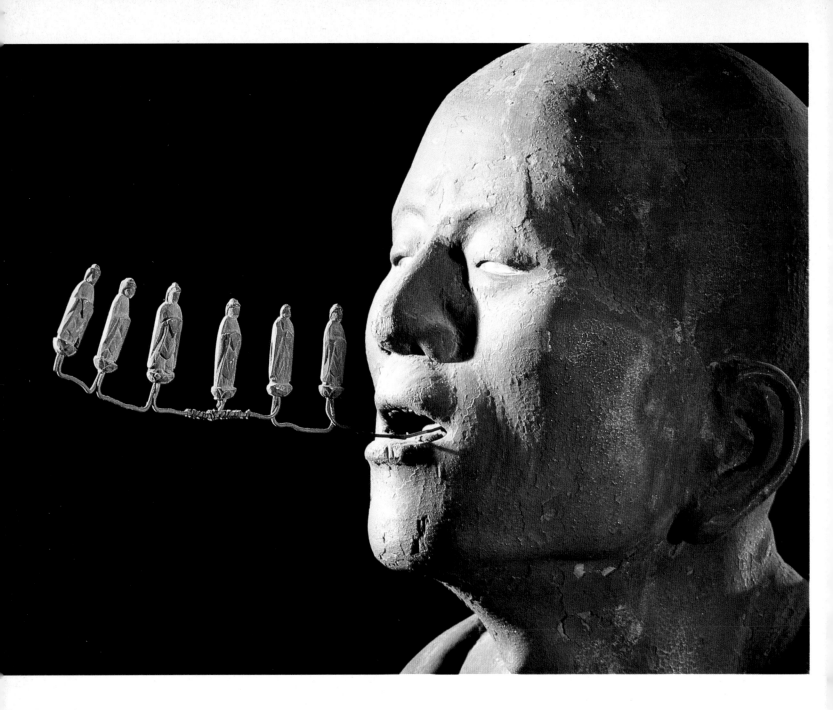

large, however, and it is here that the sculptor is clearly assimilating the familiar characteristics of the earlier statues of Buddha into the work.

In contrast, the bones and lines on Chogen's face—even the shape of his ear canals, his baggy eyelids, his sunken cheeks, the attenuated cords of his neck, and the raised veins—are all rendered in exquisite detail. Although his eyes are caught in a stare, it appears that in the next moment they could change. Both hands grasp beads and, thus, are not completely still.

The differences between the statues of Ganjin and Chogen can be attributed to the thorough rendering of details, a technical aspect of realism. Although both models are seated, it appears to the viewer that while

Ganjin will remain still forever, Chogen is caught in a fleeting stance—there is that much movement in his stillness!

Violent emotions are also captured, frozen in time, in the Buddhist sculptures of the period. For example, the statue of a *rakan* (believer in Buddhism) made of clay in the eighth century and housed in the pagoda at Horyu-ji, is shown screaming at the exact moment of the Buddha's passing. Individual emotions and the facial expressions that reflect them are mutable (diachronic peculiarity). However, the features portrayed in the statue of the priest Gien (ca 728) at Oka-dera temple are immutable, as expression of individuality is distinct and does not change with the flow of time (simultaneous peculiarity). These two peculiarities do not nec-

essarily coexist in art, yet both reflect individuality as opposed to universality. If the original intention of portrait sculpture was the pursuit of simultaneous peculiarity, then diachronic peculiarity would be the height of this pursuit. This was the stylistic characteristic of portrait sculpture of the Kamakura period, where a shift in styles occurred from the universal and the general to the more particular and individual.

The change occurred not only in sculpture but also in painting. As an example, let us consider the portrait of Priest Shinran, called the *Kagami no miei* (Mirror portrait), ca 1255, reportedly painted by Sen Amida-butsu. In this portrait, the face is drawn in great detail and superbly depicts individual features. The technique of creating details in the clothing and backgrounds used in order to attract attention to the face is also adopted in the portraits of Minamoto no Yoritomo and Taira no Shigemori (on silk, said to be painted by Fujiwara no Takanobu in the late twelfth or early thirteenth century). The background of the portraits is a subdued monochromatic plane, and the large, triangular-shaped black kimono is drawn in straight lines. At the apex of the triangular clothing is the face, drawn with a fine brush and adorned by a black headdress.

Each of the faces is turned slightly to the side; Yoritomo's to the left, showing the right side of his face, and Shigemori's to the right, showing the left side of his face. The eyes of both men are particularly vibrant, rendered in fine brush lines; Yoritomo's eyes are severe, while Shigemori's are soft and gentle. The thin mustaches, the hairlines, and the ears are quite similar in each portrait. However, although the fleeting expressions on the faces of both men are skillfully captured, there are no individual characteristics.

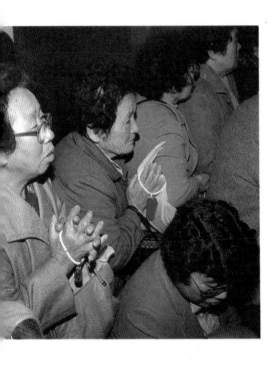

ABOVE and RIGHT: The annual ceremony of Ho-onko is held over an eight-day period from November 21 to 28 at the Higashi Hongan-ji temple in Kyoto. These days mark the anniversary of the death of the temple's founder, Priest Shinran. Worshipers come from near and far to pay their respects to the priest during this time.

Why were so many portrait sculptures and paintings made during the Kamakura period? The reason, in short, can be easily attributed to the collapse of Heian aristocratic society, which for four hundred years had been the major arbiter and creator of culture.

When the established order of the community collapses, three things inevitably occur. First, individuals must learn to rely on themselves and consequently bring ingenuity into play. Since there are many expressions of ingenuity among individuals, idiosyncratic differences will inevitably become more pronounced.

Second, with the decline of the aristocracy, local lords, farmers, samurai, hunters, fishermen, prostitutes, itinerant monks, and even thieves ceased to be objects of rule and emerged as subjects who could lay claim to themselves. Groups as "objects" do not have a face. However, common people as "subjects" have separate, individual but identifiable faces.

A third change was that the new Buddhism individualized faith. Buddhism had previously been an activity and practice of the community, but social conditions warranted a change that would adapt to issues of life and death. Such conditions were expressed in Kamakura Buddhism. The Jodo Shinshu and Nichiren sects did not yet possess large temples and lacked the economic capacity to employ Buddhist sculptors, but Zen temples that normally prohibited depictions of Buddha to be displayed within were able to commission the creation of founders' images. More than a few distinguished Zen priests were strong and individualistic, characteristics that generally appeared in their portraits and were further enhanced by the technical ingenuity of eyes carved of jade.

BELOW: On November 28, the last day of the Ho-onko ceremony, chanting is performed in the Miei-do hall at the Higashi Hongan-ji temple in Kyoto.

Images of Heaven and Earth

B rush paintings using *sumi* ink (*suiboku-ga*) are drawn on paper or silk. Sometimes color is added, but when it is not, the materials employed are the same as those used in calligraphy. What determines the nature of a line in art or calligraphy?

Brush painting begins with the outline of an object rendered in lines that can be drawn either thick or thin. The shade of the ink can vary liberally and, in itself, abounds in expression. The nature of a line is also determined by the kind of brush employed or by the amount of water added to the *sumi* ink.

There are other important factors involved, such as the point of contact between the surface and the tip of the brush, or the speed with which the brush is moved. The ink constantly seeps from the tip of the brush, so the brush must move at a certain speed to keep up with the ink. Once a line is drawn, the painter can neither alter nor erase it.

Such characteristics necessarily impose certain constraints on *sumi* painters. The brush painter does not have the leisure of discovering the object while painting it, but must have a clear image in mind before putting brush to paper. For example, the painter must be able to envision a clear image of a bamboo leaf that can then be anchored swiftly on his chosen surface with a single gesture. If the painter is copying an existing painting, however, this will generally not prove as difficult as creating an original image. In a country such as China, where the maintenance of time-honored traditions is generally valued over the expression of artistic individuality, copying or reviving classical masterpieces is one of the most respected pursuits of brush painters.

Each element of *sumi* paintings is drawn by a set method in a fixed pattern. For example, there are several set patterns for drawing rocks, and the leaves on trees are limited to several techniques that are classified and

exemplified in the picture book *(gafu)* that is used as a reference. The patterns are studied carefully, and the skillful artist will be able to draw each one rapidly and expertly once they have been mastered.

Lines in brush painting are created by moving the tip of the brush on the paper, a technique also used in calligraphy. Such lines reflect the process of drawing in that the movement of the brush is the movement of the hand, and the movement of the hand is the movement of the creator's mind. Feelings of hesitation or decisiveness, delicacy or dynamism, confidence, affectation, restraint, or grace are all revealed in the lines.

The inverse is also true: the painter's inner self, spirit, or emotional state creates an "impulse of the brush" in the lines. The painter can then emphasize either the descriptive ability of lines (realism) or their formative function (as in abstract ornamental paintings). Certain aspects relative to the conditions of *sumi* brush paintings tend to incline the painter toward a form of Abstract Expressionism.

Ink brush-painting techniques were created in China during the Sung and Yuan dynasties. Line-drawing techniques and the use of planes were added later. Such skills take full advantage of the "smudging" phenomenon of *sumi* brush-painting techniques. After outlines are drawn, diluted shades of ink are mixed. The ink is then scattered or blurred onto the drawing surface. A technique in which ink is dripped from the brush onto blurred ink (or paint) that is not yet dry, said to have been invented in Japan by Tawaraya Sotatsu (1576–1643), creates a complex blurring of shades. There is also a method of using the fingertips that makes the *sumi* lines softer and wider. When drawn with the fingernails, the lines are sharper and thinner. This technique was mastered by the *sumi* artist Ike no Taiga (1723–98) in the eighteenth century.

Techniques such as these enriched the world of brush painting, and were particularly instrumental in improving its descriptive capacity while at the same time allowing for the possibility of expressionistic creation and innovation. The mind of the painter, which can be reflected in the expression of the line, can also be reflected in the nature of the plane.

In the history of modern Western art, the term "Expressionism" is often applied to a group of specific artists known as the Blue Rider school who were working in the periods before and after World War I. These

ABOVE (DETAIL): The Niso Choshin-zu *attributed to Sekikaku. National Museum of Tokyo.*

OPPOSITE PAGE: Sumi *brush painting, originally copied from a Chinese style imported to Japan during the Kamakura period, became deeply rooted in the Japanese soul. Its profound relationship with Zen Buddhism continues to this day.*

artists had been influenced by the work of the Russian artist Wassili Kandinsky and, since their center of activities was Munich, the movement came to be known as German Expressionism. However, the meaning of the term "Expressionism" sometimes extends to include post-World War II Abstract Expressionism and, later, the Action-painting techniques of the American artist Jackson Pollock. This extension of the term encompassed an artistic stance whose primary goal was to express the inner world of the painter. Expressionism was, therefore, an expression

ures he painted that intensified the psychological impact of his work. The Blue Rider school simply expanded on the artistic tendencies of earlier artists such as these.

Description for description's sake is not a required element of Expressionism. Thus, in order to take a totally expressionistic stance, it would be necessary to dispense with concrete description altogether. In fact, Kandinsky's work moved toward Abstract Expressionism. The fundamentals of abstraction are different from those Cezanne used in his progress toward Cubism and from the

ABOVE: Shosho Hakkei-zu *(a portion of a series of eighteen works attributed to Soami) dates from approximately 1513 and is located at the Daisen-in in Kyoto. This series of paintings masterfully depicts the four seasons of the renowned Doto Lake area despite the fact that the artist had never visited the actual site. Imaginary landscapes were popular subjects among Chinese painters and Soami was undoubtedly inspired by them.*

of self rather than a description of the outer world. The world emerges in an expressionistic work in forms or colors other than those that appear in reality; we may find a rose-colored road or purple trees. If the expressionistic tendency is defined in this way, it did not necessarily follow that Expressionism as an art form began with Kandinsky and the Blue Rider school. Il Tintoretto (1518–94) of Venice apparently sometimes used colors for psychological effect rather than in a purely descriptive or ornamental manner, while El Greco (c 1541–1614) was known for the distortion of the human fig-

ones Mondrian incorporated in his progression from landscape painting to more abstract styles. Cezanne was not interested in the inner self but in the fundamental correspondence between the structures of the outside world and a two-dimensional plane, while Mondrian's abstract paintings were clear descriptions of the outside world alone.

Inherent in *sumi* brush painting and calligraphy is an expressionistic tendency recalling the work of Kandinsky but completely unrelated to that of Mondrian. Brush painters were primarily interested in the interaction between the environment and the inner self, and one aspect of this was the self as expressed in the impulse of the brush. But that self was not an individualistic self as expressed in twentieth-century Western art. Rather, it was an almost pantheistic self, a general artistic subject that became one with the environment, something akin to what is called *shikon,* or poetic spirit. In this way, the expressionism of *sumi* brush painters differs significantly from that of Kandinsky.

The goal in calligraphy, by contrast, is to draw an object as expressed through its Chinese character. For instance, brush painters that the brush painter draws the shape of the object itself, while the calligrapher writes the character that signifies the object. One is totally subjective, the other objective.

Brush painting follows set patterns for drawing particular objects, but calligraphic brush work adheres to established conventions for holding the brush when creating a particular part of a Chinese character. Calligraphic stroke patterns also had a strong influence on the brush strokes used in brush painting. Outlines and lines, folds and creases painted in light and dark shades of *sumi* ink

depict a certain cloud, whereas calligraphers produce the character for the word "cloud." There is very little relationship between the shape of the actual cloud and the shape of the character used to describe it. Both brush painter and calligrapher have to work within these given conditions regardless of their feelings or intentions. In that sense, the conditions force the artists to transcend their subjectivity, and the transcendent shapes created on paper using brush and *sumi* ink reflect the mind of the painter or calligrapher, a characteristic that may then be termed "expressionistic." The only difference is the fact are easily discerned in Kao's *Kanzan-zu* (from the first half of the fourteenth century), Josetsu's *Sankyo-zu* (from the first half of the fifteenth century), Noami's *Byakue Kannon* (1468), and Kano Motonobu's *Dharma Eka (Hui-ke) Taimen-zu* (from the sixteenth century). However, the various lines cannot be explained as mere descriptions of the object being painted; the calligraphic stroke patterns must be taken into account as well. After all, these painters came from differing schools and times, but all of them have clearly incorporated calligraphic stroke patterns into their work.

ABOVE (DETAIL): The Shosho Hakkei-zu *attributed to Soami.*

As examples of *sumi* brush paintings, the four above-mentioned works clearly have other common characteristics. First, all are portraits. Second, the painters have not drawn their patrons or high officials, but rather have depicted legendary figures who are seen as symbols of spiritual power. Those portrayed are not commoners but "exalted" figures such as Kanzan, Kannon, Dharma, and Eka. The work *Sankyo-zu* includes Confucius, Buddha, and Lao-tzu (indicating that their teachings are in accord). We can surmise then that Japanese brush painters easily adopted the brush strokes associated with calligraphy when attempting to express the spirit of a revered figure.

The spirit of a person is said to be manifest in the face, particularly in the eyes. Thus, the first means a painter would adopt in order to express spirituality was concentration on the detailed expression of the face, minimizing the body and background; Josetsu completely abbreviated background description, while Kao drew in only part of a pine tree in one corner of his composition. Although Noami placed the Byakue Kannon in a setting of water, rocks, and wild plants (on silk, colored), and Genshin drew a rocky mountain in his depiction of Dharma, the background drawings in these two paintings exist primarily as exposition; Kannon is shown making an earthly appearance, while Dharma is shown peacefully practicing meditation in front of a cliff. All four painters, however, employed extremely minimal de-

scription of the body or clothing so that the facial expression of their subjects would remain prominent.

In the cultural environment in which Japanese brush painters lived after the fourteenth century, calligraphy represented the visual expression of spirituality. It could be, then, that painters attempted to express their compassion for the spirituality of their subjects by using lines that strongly recalled calligraphy. If they believed that spirit was inherent in the calligraphic brush-strokes themselves, they must have seen the need to adopt not only the technique of drawing piercing, otherworldly eyes, but also of using lines strongly associated with calligraphy to effectively spiritualize the entire body. This was a unique fusion of description and expression, painting and calligraphy. Such fusion was possible only after technically adopting brush-painting techniques and philosophically adopting the aesthetics of *hissei,* or "the impact of the brush."

The close relationship between painting and calligraphy did not stop there, however. While calligraphic strokes influenced the line in Japanese painting, the opposite occurred in Chinese art. A special calligraphic technique, called *hihaku* in Japanese, was developed in which a picture was drawn in a space meant to contain characters. This style of drawing pictures was a clever kind of punning and might have been seen as a way of breaking tradition by Chinese intellectuals.

This technique was rarely used in Japan,

except by the priest Kukai (Kobo Daishi). He was so familiar with Chinese culture that his skill in constructing wordplay with Chinese characters in the *hihaku* style rivaled that of a native Chinese practitioner of the art. It could be that since no one else was practicing this style in Japan, he had found an arena in which to express his outstanding abilities, demonstrating that, for him, nothing was impossible.

The fundamental relationship between calligraphy and painting in China was not a case of one influencing the other exclusively; rather, they coexisted and were unified within one picture. In China, eulogies were written in calligraphy in the margins of ink-brush paintings and in other styles of painting as well. While these and the images coexist in a picture, each strongly insists on its independence. Rather than merging within a common frame, they confront each other, compete, and creating tension. If this creates a contradiction, then the painting as a whole is a unified dialectic of contradiction. Such eulogies typically took the form of poetry that connoted the intrinsic meaning of a painting.

Sung- and Yuan-dynasty brush paintings exhibited well-balanced characters in combinations of poetry and painting, some actually creating a kind of pictorial harmony. Some *bunjin-ga* (paintings in the literary style) show a tendency toward true unification rather than consolidation of the elements of poem, calligraphy, and painting; a single artist plays the part of poet, calligrapher, and painter simultaneously.

The relationship between calligraphy and painting historically became closer with the poetic *bunjin-ga* of poetry. In any case, such a close relationship between painting and letters was extremely rare in other cultures.

BELOW: View of Murnau *(1909) by Alexej von Jawlensky (1864–1941). Lenbach Haus Municipal Museum, Munich.*

BELOW (DETAIL): An early example of Japanese brush painting can be seen in this detail from the Chikujaku-zu *(Bamboo and sparrow) painted by Kao in the late Kamakura period. Yamato Bunka-kan, Nara.*

ABOVE (DETAIL): The Shosen Taishi Higaku *by Sokuten Buko (699).*

RIGHT: Highly ornamental Chinese characters in the hihaku *style were imported to Japan and can be seen among the works of Kukai (Kobo Daishi) especially in these samples from the* Junyoze *of the first half of the ninth century.*

Chinese brush paintings reached the shores of Japan in the late Kamakura period through Zen Buddhist temples, and the Ashikaga shogunate later imported a great many in its trade with the Ming dynasty (1368–1644). Even while Japan remained in isolation during the Edo period, Chinese brush paintings continued to be imported via the port of Nagasaki. In the fourteenth to sixteenth centuries, most of the imported paintings were either original Sung- (960–1279) and Yuan-dynasty (1279–1368) works or reproductions of those paintings. From the seventeenth century on, the majority were from the Ming and Ching dynasties (1644–1911).

The primary reason these particular paintings were imported to Japan is a seemingly obvious one: there was a great demand for them. The imported Sung- and Yuan-dynasty brush paintings were completely different in terms of technique, style, and subject from the Yamato-e style, a popular style developed during the Heian period (794–1185), typically Japanese in subject matter and apparent even in the scroll paintings of the Kamakura period; but the spirit of the times had changed and with it the aesthetic taste and values of the people of Japan. Soon, Chinese brush paintings were being hung by Zen monks in their quarters and by samurai in their studies. The imports were undoubtedly expensive when traded in the domestic market, but they also became the focus of investment.

We must ask who painted, or claimed to have painted, the Sung- and Yuan-dynasty brush paintings Japan imported. This is a decisively important question in the history of Japanese art. Part of the answer is that, through the copying of Sung- and Yuan-dynasty paintings, Japanese brush painting began an approach that did not fundamentally change until the end of the Edo period (1603–1868). Ming- and Ching-dynasty paintings were imported to Japan during the Edo period, but it should be noted that originally, in China, Ming works were copies of Sung and Yuan works. Since Ching paintings were painstakingly copied from Ming paintings, Japanese brush painting thus retained a connection with Sung- and Yuan-dynasty paintings brought in during the Muromachi period (1392–1568). We must also consider that if the Japanese had a certain amount of freedom in choosing which paintings to import, then those that in fact were chosen from among the Sung- and Yuan-dynasty paintings must have reflected Japanese taste, a preference that in turn must have been determined and nurtured by Japanese culture.

Judging from the available literature and number of existing works, Muxi was the Chinese brush painter who was the most popular in Japan, followed by Liang Kai. Not many works of Ma Yuan or Hsia Kuei, the most representative of the *intai-ga* (southern Sung painters) were imported. Muxi was a priest-painter of the early Sung dynasty in the latter half of the thirteenth century. He did not color his paintings, but exploited the different shades and smudging techniques of the ink to excellent effect. He did not use the line for emphasis, although he sometimes used lines in portraits, lines that were less descriptively accurate than Liang Kai's minimal strokes. He painted various objects, including flowers, plants, birds, hills, streams, portraits, and the like. *Fishing Village at Sunset,* a portion of the *Shosho Hakkei* (Eight scenes of Shosho) currently in the collection of the Nezu Museum, is attributed to Muxi. It is a gentle landscape of a river with trees and a boat floating in the water. Overlapping mountains appear far behind the clouds, yet no particular ink line stands out. *Kannon Enkaku-zu* (Kannon with gibbons and a crane), monochrome on silk (Daitoku-ji temple), combines the technique of subdued lines and the use of blurred ink to create a perfect composition. Kannon sits on a rock, while the mother and baby gibbons resting on an old tree branch seem to come alive. The Japanese crane standing in front of the bamboo grove appears to be on the verge of moving. The particularly outstanding detail of the painting is the sense of tranquillity seen in the Kannon's face, a tranquillity that probably was intended to reflect contemporary Japanese taste. Muxi's unique talent is displayed in the elegant lines of the white robe, the soft fur of the gibbons, and the balance between the dark ink on the tail feathers of the crane and the vermilion dots on its head. This is clearly not the work of an amateur.

Kaki-zu (Persimmons), which is also said to have been painted by Muxi with ink on paper, demonstrates an aesthetic use of abstract space (housed at the Daitoku-ji temple in Kyoto). Although the Japanese of the Muromachi period admired Muxi's works and imported a great many of them, he was not so highly respected in China, where the mainstream painters were of the *intai-ga* school to which he did not belong. Thus, most of Muxi's existing works (or works attributed to him) are concentrated in Japan.

ABOVE: *Kanzan, an eccentric monk of the Tang dynasty, was a frequent subject of Japanese brush painters during the Kamakura period, as exemplified in the* Kanzan-zu *by Kao.*

101

Liang Kai, also known as Liang Fushi, was a painter associated with the art academy of the Sung dynasty. Because he befriended Zen monks and was known to be somewhat eccentric, he was considered beyond the pale and deemed unclassifiable in terms of character and, by extension, in terms of painting.

In his depiction of hills and bodies of water he favored a blurred effect over the use of line. He was skilled in using different shades of ink rather than various colors. *Sekkei Sansui-zu* (Hills and water in snow) at the National Museum of Tokyo is an excellent example of his superior technique. His portraits done as rough sketches exhibit both a minimalism in strokes and an accuracy of description. Another example is

Rihaku (Li Po) Gingyo-zu, a work on paper done in ink, also in the collection of the National Museum of Tokyo.

In China, the work of Liang Kai did not belong to the mainstream of southern Sung painters but was associated with rather heretical offshoot movements. In Japan, his works were accepted by the academy along with the works of Muxi, who became close to those professional painters who were also Zen monks. Both were considered outside the mainstream, thus beyond ranking. They were seen to be outrageous and individualistic in their emphasis on the use of two-dimensional planes rather than lines, in the quality of ink they employed, and in their pursuit of the expression of inner feeling over pure description.

The standards of evaluation and the gen- eral predilection or taste were apparently different in China and Japan. One upheld a strong tradition and emphasized description or objectivism, while the other had no tradition of brush painting and an orientation toward free and unconstrained expressions of subjective feeling. This Japanese tendency revealed itself in the choice of Sung- and Yuan-dynasty paintings selected for import.

Bokuseki (sumi calligraphy) by Zen monks also had a relationship to the newly imported Chinese brush paintings. *Bokuseki* is highly valued in Japan, but was viewed as unorthodox, even heretical, in China, where Chinese calligraphy comprises a balance of rules, form/figure, and mental power. The element that was emphasized depended on the calligrapher. However, Zen monks tended to disregard the first two elements, produc-

ABOVE *(DETAIL):* The Shosho Hakkei-zu *folding screen attributed to Shubun, created in the mid-fifteenth century. Kosetsu Museum, Kobe.*

LEFT *(DETAIL):* The Kyosho Henon-zu *attributed to Li Chen of the Sung dynasty. Chokaido Bunko, Yokkaichi, Mie Prefecture.*

103

ing creations that clearly exhibited a strong psychological force.

Since China had a long tradition of calligraphy, works that completely ignored the standards and rules were not acceptable. In Japan, however, the tradition of calligraphy was relatively minor, and those works were thus easily accepted. In fact, the overwhelming psychological force this art revealed was what the Japanese pursued with the greatest enthusiasm. This, in short, is what most clearly illustrates the difference in the way calligraphy by Zen monks was accepted in Japan and China.

"Rules" and "form" are objective domains, but "psychological force" is a subjective element. The tendency of the Japanese not to adhere to formerly prescribed elements perfectly parallels their tendency not to emphasize the descriptive potential of brush painting. The lack of a long tradition in calligraphy, brush painting, or any other specific style of general artistic expression meant that confrontations and conflict between the familiar, established order and the individual rarely occurred. Under such conditions, a philosophy supporting the idea that artistic expression was assertion of self could easily prevail.

If calligraphy by Zen monks is considered the ultimate spiritualism, the same may be said of their brush paintings. The modern Zen paintings of the contemporary Japanese painter Sengai are an extreme example of such expression. Muxi and Liang Kai were not so extreme, painting in a different style than Ma Yuan and Hsia Kuei did. The difference was not altogether unrelated to "psychological force," but they never completely dispensed with descriptive techniques. How then were the brush paintings from the Sung and Yuan dynasties transformed in the process of being introduced into Japanese art?

Hasegawa Tohaku (1539–1610), in his *Shorinzu Byobu* (Pine forest screen), in the National Museum of Tokyo, attained one of the highest descriptive effects in the history of Japanese brush painting. Although Muxi does not represent Chinese descriptivism, his realism is clearly superior when we compare his work *Kannon Enkaku-zu* mentioned earlier to Tohaku's *Kareki Enko-zu* (Dead tree and monkeys) in the Ryusen-an at Myoho-ji, apparently done in Muxi's style.

The detail of the fur was probably invented by Muxi and imitated by Tohaku. However, Muxi's gibbon has bones and muscles beneath the coat of fur on its arms. Tohaku's monkey, in contrast, reveals only a touch of fur with nothing underneath. Muxi

drew the substance of the animal, while Tohaku drew the surface.

When we examine the compositions in greater detail, we can see that in Muxi's work, the gibbons are placed in the center of the picture or at the apex of a triangle formed by the tree's trunk and branches. The structure of the composition is perfectly arranged, with the dark *sumi* dots on the leaves of a vine on the old tree trunk serving merely as accents. The aim of this painting apparently was to create a composition centering on the gibbons.

Tohaku, for his part, seemed not to have

ABOVE: The Zen painter Mokuan sailed to Yuan around 1326 and died there without being able to return to Japan. He adopted the style of Muxi so successfully that the advent of his career was called "the return of Muxi." Shisui-zu from the mid-fourteenth century by Mokuan. Ikutoku-kai, Tokyo.

had much interest in Muxi's triangular composition. In Tohaku's picture of a mother monkey and her child, the trunk of the tree the two are leaning against is quite thick. Branches of the old tree and vines are roughly sketched strokes that extend vertically and horizontally. They do not exhibit any geometrically based compositional design. Still, Muxi never went beyond realism, whereas Tohaku successfully left realism behind by emphasizing the contrast between the dark *sumi* and diluted *sumi* to create a dramatic plane. We see that the objectivism (structure and realism) of Chinese paintings gave way to subjectivism (psychological force and *hissei* expressionism).

The well-known *Fukuro-jinbutsu* (Portrait of bags) by Kaiho Yusho (1533–1615) was modeled after Liang Kai's portraits. What differentiates between the way people are depicted in Liang Kai's *Rihaku (Li Po) Gingyo-zu* (National Museum of Tokyo) and in Yusho's *Chikurin Shichiken-zu* (Seven wise men in a bamboo bush) (Kennin-ji temple) is the fact that Liang Kai drew outlines of people in clothing in light ink washes that vividly captured movement. Yusho used strong, dark *sumi* lines that seem to insist upon themselves rather than the image they are creating. The outlines of clothing are drawn, but at the same time the movement of the body underneath the clothing is not captured well although it is indicated. The subject Li Po is undeniably marching forward in Liang Kai's composition, whereas the people drawn by Yusho seem to be barely moving. The difference is that Liang Kai excels in realistic depiction of the object, while Yusho is more interesting in the outward reflection of the artist's contemplation.

The same can be said of the way hills and streams were depicted. Those drawn by Soami, for instance, suggest a vast expanse of space. *Shosho Hakkei-zu* (1513, Daisen-in, Daitoku-ji temple) is one such work. But when we compare this work with the Chinese masterpiece of hills and streams *Sekkei Sansui-zu* (Hills and streams in snow) (National Museum of Tokyo), the powerful realism of Liang Kai clearly surpasses the *Shosho Hakkei-zu* of Soami with its massive snowy mountains that almost completely overwhelm the two small figures on horseback.

Liang Kai's hills and streams are essentially an expression of a human philosophy placed in the vastness of nature. The landscape attributed to Soami is a poetic sentiment, or nature reflecting poetry. Philosophy can contain poetic sentiment, but the converse is not usually true. Sentiment exists in the present, while philosophy is a function of the world order that transcends the conditions of the here and now. In the hills and streams of the paintings done by artists of the Sung and Yuan dynasties can be found a view of nature summarized by the metaphysical doctrines of Chu-tsu. That view of nature might have awakened interest in things as they exist (*kakubutsu chichi* [attainment of the ultimate reason of things]) and thus served to anchor realism.

During the Muromachi period the people of Japan practiced Zen Buddhism. The Japanese thus copied Sung- and Yuan-dynasty

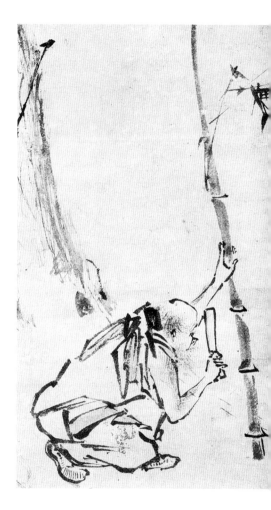

BELOW: *The* Rokuso Saichiku-zu *of Liang Kai from the Southern Sung dynasty shows Eno, the sixth founder of Zen Buddhism, about to cut a bamboo tree. National Museum of Tokyo. Zen paintings not only represented the spirit of Zen but also depicted the founders of the religion and the training required to reach nirvana.*

CENTER: *The rock garden at Ryoan-ji temple in Kyoto, where fifteen rocks are arranged in five groups within a 250-square-meter, rectangular surface covered with white pebbles. The garden is said to represent the ultimate Zen state, although a variety of interpretations of the composition have been suggested. There are two conflicting theories on the date of its origin; one holds it to be from the Muromachi period, while the other says it is from the Edo period.*

works but generally did not surpass them. The exception was Sesshu (1420–1506), whose works rivaled those of his Chinese counterparts. Sesshu was a monk who first studied Zen at Shokoku-ji and is thought to have learned painting from Shubun. He later left Shokoku-ji under the patronage of the Ouchi clan, who were active in trading with Ming-dynasty China. He lived in Undei-an in Yamaguchi, crossed the sea to China (1467–69), traveled throughout Japan after his return, and remained in Yamaguchi during most of his later days. It was then that he drew *Sansui Chokan* (Morihoko-do), *Shuto Sansui-zu* (National Museum of Tokyo), and *Amanohashidate-zu* (National Museum of Tokyo), among others. His style of calligraphy in the former two is similar to that found in the *intai-ga* school, particularly in work attributed to Hsia Kuei. The vantage point is slightly above the horizontal perspective. The figures in the *Amanohashidate-zu* sometime suggest the works of Hsia Kuei. Many creative and innovative techniques are freely employed, including strong and dark *sumi* lines, blurring, and the combined use of different shades done with fine brushes. In this third work, the perspective is extremely high, almost a bird's-eye view.

The main characteristics of Sesshu's *Sansui Chokan* (Long scroll of hills and waters) and *Shuto Sansui-zu* (Hills and waters in fall and winter) are the incomparable sense of depth created by blending straight and curved lines with the use of contrasting shades of *sumi*. The work unifies an amazing variety of individual objects in a single picture by realistically describing the differing characteristics of rock surfaces and plants. The realism Sesshu achieved in his depiction of grass or snowy sky is comparable to that of the vines and sky in Liang Kai's *Sekkei Sansui-zu*. The spacious *Amanohashidate-zu* is a solid unification of the expression of vast space and the detailed description of each component; its power is outstanding. In this respect, Sesshu is considered the exception.

The tradition of the Yamato-e school incorporated brush-painting techniques in the sixteenth century. Kano Motonobu (1476–1559) established the foundation of the Kano school under the generous patronage of the shogun. His wall paintings depict hills and water, people, or flowers and birds done in the style of Ching-dynasty line drawings combined with the brilliant coloring common in Yamato-e. It can be said that Yamato-e paintings, which had lost their vitality, were revived by brush-painting techniques.

Gyu-zu (Cow) by Tawaraya Sotatsu uses the technique of *tarashikomi* (several layers of ink or pigment applied to specially prepared paper) as do the later works of Ogata Korin (1658–1716), particularly in his delicate renderings of bamboo and in his portraits. Here, *sumi* is used as a colored plane, and the object depicted appears distorted as a result of the artist's keen observation. These detailed and calculated compositions are unique among Japanese brush paintings.

THE ORIGIN OF *BUNJIN-GA*

Approximately one century after the establishment of the Tokugawa shogunate, powerful new social classes began to emerge in a Japan that remained isolated from the rest of the world. Most significant was the rise of two new classes. One was the merchant class that focused on developing the agricultural market and spreading it nationwide; the other consisted of the intellectuals who adopted Confucian philosophy. As merchants began to define their own sense of practical ethics, the *sekimon shingaku,* the intellectual Confucianists evaluated Sung-dynasty scholarship and art in an attempt to judge it on its scholarly merit and artistic value independent of Confucian ethics.

With the rise of the new classes, the world of Japanese art was such that families connected to those in power enjoyed certain privileges subsequently passed on to their heirs. They did not have to be innovative, but only needed to follow accepted styles. Schools of art attached undue importance to their own techniques. The Kano school of art dominated the world of painting, beginning with Motonobu and ending with Tan'yu (1602–74), both of whom were active in the seventeenth century. By the eighteenth century, however, little remained of its once remarkable results except the school's inherited position and power. This naturally spawned a rush of detractors, even from within the Kano school itself. Kusumi Morikage (ca 1620–90), who painted the *Yugaodana Noryo-zu Byobu* (National Museum of Tokyo), a vivid depiction of peasant life, was disinherited by Tan'yu. Was this because he was innovative, or did he become innovative as a result of being disinherited? Either way, the stagnation of the Kano school was quite apparent by the time of Tan'yu.

The demand for new paintings by upper-class townspeople was answered by the brothers Ogata Korin and Ogata Kenzan, while anonymous street artists painted *ukiyo-e* woodblock prints for the common folk. These street artists contributed to the development of woodblock prints throughout the eighteenth century (see page 160). However, the intellectual Confucianists rejected the art of the Kano school, and once again looked to the continent for artistic archetypes. One extremely significant development in the latter half of the eighteenth century was the emergence of the *bunjin,* a group of ex-samurai and intellectual enthusiasts of literature. They composed poetry and prose in Chinese and excelled in calligraphy and painting. Some served a lord, while others were *ronin* (masterless samurai). The group retained a certain independence from samurai society and high society by establishing their own close comradeship.

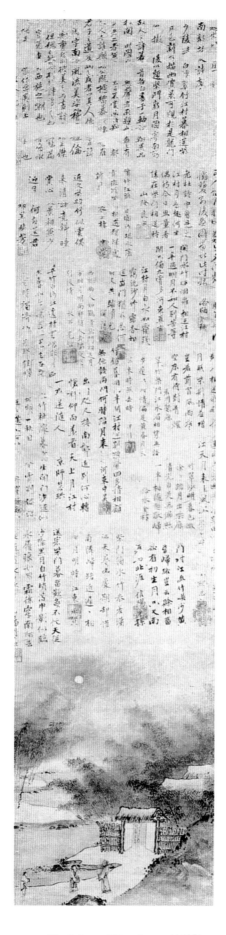

ABOVE: The Saimon Shingetsu-zu *(1405) was created by a Zen monk. Fujita Museum, Osaka.*

One thing that separated the *bunjin* from the common folk was their sophisticated schooling in foreign poetry, prose, calligraphy, and painting. At the same time, their pursuit of the fine arts set them apart from the ethics and rules of the samurai code. The works they created were called *bunjin-ga* (art in the literary artist's style).

It is probably impossible to define *bunjin-ga* in terms of particular characteristics found in the art. Rather, this style must be defined according to the characteristics of each individual painter. Edo-period *bunjin-ga* began with Gion Nankai (1677–1751) and Yanagisawa Kien (1704–58). The eldest son of a doctor retained by the Kishu clan, Nankai served the clan as a Confucianist. He was also a dilettante who mastered the *shamisen* (Japanese stringed instrument). Kien was the second son of the advisor to the shogunate, Yanagisawa Yoshiyasu, a position that he himself inherited after the death of his elder brother, who had previously taken the position upon the death of their father. Kien was a multitalented Confucianist who mastered the *tsuzumi* (hand drum), the *shamisen*, the writing of *haikai* poetry (haiku that made use of ordinary words), and the art of incense *(kodo)*. Nankai and Kien probably did not completely conform to samurai society, since in their younger days both were dismissed from their duties as a result of misbehavior. Neither was a professional painter, but both learned Chinese traditional brush-painting techniques by studying picture albums, particularly the *Kaishien Gaden*, reprinted in 1748.

The *bunjin* of this period, like the Confucianists, used classical Chinese culture as a model for education and learning. However, while *bunjin-ga* was a pastime for the previous generation of literary samurai, the next generation of *bunjin* transcended this aspect and became professional painters. They were, among others, Ike no Taiga (1723–76), Buson (1716–84), and Uragami Gyokudo (1745–1820), each of whom created his own distinctive world.

Taiga is thought to have been born in Nishijin in Kyoto, and served at Manpuku-ji temple from the age of seven. In his youth, he was educated in the *bunjin* style, and his gift as a painter was discovered by Yanagisawa Kien. Only calligraphy and paintings by Taiga remain today, as his written compositions have all been lost. He drew imaginative landscapes and brush paintings that

RIGHT: Amanohashidate-zu *by Sesshu dates from approximately 1500. Kyoto National Museum.*

were almost caricatures in imitation of the Sung- and Yuan-dynasty style. His lines are free and full of energy. He was extremely talented in depicting vast spaces with balanced perspective, while tending to exaggerate any extremely distorted object, whether it be a facial expression or a mountain. Such exaggeration often lent his work a certain departure from realism insofar as it was an expression of his inner universe. In that sense, he was highly subjective and expressionistic. Most *bunjin-ga* were small, but Taiga's works were of various sizes, from handheld fans to standing screens. His works must have been among the most individualistic Japanese paintings of the eighteenth century.

Buson was born in Settsu but moved to Edo (old Tokyo) when he was twenty years old in order to learn *haikai* poetry and to paint. He coproduced the painting *Jubenjugi-zu* with Ike no Taiga, but Buson's style was quite different. In his drawings of willows on a riverbank blowing in the wind or of a snowy evening landscape, he never departed from realism in depicting mundane objects. Buson's work also varied in size; he painted both large and small pictures. His large monochrome works contain powerful verse in the *haikai* style, reflecting his well-seasoned skills in poetry. His brush paintings, such as *Gabirosho-zu* (ca 1778), suggest an exactness of things bordering on the metaphysical. Buson's masterpieces include *Yashoku Rodai-zu, Gabi Rocho-zu,* and *Tobi ni Karasu*—a few among the series in which he took full advantage of the *sumi* effects he mastered in his later years.

Uragami Gyokudo was born in a samurai family serving the Kamogata clan, part of the Ikeda clan of Okayama. He was appointed a superintendent officer at the age of thirty-seven, but was dismissed for reasons unknown at the age of forty-three. It was then that he retired from pursuit of any other employment in favor of his deepening interest in calligraphy, painting, and poetry. Gyokudo preferred to draw mountains and trees and filled out his pictures with dark and light shades of *sumi.*

When compared to the traditional realism of the art of the Ming and Ching dynasties, these appear to be works of Abstract Expressionism, and thus more readily exhibit the painter's individualism. However, when compared to the superrealists of the late Ming and early Ching dynasties, including Sekito and Hachidaisanjin, the two most prominent seventeenth-century *bunjin-ga* painters, the *bunjin*—who apparently did not have the

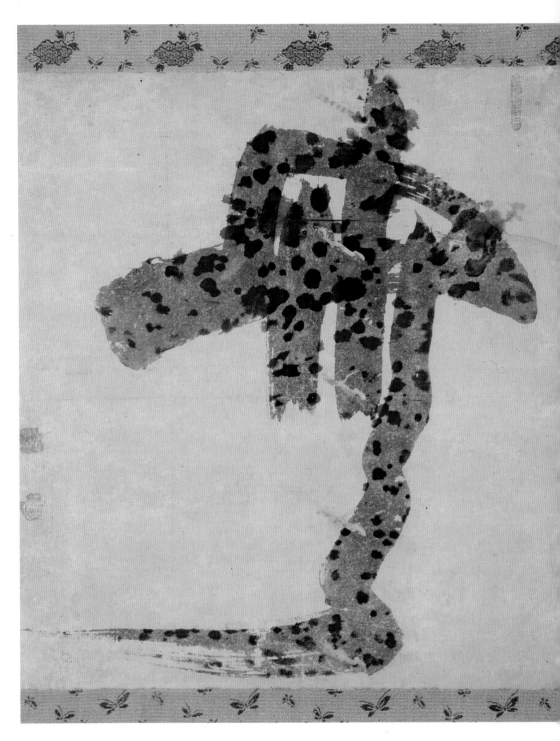

chance to see many such works—fell short in terms of outrageousness of imagery, creativity in composition, and empathy. Since such a tradition was weak in Japan, it allowed a certain freedom of expression, but the lack of restrictions against which to resist meant that each painter failed to develop his own fierce, combative, burning style. Sekito and Hachidaisanjin were descendants of the Ming imperial family, and expressed their sadness and pride over the decline of the dynasty. In contrast, the eighteenth-century Edo leaders enjoyed strong support. Thus, we find in the *sekimon shingaku* an ethical subjectivism and in the *bunjin-ga* an artistic and pictorial subjectivism that was tenderly prepared and carefully nurtured. In that sense, it inherited the aesthetic of Muromachi-period brush paintings and at the same time facilitated the rise of the last great *bunjin-ga* painter, Tomioka Tessai (1836–1924).

Tessai was well versed in Chinese classics and was an excellent calligrapher. He

drew *sumi* brush paintings in the tradition of Taiga in terms of structural composition and subject matter. However, the printed works of Tessai transcended the framework of *bunjin-ga*. His paintings were sometimes monochromatic in tone, but more often employed bright and dark emerald, crimson, and blue coloring. Samples of his calligraphy included strong lines of *ki-inseido* (noble force) and the use of blurred *sumi* for the effect produced by different shades. This effect can easily be associated with a tech-

nique similar to Abstract Expressionism as seen in his *Suiboku Seishu-zu*. If Sesshu represents Realism in *sumi* brush painting, it can be said that Tessai represents its Expressionism.

Depicting landscapes from a bird's-eye perspective is a *bunjin-ga* tradition. The perspective found in Tessai's *Seija Shuyu-zu* is a departure from that tradition, and the composition of *Kobutsugan-zu* is unique in its perspective, which is one of looking up from below. Many subjects were taken from Chi-

ABOVE LEFT: The Portrait of Daruma *by Hakuin is from the latter half of the eighteen century. Shoju-ji temple, Aichi Prefecture.*

ABOVE RIGHT: The Suiboku Seishu-zu *of Tomioka Tessai. Seicho-ji temple, Takarazuka, Osaka.*

ABOVE: *This character for* mu *(nothingness) is by Munan, an early Edo-period Zen monk.*

ABOVE RIGHT: *Painting of a circle, a triangle, and a square as seen and created by Sengai (1750–1837). Idemitsu Museum, Tokyo. This Edo-period monk of the Rinzai school of Zen Buddhism drew improvisational and abbreviated Zen paintings at the request of* audiences. *The circle is said to represent water, the triangle fire, and the square earth. Alternatively, as an expression of Sengai's worldview, the circle stands for Zen, the triangle for the Shingon sect, and the square for the Tendai Sect.*

ABOVE: Sumi on Paper *by Hans Hartung, 1937.*

ABOVE RIGHT: Variation on Sengai's Universe *by Pierre Alenchinsky (1960). Galerie van der Loo, Munich.*

nese poetry and prose, but some were sketches of real people.

What is truly spectacular about Tessai, however, is not the fact that he went beyond the *bunjin-ga* tradition. Rather, it is the fact that he painted a great many different subjects in a variety of styles. Whether in the Western or Asian hemisphere, the number of painters who could successfully accomplish a variety of styles over a relatively short period of time in their mature years is extremely limited. Tessai proved to be one exception to this rule along with, much later, the great Pablo Picasso. Tessai never at-

114

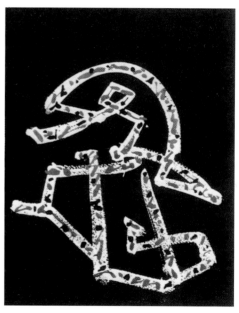

tempted to adopt other materials and techniques such as oil painting, or to take up certain more popular subjects—the nude, for example. Rather, he continued to paint with *sumi* and Japanese paints on paper or silk, following the tradition of the *bunjin-ga*. Through his constant effort to express his inner vision, Tessai exemplified the creativity and power seen in Japanese painting from the time of Hokusai to the early twentieth century. He used traditional means, and it was not in spite of this fact but rather owing to it that he was able to attain such free and bold expression.

There were three distinct periods in which Japan exerted an artistic influence on Western culture. The first occurred in the seventh and eighth centuries through the export and import of ceramic ware, the second was in the mid-nineteenth century through the popularity of the *ukiyo-e* woodblock prints, and the third occurred at the turn of the century in the areas of ornamentation and design.

The influence of Western art in Japan could first be seen in the latter half of the Edo period (1603–1868), then was felt overwhelmingly in the Meiji period (1868–1912) and thereafter. Western influences on Japan

The Rimpa School Crosses the Ocean

ABOVE: Funabashi Makie Suzuribako (*Boat bridge inkstone box) by Hon'ami Koetsu, National Museum of Tokyo.*

OPPOSITE PAGE (DETAIL): Milk pitcher with cicada and praying mantis by Emile Gallé, 15 cm in height.

encompassed broad areas of culture, including astronomy, geography and medicine, as early as the Edo period. Conversely, the aesthetic and intellectual influence of Japan on the West was limited to art and did not involve other cultural aspects.

By the Meiji period, Japanese art, music, and literature had been Westernized to a certain degree, in much the same way that scholarship, scientific technology, and the legal system had been adapted. Japan was not the only country to experience this phenomenon. Asia, Africa, and the North and South Americas all experienced varying degrees of Westernization.

While the influence of Japanese art extended westward, it did not reach China or Korea. However, the influence of Western culture could be seen worldwide during the nineteenth and twentieth centuries. For its part, Japan accepted Chinese culture first, then Western. Such reciprocal influence invites a reconsideration of the concept of influence as a whole.

On the one side are the artistic characteristics of the influencing party, and on the other are the subjective conditions of the party evaluating and receiving the influence. The adopted influences passed along through ceramic ware, woodblock prints, and certain design elements revealed the West's remark-

able capacity to judge and evaluate quality. It has often been noted that the woodblock prints of Hokusai were a result of the influence of his life in Edo, while the ability to evaluate them in terms of artistic merit was a result of the influence of the culture of Paris at the time. It is clear, however, that the ability to is create and the ability to evaluate that which is created do not necessarily go hand in hand. When evaluation serves as an inspiration for creation, as in the work of van Gogh and Degas, then evaluation itself becomes part of the creative results of conversely discovery; the two become difficult to separate. Artists created because of their discoveries of new ideas, and they conversely discovered new ideas because they were extraordinarily creative.

The aestheticism of the chinoiserie trend and Japonisme are interesting cases. Chinese porcelains were known in the West as early as the fourteenth and fifteenth centuries. In the sixteenth century, the Portuguese imported them from Macao, while in the seventeenth century, the Dutch began to import a massive amount of late Ching-dynasty blue and white porcelain amounting to several tens of thousands of pieces per year. The Dutch interest was not confined to Chinese products. Imari ware and Kakiemon ware from Japan were also popular. In the seventeenth and eighteenth centuries, the manufacture of porcelains using adapted Chinese and Japanese technologies and patterns that were derivative of Delft and Meissen developed into the chinoiserie style. People of the West did not clearly distinguish between Chinese and Japanese civilizations in those days, and as a consequence, the separate styles of both Chinese and Japanese influences became mixed together, at least in terms of pattern.

A great deal has been written about the Japonisme surrounding *ukiyo-e* woodblock prints dating from the mid- to late nineteenth century. Japonisme was centered in Paris since *ukiyo-e* had made a deep impact on the Impressionists. This impact included, among other aspects, two-dimensionality (since Japanese woodblock prints do not generally employ geometric perspectives), variation of visual angles, cropping techniques, the use of subtly harmonized colors, and an exactitude by which fleeting movements are captured.

It cannot be said that the Impressionists discovered each of the characteristics of *ukiyo-e* for the first time in the *ukiyo-e* prints themselves. What they saw in them must have been their own amazement at the fact

that such characteristics were unified in a single picture and created a unique harmony. What Claude Monet, Edgar Degas, Paul Gauguin, and Pierre Bonnard pursued so exhaustively was a two-dimensional picture that would represent the structure of the three-dimensional world.

Between the years 1890 and 1910 in Europe, a new artistic style that touched upon the architecture, interior design, furniture design, glasswork, and paintings of the period became popular. In France it was known

spaces was the basic objective of Art Nouveau and Jugendstil. This was also the fundamental principle common to the art of the Edo period in Japan.

It was not from Japan, however, that Western culture adopted the concept of turning living space into art. Such a concept existed in the West prior to the advent of Art Nouveau. William Morris promoted the development of furniture design, pyrography, and other crafts at the turn of the century. But once the making of everyday objects

BELOW (DETAILS): Kohakubai-zu Byobu *(Red and white plum-blossom screen) from the eighteenth century. This is one of the later works of Ogata Korin. MOA Museum, Atami.*

as Art Nouveau; in Germany it was known as Jugendstil. Both movements were deeply influenced by the Japanese arts and crafts of the Edo period.

Art Nouveau attempted to transform the spaces of everyday existence into art. As is apparent in the work of interior decorator Victor Horta seen in the celebrated *House on 12 Turin Street* (1883), the artist's efforts were directed toward concrete interior objects such as ceiling and window-frame design, glass, furniture, cabinetry, and household objects. Decoration of daily living

into art became the goal of artists whose interest centered on decorative design, Japanese art became a vast treasure trove of potential influences.

The artists of Art Nouveau often used motifs from the natural world such as flowers, plants, birds, insects, or water. Many of these also were the main motifs of ornamental design in the Edo period. In addition, lacquerwork and the patterns on elegant kimono all contained identical motifs. The level of perfection attained during the Edo period was nearly unparalleled in terms of mastery of the smallest details; variety of color, tone, and texture; elegant flow of the line; and subtle sophistication of composition. Designs that usually would not appear in Western pictures, such as Japanese plants and flowers, dragonflies, and butterflies began to be seen in glassware created by French artists such as Emile Gallé.

Art Nouveau revived the line. This is made immediately obvious when one observes the absence of straight lines and the use of delicate curves that characterized the work of sionists, however, were inspired in quite a different way by the same set of woodblock prints.

Which designs of the Edo period exerted the strongest influence on the Western masters of Art Nouveau? Most of the fundamental design elements were created by the Rimpa school of Japan whose decorative, evocative elements became popularized as patterns that spread throughout Japan and became widely used by the artisans of the Edo period. The Rimpa school began with

this period. The Impressionists of the late nineteenth century were greatly influenced by *ukiyo-e*, but unlike the *ukiyo-e* painters, they did not incorporate the use of an outline in their pictures. It was probably owing to the influence of Japanese woodblock prints that two masters of Art Nouveau and Jugendstil, Aubrey Beardsley in London and Gustav Klimt in Vienna, respectively abandoned the use of three-dimensional perspective in their attempt to maximize the sensual effects of flowing lines on a two-dimensional plane (see page 160). The Impres-

the master painter Hon'ami Koetsu (1558–1637), the creative genius Tawaraya Sotatsu (1576–1643), and several of their colleagues working in the late sixteenth and early seventeenth centuries. Koetsu and Sotatsu did not influence the general public at the time, but did influence Ogata Korin (1658–1716) and his brother Kenzan (1663–1743) one hundred years later. Perhaps it would be more accurate to say that the earlier artists Koetsu and Sotatsu essentially produced Korin himself and that it was Korin who finally determined the aesthetics of the Edo

ABOVE CENTER: Sekiya-zu, *the right section of the* Genji Monogatari Sekiya Miotsukushi-zu Byobu *by Tawaraya Sotatsu. This section depicts scenes from Chapter 16 of* The Tale of Genji *where Genji is shown in a chance encounter with his former lover and her husband. The rhythmical arrangement of the oxcart, people, and trees is depicted against a background of one-dimensional hills, creating a well-balanced contrast. Seikado Bunko, Tokyo.*
ABOVE RIGHT and BELOW (DETAILS): From the Genji Monogatari Sekiya Miotsukushi-zu Byobu *by Tawaraya Sotatsu.*

period. It was this sense of aesthetics, if we might be allowed exaggerate slightly, that was transformed into the Art Nouveau of the West at the turn of the century.

THE AESTHETICS OF THE RIMPA SCHOOL

The first characteristic that brought attention to the aesthetics of the Rimpa school was the way a variety of spaces were dealt with so effectively. The size of objects ranged from very small (fans, cards, and plates) to very large (folding screens). Shapes were not limited to rectangles, but included peculiar forms. In addition, the Rimpa painters drew not only on flat surfaces but also on curved surfaces (e.g., the lids of inkstone boxes). They, or rather Sotatsu himself, since all the Rimpa painters learned from him, must thus have been extremely conscious of the structure of various spaces.

ABOVE: Bugaku-zu Byobu, *screen from the late seventeenth century. The dancers are placed in simple side-by-side formations, giving the impression of a flat plane. Rinno-ji temple, Nikko, Tochigi Prefecture.*

It can be said that a painter's work starts with perception of space. The second characteristic of the Rimpa school, which can be termed a kind of structuralism, must have emanated from such specific perception. For example, an equilateral triangle can be created in a picture by placing three objects (e.g., three individuals or three flowers) in such a position. The structure will not change according to the type of object placed at the apex since it is the positional relationship of the three objects that determines the structure and not the characteristics of the objects themselves. Painters can emphasize either the positional relationship or the structure exclusively, regardless of the characteristics of individual objects. Alternatively, they can

set the positional relationship aside to concentrate on the characteristics of the objects. The former is a type of structuralism. If one wants to emphasize the structure and to accentuate the equilateral triangle, three objects (e.g., a person, a stone and a flower) will suffice. However, three objects (e.g., three mallow flowers) similar in shape, size, and color, and different only in position would provide a greater visual impact thereby proving that pictorial structuralism prefers the arrangement of multiple similar objects in a homogeneous plane. Let us look at one simple but excellent example.

The Rimpa school is known for its *Senmen Harimaze Byobu,* folding screens in which fans (*senmen*) are pasted onto a background surface that is usually of a single color lined with gold leaf. When the screen is seen from a distance, only the positional relationship of the fans stands out, as the detailed patterns of their surfaces generally cannot be seen.

One such case is the *Senmen Harimaze Byobu* of Sakai Hoitsu, in which a large screen is divided into right and left sides, presenting a total of twelve rectangular, vertical surfaces and thirty-six fans. Each rectangle contains fans placed singularly or in pairs either slightly to the left or to the right. The irregular placement of the fans helps give the impression that the entire arrangement is swaying.

The fans vary in position and shape from the top or bottom of each rectangle. When viewed as a whole, the shapes begin at approximately the middle of the work, descend slightly, ascend abruptly, descend once, and ascend again. The gradual descent, counterpoised with an abrupt ascent, eventually settles in the middle of the work. One may experience the feeling of rising and falling when viewing the screen, an effect created simply by the positional relationship of fans of the same shape and size. Each fan picture depicts hills, streams, plants, flowers, or animals, but these images are quite simple and are certainly not the major feature of the work. In this way, Hoitsu's masterly screen is an unusual example in the Rimpa school although the structuralist tendencies that helped create such a screen can be found in all the works of the Rimpa school. Such tendencies did not appear previously in either the Tosa or Kano schools of art, nor were they found among *sumi* brush painters.

The point of achievement, however, is often also the point of departure. For instance, the *Shozu Byobu* (Pine tree) picture screen, stamped with the name Teiseiken but attributed to Hoitsu, depicts an arrangement of dark green pine trees, each of a different shape but bearing the same color and foliage and placed against a background of gold leaf. Near the left side of the screen, two trees are placed at about medium height. Slightly apart from this pair are seven trees in a line that starts from the lower left corner and rises toward the upper right corner. A large, open space exists between the grouping of trees and a tree in the lower right corner. This positional relationship is the crucial element of the composition, in which a subtle and stable spacial order is created by the irregular, asymmetrical rise and fall of the pine trees.

necessary means of structuring the background of sheets of gold leaf along the axis line from the upper left to the lower right corners of the composition. This technique, incidentally, was used by the *ukiyo-e* artists two hundred years later and became internationally well known. Description of the pine tree or the ornamental object is not the goal here. Four figures are drawn along the axis line, two in red and two in a deep, dark color, dancing with their robes floating in the air. To the left side of this dynamic central arrangement of figures is a group of four people clad in masks and dark blue clothes standing beneath a pine tree. To the right is a figure dressed in white looking toward the center.

The most representative work of Sotatsu is the *Bugaku-zu Byobu*. The lower half of a pine tree is found in the upper left corner of this composition, while the upper part of an ornamental object protruding from behind drapes can be seen in the lower right corner. The extreme trimming of the pine tree, coupled with the hint of the objet d'art was a

Both contribute to the balance of the composition of the picture. The gold background is bare, but is also vibrant to the extent that some depth can be perceived. The movement created by the dancing figures, the sense of balance between the figures on the left and the figure on the right, and the stability of the entire picture as it is set along its

ABOVE LEFT, RIGHT (DETAILS): Bugaku-zu Byobu *by Tawaraya Sotatsu. Although all the dancers are taken from other existing* bugaku-zu, *their skillful arrangement here gives the picture a unique rhythmical movement. Daigo-ji temple, Kyoto.*

horizontal axis, are all effects Sotatsu created by calculating the distance and positional relationship of the figures as they are arranged on a homogeneous background plane. He further enhanced these effects by masterful choice in the selection of colors.

If one scans the picture following a horizontal line from left to right, the mass of four dark-colored figures on the left and the white-clad figure on the right appear extremely well balanced, as if they were "weights" of color. This use of color was not simply manipulated for the sake of being ornamental or functional, but as a visual realization of motion and stillness, fluctuation and harmony, variety and unity, and lightness and darkness. It is also a skillful, individualistic, graphic expression.

One of Korin's most representative works is the *Kakitsubata-zu Byobu* (Irises), a six-fold screen located at the Nezu Museum in Tokyo. Blue irises and their clusters of green leaves are drawn against a gold background. Two dark and light shades of blue are used in the flowers, but smooth leaves with no visible veins are painted in a single, dark green

tone. Korin's incomparable skill in sketching the irises and leaves is particularly evident in the patterns of the leaves. His masterful utilization of abstract space enabled him to create infinite variety in the clusters of plants. This technique helped lend a certain liquid quality to the structure of the composition. In this painting, the collective shape, rather than the individual form of a particular flower or leaf, is called into question. The structure and lyricism of the space is determined by the position of each plant cluster in the composition.

The abstract use of space found in other works of the Rimpa school was not always accomplished by arranging similarly shaped objects on a homogeneous background. The method of drawing a large, colored plane in the tradition of the Yamato-e school was also employed. For example, low hills or mounds were utilized, dividing the picture with the smooth curves of their outlines. Typical of such usage is the *Tsuta no hosomichi-zu Byobu* (Footpaths in vines), a six-fold screen. In the lower half of the composition on the left-hand side is a dark green plane which

ABOVE: Fujin Raijin-zu Byobu *(Wind and thunder gods screen) by Tawaraya Sotatsu. The powerful and almost humorous gods are placed on either side of the work, allowing the large golden space in the middle to create a sense of dynamic movement. Kennin-ji temple, Kyoto.*

123

gradually descends, disappearing into the bottom of the work at a point about two-thirds the length of the picture. Slightly over-lapping this and beginning at a point higher than the other is another dark green plane that gradually increases in width and extends to the right side of the picture. In this extremely creative composition there is nothing but green and gold planes, vines, and characters. Indeed, the space is so perfectly structured with those few elements that there is no room left for interference by any other figurations.

The use of a green plane reappears in the upper half of the large picture called *Sekiya-zu* in Sotatsu's *Genji Monogatari Sekiya Miotsukushi-zu Byobu* as highly abstracted background hills. This technique was used almost directly by Sotatsu again in his *Akikusa-zu Byobu* (The grasses of autumn screen) dating from approximately 1641 and located in the National Museum of Tokyo.

Among smaller pictures, Koetsu's *Kikori-zu Suzuribako* (Inkstone box with picture of a woodcutter) from the early seventeenth century contains the same sort of plane on the ground on which the woodcutter stands. An eloquent line gently arcs from the mid-left-hand side to the lower right corner of the slightly bulging surface of the box's lid, di-viding the surface into a lower third of gold (soil) and an upper two-thirds of dark color (background). The woodcutter's figure is placed over the dividing line. He is depicted in a completely realistic style, in contrast to the thoroughly abstract handling of the space in which his figure is placed.

The Rimpa school was also responsible for creating incomparable formative harmony in design and in the kana (Japanese syllabary characters) used as design elements. Kana characters were developed during the Heian period when beautiful works of *waka* (thirty-one-syllable Japanese poems) were being written in continuous lines on patterned writing paper. Koetsu took the formative aspect of kana characters to the limit in terms of originality. In his renowned, calligraphic de-sign of deer, the *Shiki Soka Waka-kan* (Plants and flowers of the four seasons *waka* collec-tion) (stamped with the name Inen), he scat-tered writings composed of songs from the poetry anthologies *Shin kokin Waka-shu* (New collection of ancient and modern po-ems) and *Senzai Waka-shu* (1187, compiled by imperial command). These he did not simply write in the usual form of vertical lines with equal spaces between them. Rather, he chose the position of each character with exquisite care, and also used different shades

of *sumi* and different thicknesses of line to achieve this masterly effect. Further, he ad-justed the number of strokes of each charac-ter with a purely formative point of view whenever he saw the need.

For example, a kana character composed of strokes written in thick lines would pro-duce a strong accent, while simple letters written in thin lines of light ink would in-hibit the visual effect, as that portion of the composition would be comparatively weak, a technique that works like musical notation. This arrangement of strength and weakness was deliberated with full consideration to the overall balance of the design in creating

ABOVE (DETAIL): Genji Monogatari Emaki *(Picture scroll of* The Tale of Genji)*, twelfth century. Goto Museum, Tokyo.*

ABOVE (DETAIL): Tsuru Shitae Sanjurokkasen Waka-kan. *Background painting by Tawaraya Sotatsu with calligraphy by Hon'ami Koetsu. National Museum of Kyoto.*

a unique visual rhythm. Kana became part of the picture, and the rhythm of the charac-ters was enhanced by the design. What Koetsu discovered was a method of attaining a subtle unification between the structuralism of cer-tain scattered writings and the concrete forms of artistic design.

A third characteristic of the Rimpa school concerns the manner in which individual objects were treated. One such treatment involved the unabashed utilization of distor-

OPPOSITE PAGE (DETAIL): Matsu-zu *(Pine tree) by Tawaraya Sotatsu painted on* fusuma *(sliding doors). Yogen-in, Kyoto.*

Nanban Byobu (*Southern barbarians screen*), dating from the sixteenth to seventeenth centuries, Toshodai-ji, Nara..

tion. Another treatment illustrated interest in detail independent of the whole, a method often used in miniatures.

Examples of distortion are seen in the *Karajishi-zu* (Chinese lion) and *Hakuzo-zu* (White elephant) attributed to Sotatsu and painted on cedar doors in the main hall of the Yogen-in in Kyoto. The curls of the lion's mane and tail are patterned in an effect that was apparently created for decorative purposes only. The round body of the elephant is washed fully in white, and thick *sumi* lines are added that produce a sense of great mass. The extreme abbreviation in stroke and the distortion of the image emphasize the presence of the subject.

Shohitsu (abbreviated strokes) were later adopted and fully utilized by Korin, but this

technique was not necessarily unique to the Rimpa school. The use of *sumi*, as in the *tarashikomi* technique, a technique in which several layers of ink or pigment were applied to specially prepared paper that is attributed to Sotatsu, is more characteristic of the Rimpa artists. *Ushi-zu* (Cow) by Karasumaru Mitsuhiro at the Chomyo-ji temple in Kyoto did not employ lines, but the weight and movement of the cow's heaving neck and belly were captured through the *tarashikomi* technique. In short, these artists were able to transcend details and to discover the true nature of individual objects based on the newly discovered realism.

The artists of the Rimpa school also had an interest in details painted in the Yamato-e style. It was in this style that Sotatsu painted

fine flower patterns on the wheels of a cart in the *Sekiya Miotsukushi-zu Byobu* mentioned earlier. Korin added green moss to the trunks of plum trees in his *Kobai Hakubai-zu Byobu* (Pink and white plum tree screen) using the *tarashikomi* technique. The fanned feathers of a peacock's tail seen in Korin's *Kujaku Tachiaoi-zu Byobu* are drawn in a fine brush. Such attention to minute detail cannot be seen from the distance required to view the whole composition. If one approached the picture in order to see such details at close range, one could not see the picture in its entirety. Thus, the miniatures contained in large paintings show the painters' interest in the detailed portions themselves apart from the composition as a whole.

The fourth characteristic of the Rimpa school has to do with the use of color. The deep green of the pine trees painted on a gold background can also be seen in the works of the Kano school, but certain elements are seen only in the work of the Rimpa painters who possessed a unique and masterful sense of color.

Fifth, it should be mentioned that the above-mentioned characteristics do not necessarily appear independently in individual works. Rather, representative paintings unify some of those characteristics in the same work. This comprehensive harmony of the whole created through the employment of various techniques may be the Rimpa painters' strongest characteristic.

For instance, in the work called *Fujin Raijin-zu* on display at Kennin-ji temple in

Kyoto, the white Raijin (god of thunder) and the green Fujin (god of wind) are positioned at both ends of a wide, golden space. One is bearing down on a cloud, while the other is running across one. The details of their bodies are abbreviated and their muscles are contorted, yet the depiction of their postures in motion, incorporating a sense of strong force and vigorous movement, is quite accurately captured.

How is the golden background employed? As a technique, it is quite ordinary. Contemporary screens and *fusuma* (sliding doors) are often seen painted in this style. As an early artistic expression, however, it represents heaven and the sky, and is quite possibly the largest space ever depicted by a Japanese painter.

In the *Kobai Hakubai-zu Byobu* mentioned earlier, the highly abstract pattern of water flows through the middle of the picture. This original flowing pattern, later adopted by Sakai Hoitsu, was infinitely repeated in Edo-period crafts and became almost a Japanese folk art still seen in some of today's mass-produced lacquerware. However, when Korin drew it in the early eighteenth century, it was not a mere decorative pattern but rather a brave adventure by an audacious artist. It was also an unprecedented approach to abstract painting.

The flowing water creates a perfect balance with the detailed pink and white plum trees on both sides of the river. These plum trees, masterfully cropped and painted in a subdued yet brilliantly musical arrangement of small pink and white flowers, create a perfect harmony by their contrast.

Finally, the sixth characteristic of the Rimpa aesthetic is theme. The artists were thoroughly worldly. They did not paint the Buddha, Bosatsu, gods, nor any mixture of the theistic elements found in Shintoism and Buddhism. With the exception of Sotatsu's Fujin, Raijin, and Karajishi, legendary animals such as dragons do not appear. Instead, scenes from Heian-period literature, such as *The Tale of Genji* and *Ise Monogatari,* were repeatedly chosen. *Waka* poems were sometimes scattered throughout a composition. Plants, flowers, and flowing water were also depicted. These worldly themes remained unchanged from the late sixteenth century until the early nineteenth century. The Rimpa painters were not alone in using these themes, so it may not be appropriate to say that the worldliness of their recurring themes was an inherent characteristic of the Rimpa school. Nevertheless, they were consistent in their choices, and thus represented the features of typical Edo-period culture in the world of painting.

Hon'ami Koetsu lived in a period marked in the beginning by the battle of Okehazama (1560) and in the end by the Shimabara Uprising (1637). In 1573 the feudal system centering on the Muromachi shogunate collapsed, precipitating a series of brutal civil wars through which the military dictatorship attempted to maintain hegemony and unify the nation. This concentration of power also meant the control of provincial feudal lords known as daimyo and restrictions on court nobles and Kyoto merchants who had developed their own economic power bases since the Muromachi period. The policy of Sakoku (national seclusion) was instituted in 1639. The nation was closed to the outside world and foreign trade was severely restricted by the ruling samurai. Sakoku and the earlier limitations placed on overseas trade (1633) were of obvious detriment to the powerful merchant class of Kyoto. Many of the wealthier families, such as the Chaya and Suminokura, had built economic empires through their participation in foreign trade.

Furthermore, Sakoku had a direct relationship on the suppression of Christianity that had been introduced in the sixteenth century. Prior to the creation of this policy, there had been a great many religious struggles in Japan including conflicts with the priests of the Hongan-ji temple, the suppression of the Ikko riot, and the repression of the Nichiren sect. During this period the Tokugawa shogunate exerted control over temple organizations, essentially suppressing organized rebellion by people of particu-

BELOW LEFT (DETAIL): Kimono fabric in a design of iris and flowing water on white by Ogata Korin. Courtesy of Kanebo Co., Ltd., Tokyo.

BELOW RIGHT (DETAIL): A work depicting the flowers and birds of four seasons by Sakai Hoitsu (1751–1828). National Museum of Tokyo.

lar religious faiths. Religious rebellion has never occurred since in Japan.

The Hon'ami family, into which Koetsu was born, was one of the most distinguished and powerful families in Kyoto. Suminokura Soan (1571–1632) was a wealthy merchant

and scholar, expert in the Chinese classics, and known as a man of refined taste. Soan studied under Furuta Oribe (1543–1615), one of Koetsu's disciples in calligraphy, and collaborated with Koetsu in reproducing and publishing beautiful reprints of classic literature. Chaya Shirojiro (ca 1545–96), a renowned merchant, joined Koetsu in building an artistic colony when Koetsu moved to Takagamine with his family. We can surmise from these facts that a close relationship existed among the Kyoto upper-class towns-

LEFT: Gunkaku-zu Byobu (*Flock of cranes screen*) *by Suzuki Kiitsu (1796–1858). The work is a copy of a Korin original. Shinenkan, USA.*

BELOW LEFT (DETAIL): From Sakai Hoitsu's Flowers and Birds of Four Seasons. *Uomachi Noraku-kai, Aichi Prefecture.*

BELOW RIGHT (DETAIL): Moon and Autumn Grasses kimono fabric by Ogata Korin. The second son of a renowned kimono merchant in Kyoto, Korin designed kimono fabrics that came to be known as the "Korin pattern" and were very popular.

people. This was the social milieu in which Koetsu existed.

The Hon'ami family was well known among the wealthy families in the imperial cultural circle. The family trade brought them close to the level of upper-class samurai. In fact, since Koetsu's father's generation, the Hon'ami family had received a stipend from the Maeda clan in Kaga. Koetsu was also deeply connected to the imperial court, and was a close friend of Karasumaru Mitsuhiro (1579–1638), a renowned calligrapher who highly praised the paintings of Sotatsu and who helped Koetsu maintain a strong connection to the nobility.

When Tokugawa Ieyasu granted him a large tract of land in Takagamine north of Kyoto in 1615, Koetsu essentially had no choice but to move there. As he had known many artists and craftsmen, Takagamine became a kind of artists' colony and workshop after his relocation. Koetsu moved his family there, and also brought the paper merchant Sojin, the brush merchant Myoki, Ogata Sohaku, a son of Koetsu's older sister (who was a kimono merchant), and other artisans. In addition, since a piece of poetry-based artwork combining Sotatsu's designs and Koetsu's calligraphy has been discovered, it seems likely that Sotatsu as well was nearby. Koetsu copied the *Rissho Ankoku-ron (A Treatise on Pacifying the State by Establishing Orthodoxy)* by Nichiren at the request of the priest at the Myoren-ji temple. Thus, Koetsu's milieu consisted not only of upper-class townspeople but also of followers of Nichiren.

In the early seventeenth century, court nobles and upper-class citizens of Kyoto became dissatisfied with the policies of the Tokugawa shogunate. It was only natural then that the shogunate regarded them, in turn, with some apprehension. Although the shogunate never forcefully oppressed Nichiren believers, it exiled Nichioku, the leader of the Fuju Fuse branch of the Nichiren sect, to a remote island (1599). Given such an atmosphere, what attitude did the shogunate take toward the alliance of Suminokura Soan, Karasumaru Mitsuhiro, and Hon'ami Koetsu?

The Suminokura family had a history of supporting the Fuju Fuse. Naturally, then, the shogunate was suspicious of the Hon'ami family's faith in Hokke. On the other hand, Karasumaru Mitsuhiro (along with other court nobles) was once convicted of adultery (1609) and punished for the offense. Since Koetsu was a close friend of Karasumaru, it is quite likely that the shogunate gave him the land in Takagamine in order to remove him from Kyoto.

Seen from the perspective of Soan, Mitsuhiro, and Koetsu, the move must have served to further strengthen ties between and among the aristocrats and upper-class townsmen united against the Tokugawa shogunate, at least in the cultural domain. The effect of this united front was a revitalization of the tradition of Heian culture rooted in Kyoto.

It has already been noted that the writing paper, designs, and particularly the poetry-based artwork developed by Koetsu's group had a distinct style. Koetsu's work was a combination of conservative themes and innovative styles. For example, the theme of the design of the *Funabashi Maki-e Suzuribako (Boat Bridge Inlaid Inkstone Box)* at the National Museum of Tokyo was taken from the Heian period. The form of the box is innovative and unique; the lid is raised and

ABOVE: The Woods (*1886–1888*) *is an example of Japonisme by Vincent van Gogh. Van Gogh Museum of Amsterdam.*

ABOVE: Kameido Umeyashiki *(Kameido Garden) by Utagawa Hiroshige (1787–1858). Van Gogh Museum of Amsterdam.*

gracefully arched and there is a wide lead plate inserted diagonally across its center. The design of the inlay work is of a wave and a boat with the kanji characters of a song scattered around them. The proportions of the characters on the lead plate, the contrast between the dark color of the lead and the silver used in the inlay work, and the care-

Yamato-e painting, lacked creativity to the point that no one expected its artisans to revive the tradition. Although Sotatsu began his training in the Yamato-e style, handling the same themes as those in the Tosa school, he was able to create a completely unique style. Among Kyoto noblemen and upper-class society there was an interest in impe-

fully conceived design of the inlay work itself are particularly masterly, reflecting the ultimate sophistication in aesthetic perception.

The same can be said regarding the paintings of Tawaraya Sotatsu. The Kano school enjoyed the patronage of the ruling samurai. The Tosa school, though connected to aristocratic culture in keeping to the tradition of

ABOVE LEFT: Ohashiatake no Yudachi *(1857) by Utagawa Hiroshige. Keio Gijuku, Tokyo.*

ABOVE: Bridge in the Rain *(1887) by Vincent van Gogh. Van Gogh copied Japanese* ukiyo-e *woodblock prints. Van Gogh Museum of Amsterdam.*

ABOVE: Vase with seaweed pattern, 23.5 cm in height, by Emile Gallé.

RIGHT: Vase in the shape of an eggplant, 29 cm in height, by Emile Gallé.

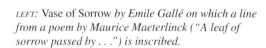

LEFT: Vase of Sorrow *by Emile Gallé on which a line from a poem by Maurice Maeterlinck ("A leaf of sorrow passed by . . .") is inscribed.*

rial styles and a tradition of imperial culture as a basis for self-identification. Themes were determined by this environment, and the particulars were determined by the genius of the artist.

Sotatsu's materials were always taken from Bugaku (court dance and music) and traditional tales. He never drew Chinese-style landscapes or portraiture, nor did he depict animals such as dragons and tigers. He did not adopt themes from popular culture that were drawn even by the Kano school painters and he did not choose to depict contemporary beauties, bathing women, or foreigners. In short, Sotatsu was thorough in his choice of themes and exclusively emphasized imperial styles.

In contrast to what is known of Koetsu's life, we can say little about that of Sotatsu. It has been assumed that he might have been a fan merchant in Kyoto. The only thing that is certain is that a painter by the name of Sotatsu was around at the same time as Koetsu and was painting for major temples and people in the same area.

Noted earlier, Ogata Korin and Ogata Kenzan were the sons of a respectable old Kyoto family of wealthy kimono merchants. Their great-grandfather married Koetsu's older sister, and their grandfather lived with Koetsu at Takagamine. Korin initially squandered his fortune and later became a painter, while Kenzan loved studying from an early age and eventually produced pottery for a living. Both profligacy and study would have been difficult without the benefit of an inherited family fortune.

Korin learned painting from Yamamoto Soken of the Kano school but later became devoted to Sotatsu. Kenzan studied pottery with Koho, a grandson of Koetsu, then later studied under Nonomura Ninsei, adding his own styles. He also painted screens in his later days. Most of the subjects of Korin's paintings were ordinarily encountered scenes: plants, flowers, flowing water, trees, and *yatsuhashi* (eight-fold plank-bridge) designs. He did not paint landscapes. Particularly skilled in *sumi* brush painting, he painted *Yuima-zu* (Vimalakirti) and *Kemari Hotei-zu* (Hotei, one of the Seven Deities of Good Fortune) in a superb brush-painting style. Flowers, birds, and streams were by far his most common subjects.

In the world of the Genroku era (1688–1704), *chonin* (townspeople) did not harbor as much resentment against the ruling power as those in Koetsu's community did. By then, the shogunate was well established and the economic power of the townspeople was

ABOVE: *Milk pitcher with cicada and praying mantis, 15 cm in height, from the Gallé workshop.*

increasing. In this atmosphere, a philosophy affirming the reality of everyday life developed, rather than the desire to revive Heian culture. Their personal immersion into the world of art must have been a particular source of pride for Koetsu and Sotatsu. This feeling of pride might have been the basis on which they established individualism within the tense environment caused by their relationship to surrounding society. Korin and Kenzan painted screens and hanging scrolls, and made ceramic ware and mosaic boxes to beautify the life of the upper-class townspeople and to incorporate art as ornamenta-

ABOVE: *Perfume bottle in the shape of a figwort, 15 cm in height. Lines from a poem by Pierre Dupont are engraved on the vessel's surface.*

tion into their culture. This was not an attempt to make life into art, but rather to make art into life.

Up to this point in time, the determining factor in artists' themes was the times in which they lived and the way their works were used by members of society. What actually determined the artistic quality and originality was individual will and talent. Korin and Kenzan came from upper-class society, but the era eventually assimilated their art into everyday life. Their signature flowing waters and *yatsuhashi* would eventually become commonly seen patterns.

After Korin and Kenzan, the Rimpa school experienced a revival during the late eighteenth and early nineteenth centuries in the painter Sakai Hoitsu (1761–1829). One of his masterpieces is the *Natsu Akikusa-zu Byobu* (Summer and autumn grasses screen) at the National Museum of Tokyo. On the lower half of the left screen are blades of eulalia grass with *hirugao* (bindweed), lily, and *ominaeshi* (valerianaceae). A tiny stream of flowing water is depicted in the upper right corner. Eulalia and kudzu leaves sway in the wind, and three reddened grape leaves fly in the sky in the screen on the right. Here,

ABOVE: Flower vase with jellyfish pattern, 30.5 cm in height, by Emile Gallé.

ABOVE: Lamp with pattern of waves and fish, 33 cm in height, from the Gallé workshop. Kitazawa Museum, Nagano Prefecture.

OPPOSITE PAGE (DETAIL): Flower vase with jellyfish pattern.

RIGHT: A poster for La Traviata *starring Sarah Bernhardt at the Renaissance Theatre in Paris, 1896, by Alphonse Mucha (1860–1939). Kyoto University Industrial Art and Textile Museum.*

ABOVE: Hyginea *detail from* Medicin *by Gustav Klimt (1862–1918), ca 1907, destroyed in 1945.*

the gold background that Korin employed is transformed to silver, and his wide iris leaves are transformed into the narrow leaves of eulalia with edges as sharp as blades. This screen does not show a self-satisfied, affluent, and forever stable world. Rather, as the contrast between summer and autumn well illustrates, it is a fleeting, perceptual world, sharp and filled with tension. One could call it a symbolical expression of the disappearing social and political order. In this screen, Korin may well have captured the most profound expression of the period.

If Korin related well to noble culture, Hoitsu held himself in opposition to it. Suzuki Kiitsu (1796–1858) was a disciple of Hoitsu who employed new devices and explored many new concepts. However, his pictures do not vibrate beneath the surface as do Hoitsu's. They do not exhibit a sense of being sharp as a knife blade yet fragile, nor do they reveal an intrinsic sense of the present. With the final glow of the Rimpa school radiating from his work, it was the incomparable Hoitsu himself who seems to have foreseen the end of the Edo period.

139

A Universe in the Palm of the Hand

The irregularly shaped tea-ceremony bowl was born out of a combination of imported technology and a unique aesthetic. Raku-yaki (low-fired, lead-glazed, hand-molded earthenware) tea bowls made by the tilemaker Chojiro (1516–92) are perfect examples of this aesthetic (Raku is the name of the pottery made by the Raku family in Kyoto, *yaki* is the generic term for all types of ceramic ware). One might imagine that the ceramic ware of Chojiro's time exhibited a certain lack of uniformity in shape as a result of the limitations of the available technology, but in reality artisans in sixteenth-century Japan intentionally created irregular and contorted shapes despite the fact that highly developed manufacturing techniques were available.

Pottery was imported to Japan from the continent; Chinese and Korean cultures were both highly developed in this craft. By the Tang dynasty (618–907), China had perfected porcelain technology and was manufacturing ceramic ware of glossy surfaces and sophisticated shapes. However, while China developed several complex printing techniques during the Ming dynasty (1368–1644), Chinese potters did not pursue the art of creating complex, contorted shapes by hand. Although slightly irregular tea bowls can be found among the Korean ceramic ware of the time, these were originally folkcraft intended for the everyday use of commoners. Technologically developed societies tended to create regular shapes such as those seen in the perfect, smooth shapes of Sung-dynasty (960–1279) celadon and white porcelain. Chojiro rejected those techniques in favor of a more simplified aesthetic, and the fact that the ruling class and artistic leaders preferred irregularly shaped or contorted tea bowls, at least from the Momoyama period (1568–1600) to the Edo period (1603–1868), is a distinctly Japanese phenomenon. The design of the shape of pottery originally imported from the continent can, therefore, be said to have been Japanized due to this preference.

Another distinctive characteristic of tea-ceremony bowls is their expressive, tactile quality. In addition to their purely visual attributes, they open up the world of touch. Sung-dynasty porcelain dishes and vases were virtually flawless in terms of their evenly balanced shapes and were considered the height of elegance. The coloring of the luminous surface of these porcelains is perfect and uniform. After all, they were meant to be viewed and admired again and again.

On the other hand, tea-ceremony ceramic ware, especially tea bowls, were meant not only to be viewed, but also to be touched and held. The movements of the fingers of the artist who worked the clay speak through the weight and surface of the tea bowl so that when one holds a tea bowl, turning and handling it, the tactile sensation draws one nearer to the emotional state of the artist at the time the work was created. The shape of the tea bowl simultaneously represents completion as well as the process of creation. The surface of a Raku-yaki tea bowl is uneven, some parts rough and others smooth, and the coloring of the glaze corresponds to the surface. The touch, color, and luster differ on various portions of the tea bowl, so that if one admires a tea bowl while turning and handling it, a new and unexpected perspective will arise at each angle.

This aesthetic is based on fundamentally different principles than those used in the creation of Sung-dynasty porcelains. The aesthetic of tea-ceremony ceramics does not appeal to the order of the object in its entirety, but rather can be experienced through its infinitely complex parts. It is not a beauty of perfection but an embodiment of movement and process.

One red tea bowl created by Chojiro is named *Sunset* (Goto Museum, Tokyo) after the custom of giving a *mei*, or inscription, to one-of-a-kind works. This tea bowl conjures a variety of images for those who use it. One is the image of the western sky at dusk, with a burning crimson cloud and a fading gray cloud silhouetted against a slightly rose-colored sky.

In other instances, the green powdered tea used in the tea ceremony, after being whipped into a foam in the bottom of a black Raku-yaki tea bowl, may appear particularly bright. The color can be reminiscent of a larch grove in early spring or of the Mediterranean seen from a cliff on the Côte d'Azur. Shino tea bowls are milky white with a smooth but

ABOVE: Kinoshita, *a black tea bowl by Donyu (1599–1656), 11.6 cm in diameter. Raku Museum, Kyoto.*

OPPOSITE PAGE: The entrance to the Shokokan teahouse dating from the Edo period. Daitoku-ji temple, Kyoto.

subtly uneven surface and a matte finish, quite different from the cold luster of white porcelain. The novelist Kawabata Yasunari once compared the feel of a Shino tea bowl to the skin of a woman.

Tea bowls used in the tea ceremony were one-of-a-kind with distinct, individual characteristics. Such characteristics are not to be found among mass-produced porcelain, but neither are they exclusive to Japanese culture. There are many examples of one-of-a-kind pieces of porcelain seen in China. However, the custom of giving a special name or *mei* to tea bowls is not seen in China or in the West.

Some names are given simply to identify a precious item. For example, a large black tea bowl may be called *Oguro* (large black). Some tea bowls were named after their original owners, and the names themselves can resonate with meaning. One is *Shibata,* origi-nally owned by Shibata Katsuie, a renowned samurai. Another is *Kizaemon,* which once belonged to Takeda Kizaemon, who would not give up his *Ido-jawan,* an extremely precious tea-ceremony bowl imported from Korea, even after he suffered financial ruin. Such names not only identify certain tea bowls but endow them with a certain legendary and literary quality. Other names were not assigned for purposes of identification, but rather to give the bowl a certain image or association. For example, the naming of the previously mentioned Raku-yaki tea cup *Sunset* expresses creative judgment. Chojiro's red tea bowl *Dojo-ji* is shaped like the famous bell at Dojo-ji temple turned upside down. Hon'ami Koetsu's (1558–1637) Raku-yaki tea bowl known as *Mount Fuji* has a whitish glaze on its upper portion that dark-ens toward the bottom, representing Mount Fuji covered with snow.

The names themselves resonate beyond their evocations of the actual places or images. *Dojo-ji* prompts recollection of a famous Noh play, while the words "Mount Fuji" harken back to the many poems composed on the theme throughout Japanese history. The effect of this kind of creative judgment or comparison, known as *mitate,* was also a preferred technique of eighteenth century *ukiyo-e* artists because of its traditional literary associations.

Mitate usually reflects the formal characteristics of the object, but sometimes does not have any direct relationship to the object's form. The tea bowl inscribed *Shunkan,* after a monk exiled to the island of Kikai-jima at the end of the Heian period (794–1185), has a very interesting story. A man in Satsuma demanded that Sen no Rikyu (1522–91), the wealthy Sakai merchant classes' most distinguished tea master, send some tea bowls

made by Chojiro to him. Apparently, the man in Satsuma then kept only one out of the three that Sen no Rikyu sent and returned the other two. If Satsuma is seen as a kind of parallel to Kikai-jima island, then the bowl that stayed in Satsuma must be like Shunkan (i.e., exiled). This is a form of wordplay and has no relationship to the formal qualities of the bowl in question. However, the name *Shunkan* also brings to mind the names and plots of Noh, Kabuki, and puppet plays of the period.

This kind of intricate literary effect was used in a black Raku-yaki tea bowl called *Akujo (Ugly Woman).* The fact that the bowl is deep plays upon the expression "*akujo no fukanasake*" (an ugly woman has deep compassion). Although it is not clear who named the tea bowl or when, the combination of such a precious item and a name like *Akujo* is jarring, wrought with black humor.

Preference for the literary effect of a name regardless of the nature of the item being named is one distinctive characteristic of Japanese culture. The reason why *waka* (thirty-one-syllable Japanese poem) anthologies compiled during the Heian period by the imperial court on the emperor's orders contain so many songs about *hototogisu* (cuckoo) and *uguisu* (Japanese nightingale) is not that they were the birds most commonly seen singing in hills and fields at that time, or that their songs were particularly beautiful compared to the songs of other bird. Rather, it was because the words *hototogisu* and *uguisu* came from traditional poetic vocabulary.

The creativity of Japanese pottery is probably best represented by the irregularity in shape of Momoyama-period tea-ceremony ceramic ware, but the history of Japanese pottery is a long one, and tea-ceremony objects are but a small part of it. There are perhaps two outstanding characteristics in the development of Japanese pottery as a whole. As we have discussed, one is the fact that technological innovations occurred in China and not in Japan. Innovative technologies were always imported from the continent. The second factor is that, once imported, new technologies were assimilated in a relatively short period of time and were often improved in the process. However, production using old technology was never abandoned in lieu of newer, incoming technology. In Japan, both were used simultaneously, leading to enormous variety in pottery and porcelain.

Some of the painting on ceramic ware created during this period was done in the

ABOVE and DETAIL: Powdered green tea is slowly whisked into foam with a bamboo chasen *before being served.*

Chinese style, but objects decorated with plants and flowers show the clear influence of Yamato-e or the Rimpa schools. In some, a large area of white background has occasionally been left untouched. In others, the background is either completely or partially painted solid black. Gold and silver leaf has been scattered on the surface, and bright red, yellow, purple, and green spots of glaze appear in a delicate arrangement. The *Iroe Fujizu Chatsubo* (Tea jar with painted wisteria) in the MOA Museum in Atami and the *Iroe Keshizu Chatsubo* (Tea jar with painted poppies) in the Idemitsu Museum in Tokyo are further examples of how ornamental plant and flower paintings of the Sotatsu workshop were masterfully translated onto the surface of ceramic ware.

Ceramic ware made in the Omuro family kilns in Kyoto exhibited unique ornamental designs and sophisticated ceramic-painting

Kenzan abstracted his designs and made them into patterns. For instance in the *Iroe Tsubakimon Shiho Mukozuke* (Square dish with camellia pattern) now owned by the Tokio Fire and Marine Insurance Company, the simple eight-petal white flowers with yellow centers are painted against a solid, dark green background. The outstanding features are the vivid contrast, the large size of the flowers compared to the size of the dish, and the repetition of flowers of the same size and pattern. The comparatively large, colored elements of a set shape are arranged in a small space to appear as if bulging out of it. The contrast of colors is so distinct that the work of Kenzan can be recognized immediately, even from a distance. The effect is not elegant and delicate but dynamic and powerful. His *Iroe Matsu-zu Chawan* (Tea bowl with painted pine) at the Shinji Shumei Club in Kyoto brilliantly expresses a pine tree

techniques from the mid-seventeenth century. A pottery kiln was established in front of Ninna-ji temple in Kyoto and mainly produced tea-ceremony ceramic ware by Nonomura Seiemon (date unknown), called Ninsei, a name taken from the first syllable of the temple's name and the first syllable of the potter's given name.

After Ninsei, Ogata Kenzan (1663–1743), the younger brother of Korin (1658–1716), created distinct, colorful ceramic ware in Kyoto. Later in his life, when he was about seventy, Kenzan moved to Iriya in Edo, where he dedicated the rest of his life to ceramic ware and painting. His work can be divided into two types. One includes square dishes and trays decorated with *akasabi-e* (red rust painting) flowers and birds, hills, streams, or calligraphy. The other group includes glazed dishes, bowls, covered containers, and tea bowls. Unlike any other Japanese potter,

with three colors: light gray, green, and blue. This certainly would not have been Rikyu's favorite piece of ceramic ware since his ideal was *sabi*, an aesthetic ideal related to the word *sabi* (rust) or to *sabireru* (to become desolate). Nor would it have appealed to the unorthodox taste of the master ceramist Furuta Oribe (1544–1615). Rather, a kind of brightness prevails in Kenzan's patterns and designs that differs from the aesthetics of tea-ceremony ceramics exhibiting the characteristics of *wabi*, an artistic expression of the awareness of the Zen "void.". Although the aesthetics of *wabi-sabi* had existed since the Genroku era (1688–1704), it demonstrated a completely different sensibility.

145

As we have seen, Japanese Neolithic culture produced creative and sophisticated ornamentation on Jomon earthenware, but it did not create any innovative technology since the culture remained isolated. Encounters with the outside world facilitated a process whereby new and old technologies coexisted; the old were not simply replaced by the new. The aesthetics of the tea ceremony and *chado* or *sado,* the Way of Tea, with its penchant for the simple and quiet, were established through this sort of technological progression.

AN AESTHETIC REVOLUTION

The custom of drinking tea became preva-

lent in Zen temples during the Kamakura period (1185–1333). In the early thirteenth century, Eisai imported the Rinzai Sect of Buddhism from China, and along with it brought Chinese tea. Writing in the *Kissa Yojo-ki (Book of Tea and Health),* he praised tea for being "a miracle elixir for health." The custom of drinking tea soon spread beyond the temples. During the Muromachi period (1392–1568), entertainment such as *rinkan chanoyu,* a combination of bathing and tea drinking, became popular among

commoners, while members of the upper class competed in collecting tea-ceremony utensils, calligraphy, and paintings. This fashion was so popular that when the tea master and connoisseur Murata Juko (ca 1432–1502) first rose to eminence in the fourteenth century, it was thought that "those who do not enjoy *chanoyu* (the tea ceremony) are not human." This saying demonstrates that participation in the tea ceremony was regarded as one of the new forms of entertainment at the time, and that it was thought to be even better if, in addition to its pleasures, it was useful in propagating the spread of Confucianism or Buddhism.

"The tea ceremony is singularly preferred not only among daimyo, but also among commoners in the southern capital of Kyoto, and Sakai [an important port city during the mid-fourteenth to mid-seventeenth centuries]," says the *Book of Tea and Health* which also relates how the feudal lord Ashikaga Yoshimasa, who retired at Higashiyama Sanso (present-day Ginkaku-ji in Kyoto), supposedly enjoyed every form of entertainment available as "he played day and night, during all four seasons." Yoshimasa reportedly asked the painter Noami (ca 1450) if he knew "any unusual entertainment." Noami recommended the tea ceremony and introduced Yoshimasa to Juko since, as a tea master, "Juko had devoted himself to the tea ceremony since thirty years of age" and was also educated in Confucianism. Also, Zen Buddhist *bokuseki* (*sumi* calligraphy) brush paintings are sometimes used as elements of the tea ceremony, leading Juko to reportedly say, "Buddhism is in the tea ceremony."

Juko was one of the most outstanding among the first generation of masters of the three art forms: calligraphy, painting, and tea ceremony. In his time, the objects of choice in calligraphy, painting, or tea-ceremony utensils were always *karamono* (Chinese) Tang-dynasty items such as *bokuseki* brush paintings, and porcelain imported from China. The Japanese learned *bokuseki* from Chinese calligraphy, and they had a certain aesthetic preference for the paintings of the artists Muxi and Liang Kai. These preferences were passed on to the tea-ceremony connoisseurs who came after Juko, who is said to have owned a treasured *bokuseki* received as a gift from the great Zen master Ikkyu (1394–1481).

Sen no Rikyu also used *bokuseki* by Ryoan (1425–1514) in his tea-ceremony rooms. The collection of Tang paintings owned by the shoguns Yoshimitsu and Yoshimasa, Juko, and the tea-ceremony master Takeno Jo-o (1504–55) exhibit a perfectly consistent preference for this artistic style. The most cherished tea-ceremony utensils were celadon porcelains and *tenmoku* (tea bowls) from China. Later, various kinds of dazzling *tenmoku* came to be valued. It is not clear in what way Juko evaluated Japanese ceramics in terms of their use as tea-ceremony utensils or to what extent he might have used them himself. The close attendants of the Ashikaga shogunate used to prepare tea in a separate room and serve it in the guest room, but Juko apparently invented the practice of preparing tea in front of his guests. It is not clear, however, whether the tea room was expressly invented for the purpose of preparing tea for visitors. Basically, it can be said that the tea ceremony of the fifteenth century was a form of luxurious entertainment with Tang-dynasty art and objects the preferred accessories and utensils.

In the sixteenth century, the tea ceremony became popular among rich merchants in Sakai. Rather than having their attendants prepare tea, they themselves used the utensils to make tea, sitting with their guests. Takeno Jo-o, who came from a merchant family in Sakai and later served the Ashikaga family, created a small room of four-and-a-half tatami mats (tatami mats are generally 1.76 meters long by 0.88 meters wide) for the purpose of performing the tea ceremony therein. This room was the prototype of teahouse design and became known as the *Jo-o yojohan* (four-and-a-half-tatami-mat room). The entrance had a small veranda, and the room contained a square pillar, a white wall, and an alcove. Utensils were not limited to items of Chinese origin but also included common tea bowls from the Korean Peninsula, Shigaraki (ceramic ware made in Shiga Prefecture during the Kamakura period, 1185–1333) and Bizen ceramic ware (made in Okayama Prefecture at the same time), and sometimes Seto-yaki (made in Seto, Aichi Prefecture) *tenmoku*. This diversity marked the discovery of a new kind of beauty that exhibited a clear inclination toward the *wabi* tea ceremony of the *so-an* (a word for hermitage or hut, used to describe the attendant solitude) and the aesthetics of *wabi* that were soon to be firmly established.

Rikyu made his tea room even smaller (two tatami mats), did away with the small veranda at the entrance, and emphasized bare ground as flooring. He used a round pillar with an intact natural surface instead of a square pillar. His tea room had a roughly textured wall instead of a smooth white one, and the tea bowl he employed was the Raku-yaki bowl he had requested the tilemaker Chojiro to create for him. Rikyu's ideal for the tea ceremony was simply holding a Raku-yaki tea bowl while sitting in a two-tatami-mat room. This simplicity marked an aesthetic transformation from one extreme to the other.

First, the teahouse as a structure was anti-monumental in that it rejected the prevailing notion of the times that bigger was better in favor of a more minimalist, austere approach to style. Toyotomi Hideyoshi's grand hall of a thousand tatami mats, created at the same time, represented the former value while Rikyu's two-tatami-mat room represented the latter.

The highest structure in Japan at the time was the tower of Osaka castle, while the

ABOVE: Celadon porcelain flower vase, 35.5 cm in height, Southern Sung dynasty. Fujita Museum, Osaka.

lowest was the lintel of a teahouse entrance. From the point of view of comparative cultural history, Japanese monumental architecture achieved its largest scale during the Momoyama period, although it never paralleled the massive castle structures created by Chinese and European rulers. There may actually be no Chinese or European counterpart for the smaller structure that was eventually perfected in Japan. Drinking tea in a room whose entrance was so low that upper-class officials had to bend over in order to enter it was particularly Japanese.

ABOVE: Incense burner with lotus pattern, 7.7 cm in height, dating from the Kamakura period. As Tang-dynasty pottery gained popularity, less expensive substitutes were produced.

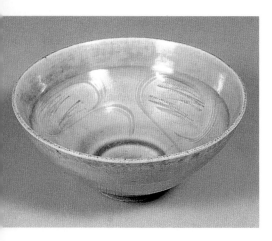

ABOVE: *Celadon porcelain tea bowl, 15 cm in diameter, Southern Sung dynasty. With the advancement of the* wabi-*style tea ceremony, more subtle colors were preferred. Idemitsu Museum, Tokyo.*

Secondly, teahouses modeled in the small *so-an* style are characteristically impermanent. Although most buildings are generally built to last, teahouses are deliberately designed to remain fragile and certainly appear temporary. Flimsy but resilient, they might not be destroyed in an earthquake, but a typhoon could easily blow them away.

Another facet of the teahouse is that it provides no protection against the elements. It is not meant to be a durable structure offering a protected inner space that resists nature and the environment. Rather, it is intended to facilitate the discovery of positive values through the acceptance of natural forces and environmental changes, even to the extent of letting them destroy the structure and encroach upon or dominate the inner space itself. Sen no Rikyu's philosophy might have been that life was uncertain, therefore architecture should reflect that uncertainty. If so, this was a unique approach to design and construction.

Thirdly, that which was rich and luxurious offered a contrast to that which was poor and simple. The *so-an* hut itself and the common objects inside it, such as ceramic water pitchers and the quiet and subtle detailing of a rough-hewn wall, were noticeably different from golden *fusuma* (sliding door) paintings and precious items such as Tang-dynasty tea cups. *Wabi* aesthetics, passed on from Jo-o to Rikyu, were an attempt to recognize beauty in simplicity.

Why did such a change of values occur? From Sen no Rikyu's time to the present day,

most writers touch upon Zen when describing the "tea ceremony of *wabi*." How did Zen relate to the tea ceremony, and what caused the shift in aesthetics?

It would be inaccurate to say that the tea ceremony originated from Zen Buddhist sects. The truth is that it came from Zen temples, and Zen sects and Zen temples are not necessarily synonymous. The custom of drinking tea became popular due to the belief that tea was medicinal. Soon afterwards tea drinking was considered entertainment. The *so-an* tea ceremony and its connection to Zen came at a much later age. The influence of Zen on the tea ceremony did not occur while Zen was becoming a powerful religious persuasion. Rather, it occurred when Zen was secularized during the Muromachi period after having enjoyed a long connection with political power, during which time it lost most of its religious force.

Sen no Rikyu is said to have used Zen vocabulary when explaining the Way of Tea. This does not necessarily mean that the characteristics of the object, the tea ceremony as performed by Jo-o and Rikyu, relate to Zen. However, in the Muromachi period, the playwright Zeami (1363–1443) used Buddhist terms and Zen vocabulary in his theories describing the subtle ideas connected to the performance arts and to Noh. It could be that he was unable to find other suitable terms with which to analyze his subject. However, *mugen* Noh is structured around the axis of the relationship between this world and the other world, a structure that parallels Bud-

RIGHT: *The* Kizaemon *tea bowl, 15.4 cm in diameter, from the sixteenth century. Daitoku-ji temple, Kyoto.*

dhism but in no way resembles Zen. The themes of his plays are often closely related to the tenets of the Jodo sect of Buddhism, but rarely relate to Zen. When Zeami speaks of aspects of the actors' performances, it is quite clear that he learned these elements from his experience on the stage and not from Buddhism or Zen.

What of the *so-an* tea ceremony? No theoretical writings exist that could offer a means of comparison to Zeami's Noh theory. However, the physical characteristics of the teahouse, such as the fact that it is small rather than large, fragile rather than sturdy, and simple rather than ornate, point to a certain denial and disregard of the value systems of the times. Zen, too, includes the aspect of absolute denial of existing value systems, including those found within Buddhist temples, such as the belief that impurities could be eradicated through the chanting of Buddhist sutras. In this, the tea ceremony bears a resemblance to Zen, but a cause-and-effect relationship cannot be established by this correlation alone. A shift in value systems occurred in both the new Jodo and Zen sects, but the area of change related to how the absolute being was seen in a religious sense. It was not a cultural or aesthetic shift in values. The *so-an* tea ceremony revolutionized aesthetic values. Zen, which was ethically conservative, could not very likely have taken a revolutionary position in terms of culture. What, then, was the driving force behind the aesthetic revolution brought about by Sen no Rikyu that influenced Japanese culture so decisively in the years to come?

Rikyu's age was one of civil war. Peasants staged repeated riots against the samurai ruling class, and samurai were engaged in power struggles employing a variety of strategies, fighting, confederations, and betrayals among themselves. Merchants in Sakai provided arms (guns and powder, or materials with which to create them) in order to make money quickly. Jo-o and Rikyu emerged from the merchant class and observed the collapse of the traditional political, economic, and ethical order in particular, and the decline of feudalistic society as a whole. Therefore, it is not surprising that Jo-o and Rikyu were not bound by any particular value system. This must have been an ideal condition in which to reverse existing aesthetic standards.

Rikyu served as tea-ceremony master to the warlord Toyotomi Hideyoshi, who often held luxurious tea parties in an immense hall. Ironically, as the tea-ceremony master serving the politically powerful, Rikyu ran enormous tea parties on the one hand, while preparing tea in his own rather humble two-tatami-mat room for different guests on the other. One world was probably the most elaborate and ostentatious existence possible, while the other was the smallest and most austere. Rikyu lived and worked in both worlds, and as there was no room for compromise between the two extremes, each side must have become more and more pronounced in its opposition. To counterbalance the gorgeous room in the warlord's castle, the tatami-mat room had to become even more severe, and so it went from four-and-a-half mats to two. If Hideyoshi's tea room was made of solid gold, then Rikyu's would need to have a rough wall. What, then, could be superior to the Tang-dynasty porcelain used by Hideyoshi? Only the handmade, simple pottery of the Raku kiln. The challenge this posed for Rikyu evolved into a difference of principle and degree. Putting these principles into concrete form made the differences between the two worlds and the aesthetics they represented even more pronounced.

Challenging a dictator, even in the area of aesthetics, was not without clear danger. A disciple of Rikyu, Yamanoue no Soji (1544–90), was also a tea-ceremony master for Hideyoshi but was discharged. Before he was finally killed by Hideyoshi, he wrote, "I truly regret that Rikyu and I practiced the tea ceremony for a living." This inscription was found on the back of a version of *Yamanoue no Soji-ki* given to his son, Iseya Doshichi. It is dated January 1588, two years before he was killed. Rikyu died soon afterward, forced to commit suicide in 1591. The two must have been well aware of the dangers of their way of life, and might have suspected that performing the tea ceremony was a potentially lethal enterprise that could very well cost them their lives.

Traditionally, guests left their swords outside before entering the teahouse, and the waist-high, small opening made it difficult to enter, especially with a sword. However, the two tea masters must have been constantly aware that their lives could end some day in the slash of a sword. Perhaps if they had not existed on the edge of death, they would not have been able to drive one of the sharpest wedges of change into the history of Japanese culture, successfully challenging the aesthetic values of the times. The untimely death of Sen no Rikyu brought an end to the aesthetic revolution that tea con-

ABOVE: Red Maple on the Hill, *Nezumi-Shino tea bowl, 14 cm in diameter, Momoyama period. Goto Museum, Tokyo.*

BELOW: Oguro, *Raku-yaki tea bowl by Chojiro, 10.9 cm in diameter (1586). Under the guidance of Sen no Rikyu, the Chojiro group crystallized the aesthetics of* wabi.

RIGHT: *The entrance to the* En-an *teahouse, early Edo period, Kyoto. The small doorway is characteristic of the* so-an *teahouse where guests must lower their heads to crawl into the space, an action that is clearly separate from those of everyday life.*

ABOVE: *The outside view of the* Teigyoku-ken *teahouse at Daitoku-ji temple in Kyoto, said to have been a favorite site of Kanamori Sowa, a tea master active in the early Edo period.*

OPPOSITE PAGE, RIGHT: *The interior of Hassoseki (House of eight windows) teahouse (1628), attributed to Kobori Enshu. Nanzen-ji temple, Kyoto.*

noisseurs from Sakai had begun, but Raku-yaki tea bowls continued to be made, and the four-and-a-half-tatami-mat tea room survived to later become an accepted symbol of traditional Japanese beauty. Hideyoshi killed Rikyu, but he could not extinguish the aesthetic and cultural values Rikyu had so firmly and irrevocably instilled.

A FIVE-POINT GRAMMAR OF JAPANESE CULTURE

The leading figures in the world of tea had dramatically changed by the Edo period. Tea connoisseurs, such as Furuta Oribe, Hosokawa Tadaoki (1563–1645), Kobori Enshu (1574–1647), and Kanamori Sowa (1584–1656), were no longer men from merchant families, but rather were descendants of the daimyo or members of samurai families. The style of the tea ceremony also changed, and tea-ceremony utensils became more diversified. For instance, Oribe favored extremely contorted and irregularly shaped ceramic ware, while Sowa preferred the lavish paintings of Ninsei. However, this diver-

sity did not change the fundamental framework established by Rikyu. To this day, teahouses and tea-ceremony utensils continue to be small, complex, and delicately arranged in terms of space.

There may have been another reason why the tea-ceremony tradition continued to flourish, and which may have something to do with elements of Japanese culture discovered by Sen no Rikyu as revealed in the following five aspects. Had Rikyu not touched a deep nerve in the national psyche of Japan, the strong tradition of the tea ceremony could never have been established or have survived as long as it did.

POINT ONE: SHIGAN (THIS WORLD)

The idea of an afterworld typically is not found in Japanese religious beliefs. The influence of the gods can be felt in the here and now, not in the afterlife. If we call this a Shintoistic world view, then the fundamental characteristic is that it relates to this world. Buddhism introduced the concept of an

ABOVE: A tsukubai *set in the garden at Juko-an teahouse, Shomyo-ji temple, Nara.*

afterworld, but the practice of mixing Shintoism and Buddhism and the emphasis placed on profit to be made in this world took precedence over the notion of life in the afterworld. Kamakura Buddhism was an exception, since the pursuit of Jodo paradise was emphasized through the worship of Amida, although this transcendent aspect of Kamakura Buddhism was slowly but surely diluted over time. Even now, Japanese interests are turned more strongly toward this world and the present than to the afterlife. This focus is overwhelmingly apparent in the literature and art of the Edo period. Even during the Momoyama period, the Sotatsu workshop, which produced extremely cre-

ative paintings, dealt with commoner's themes from *The Tale of Genji* and *Ise Monogatari,* and depicted plants and flowers, birds and deer, none of which alluded to the existence of an afterlife. The *so-an* tea ceremony also existed completely in this world, marking the beginning of Edo-period art designed for entertainment.

POINT TWO: GROUPISM

Stated in concrete terms, *shigan* (this world) is a base or group with which one is affiliated. A classic example of a group is the *mura* (village) community. It is characteris-

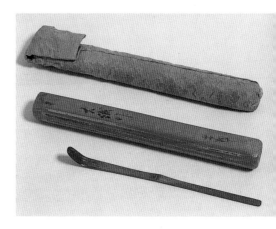

tically regional, has a clear boundary between inside and outside, the community members know one another's faces, and there is a sharp difference in the pattern of behavior between the inner circle of community members and between community members and outsiders. The smaller the community, the more distinct these characteristics become. When seen in this light, the tea ceremony becomes a symbolic action within a group. By making the scale of the tea ceremony smaller, these elements became clearer. The tea ceremony to which only a few guests are invited, held in a four-and-a-half- or a two-tatami-mat room, is an extreme example of the psychology of the

group. The interior space of the tea room or teahouse is separated from the outside space and social order. The whole atmosphere within is arranged according to a completely different value system.

When looking at the parameteres of the tea ceremony and its domain, it becomes clear that the need to regulate the participants' behavior in order to sustain internal order increased as the space became smaller. People can go in any direction in a large, open field, but this type of freedom cannot be exercised in a small tea room. The structure of the etiquette of the tea room is based on a system of agreed-upon rules. The more detailed the acceptable pattern of behavior,

ABOVE: *The first part of the scroll of* Sairei Zoshi *(illustrations of the tea ceremony), Muromachi period. A scene is depicted in which people are gathering for the tea ceremony. Tea is being prepared for guests in the lower left-hand corner. Maeda Ikutoku-kai, Tokyo.*

RIGHT: Tenmyo Semehimo *kettle, 24 cm in height, Muromachi period. Hatakeyama Kinen-kan, Tokyo.*

BELOW: *A Chinese tea canister, 6.1 cm in height, Southern Sung to Yuan dynasties. Eisei Bunko, Tokyo.*

the easier it becomes to predict the behavior of others in order to avoid confrontation and confusion, and thus achieve efficiency. Making tea rooms small and limiting the number of participants was not only an aesthetic decision, but also effectively made the tea ceremony a microcosm of the structure and function of larger groups.

POINT THREE: THE PERCEPTUAL WORLD

The world of the here and now is given to us through our perceptions. If a culture evolves without having to relate to anything beyond itself, if it remains isolated from outside influences, it could become increasingly sophisticated as a result. For example, perception of colors could sharpen, as demonstrated by the abundant variety of names signifying colors in Heian-period Japanese; the sense of smell could become more acute, as seen in the refined game of *ko-awase,* or fragrance matching; and the ear could learn to distinguish complex harmonics, such as those of the *tsuzumi* drum of the Noh theater.

Such sophistication in perception culminated in Sen no Rikyu's tea ceremony. Rikyu never alienated himself from culture but embodied and encapsulated a form of perceptual culture in the tea ceremony. The spiritual elements in his teahouse are not entirely clear, but there was definitely a balance between the unlimited number of colors and shapes he employed. This balance was essentially the result of a long history of the pursuit of perceptual pleasure. The whole of Momoyama-period art exhibited a fascination with the perceptual world. The tea ceremony emphasizes the view of "life as art." The tea-ceremony room is almost rustic in its simplicity. The accouterments found within the monochromatic walls are subtle, tasteful, and deliberately chosen. For example, the calligraphy scroll hanging in the alcove, the flower arrangement tastefully chosen according to the season and tenor of

tectural understatement. It is small, light, low, and fragile. A tea room is moderate, unpretentious, and does not stand out among the trees that surround it. Everything inside is understated. Stepping stones embedded in the bare ground are arranged one by one in the green moss. There is breathtaking beauty in the spontaneity of the red maple leaves scattered haphazardly on the green moss, and this atmosphere creates a world of its own regardless of the environment surrounding the teahouse as a whole.

There is harmony in the space inside the teahouse. What is particularly stunning is the visual balance of the vertical line of round pillar and the plane of rough wall. There is a complex shift of color and texture observed in the surface of the rough wall, which can be appreciated on its own, inde-

LEFT: Ko-Ashiya Enjo-ji *kettle, 25.8 cm in height, Muromachi period. National Museum of Tokyo.*

BELOW: Kochi *incense case of a cow and hat, 5.5 cm in height, sixteenth to seventeenth century. Tekisui Museum, Hyogo Prefecture.*

the intended ceremony, the incense chosen, the bowls that will be used, and the type of sweet to be given to the guests all demand of the tea-ceremony practitioner a very specific predilection. These choices necessarily reflect the tea master's attitude, not only toward the tea ceremony but also toward everyday life. The tea ceremony literally could not exist without this attitude.

POINT FOUR: PARTIALISM

As we have seen, the teahouse is an archi-

pendent of the round pillar. A diverting and extremely complex world independent of the world at large exists in this small space, a world similar to the diversity of perceptions arising from the surface of a Raku-yaki tea bowl held in one's hands.

Interest in the part rather than in the whole is an aspect that is consistent with the history of Japanese formative art, beginning with the miniaturized portions of Yamato-e and ending in the detailing of the hardware found on *fusuma*. The grandeur of the whole was accomplished by the accumulation of its many parts, while the whole itself could not

RIGHT: *Raku Kizaemon (1949–), fifteenth heir of the Raku family, is shown making a Raku-yaki tea bowl. Raku technique does not require the use of a potter's wheel. Here, Kizaemon scoops clay out of a handmade prototype.*

TOP, CENTER, *and* ABOVE: *Omokage (Visage), black Raku-yaki tea bowl by Chojiro, 10.5 cm in diameter, Momoyama period. Raku Museum, Kyoto.*

be divided. The study of the Detached Palace alone consists of complicated extensions and additions.

The mansions of the daimyo of the time were even more extreme in their disjuncture. Their complicated floor plans suggest that the architect probably had no sense of the layout of the entire building, even as he worked. First a room was made, then more rooms were added when necessary. This was a process that was repeated until for some reason—space or budgetary limitations, fulfillment of the intended purpose, carpenters' illness—the construction of the building was either completed or interrupted. Such a phe-

nomenon is rare among large structures built in China and Europe, although those cultures produced details on ornamental portions of large structures. The detailed ornamental sculptures on the stone stairs at the Kogu palace in Beijing and the sculptures on the capitals of the columns in Romanesque churches are examples. However, unlike Japanese architects and artisans, the Chinese and Europeans never began with such details and worked outward; they always started from the structure as a whole and worked down to the details.

Towns naturally developed as roads were built or castles were established. However,

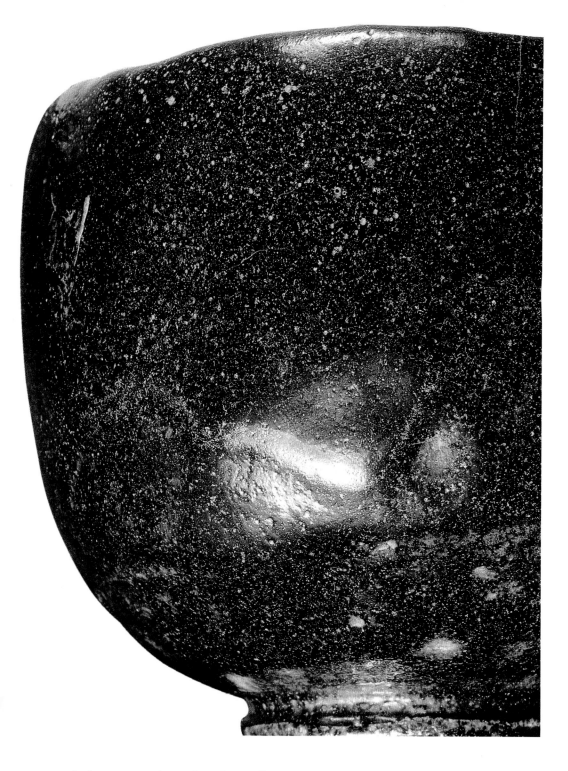

symmetrical structures depend on the available space and do not come about naturally but through intentional planning. They must be conceived in the first stages of planning, and the predilection for working out from the details to the larger space must be the primary reason Japanese culture loathes symmetry in terms of delineating space. The stepping stones on the bare ground leading to the teahouse are a perfect example of convenience sacrificed for aesthetics. The stones are not arranged in a straight line, but rather are placed in an intentionally complex manner with the intention of purposely violating symmetry. The stones in the bare ground and the teahouse itself are artifacts used to create an impression of natural space. The actual purpose of these arrangements is not to eliminate or to imitate nature and the natural environment, but to create a space that is more natural than nature itself.

POINT FIVE: THE CULTURE OF THE HERE AND NOW

Human rationality insists on attempting to give structure to the entire universe. Abstract intellectual achievement defines the present through its relationship to the past

and to the future in order to structure time. A perceptual culture pays attention to the present without regard to the past or future, just as it focuses interest on the part as distinct from the whole. Time is, after all, the infinite occurrence of the present moment. Thus, the issue becomes one of how to adapt to both environments, social and natural. The past and the present must be examined in relation to each other, but since in reality we live in the present, this is impossible. Therefore, the only choice is to adapt to changes. Adaptation can be swift, clever, and practical. It can also be subtle, sophisticated, and artistically productive—as perfectly realized in the *so-an* tea ceremony.

The tea ceremony invests the whole of life in the present moment. Ii Naosuke (1815–60), a late Edo-period tea connoisseur, used the famous Japanese saying "*ichigo ichie* (one chance to meet)" in the *Chanoyu Ichie-shu* to express the idea that each occasion of extending hospitality to another person is one that will never occur again, so the host should make his offering a perfect one by carefully considering every detail. Although Naosuke put it into words in the nineteenth century, this awareness has existed since the sixteenth century, particularly among first-rate tea connoisseurs. It means that if there is meaning in life, it happens at this moment and in this place. If it does not exist here and now, it does not exist at all. The tea ceremony continues to be immensely popular both in Japan and abroad today. While the benefits of green tea are now known to range from inhibiting cancer cell growth to preventing high blood pressure to aiding weight loss, the tea ceremony itself continues to serve an important aesthetic junction in society.

While the tea master has, in the twentieth century, become an instructor, this art has basically remained unchanged since Sen no Rikyu's time. The tea ceremony was originally an aesthetic experience transcending the boundaries of aesthetics. Life and art become one and the same thing in the tea ceremony. The tea ceremony has survived to this day against all odds because the highest expression of the Japanese belief in the present moment can be found in this ultimate aesthetic experience.

RIGHT: *A black Raku-yaki kiln at the moment a tea bowl is taken out of the charcoal fire. The timing determines the coloration on the surface of the bowl. The bellows become less active as time passes, and the moment is filled with the tension of perfect timing.*

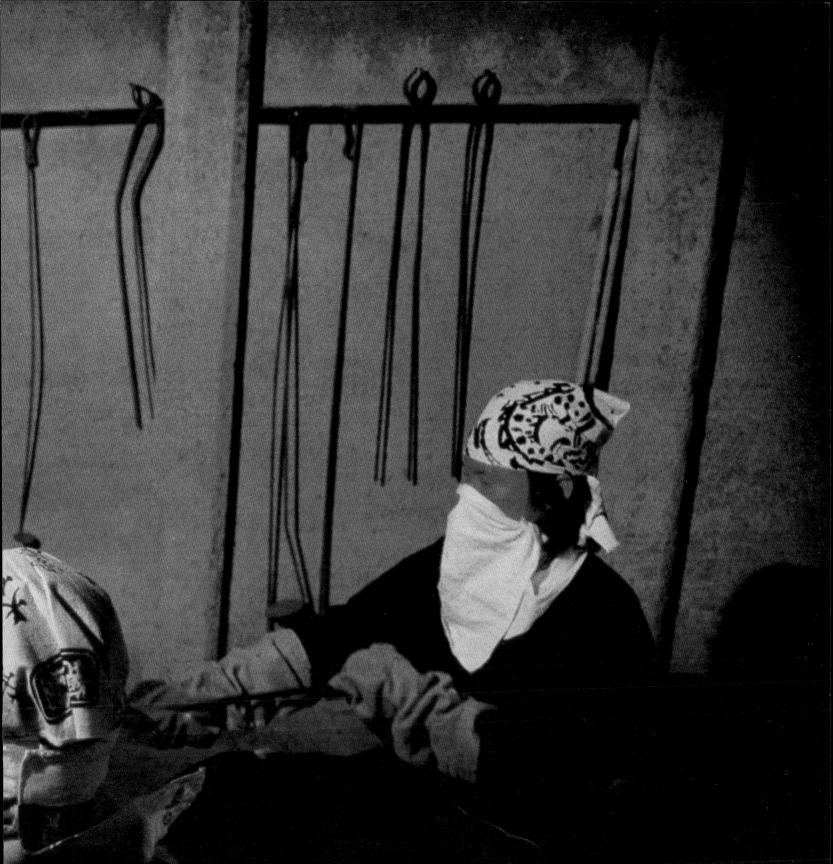

BELOW (DETAIL): Setchu Aiaigasa (*Sharing an umbrella in the snow*) *by Suzuki Harunobu. Medium-size* nishiki-e *(colored woodblock print) showing a couple strolling through a world enveloped in tranquillity. Such calmness is in marked contrast to the stark contrast in the colors of their clothes. The couple's intimacy is revealed by their subtle, raised eyebrows and very slight smiles.*

The Women of *Ukiyo-e*

OPPOSITE PAGE (DETAIL): Hokoku Sairei-zu (*1606*) *by Kano Naizen. Depiction of the grand festival dedicated to Toyotomi Hideyoshi. Hokoku Shrine, Kyoto.*

From ancient Greece to the present day, the human body (and the female nude in particular) has been one of the main themes of Western art. Nude or seminude figures can frequently be found among both Buddhist statuary and Indian religious sculpture in India and on the Indochinese continent. However, artistic representations of the human body are rare in Islamic art, and nude figures or paintings are seldom seen in Chinese and Japanese art. Clearly, some civilizations have abundant formative expressions of nudity while others do not. This can be seen, perhaps, as a reflection of different cultural attitudes toward the human body. How do such attitudes vary from civilization to civilization and from culture to culture? Instead of asking why the nude is not historically represented in Japanese art, let us first examine why nude figures were represented in the art of ancient Greece.

The ancient Greeks installed a myriad of local gods in a grand system of polytheistic mythology centering on their chief god, Zeus. They both humanized gods and semideified human beings through intermarriage between gods and humans. The gods had human spirits and minds, and their appearances were similar to human beings'. In Greek mythology, unlike Christianity, humans were not created to resemble gods; gods were created to resemble humans.

Figures depicting gods were more idealized than conceptions of ordinary human beings however. Among the ancient Greeks were sculptors, architects, and musicians who invented musical scales in which intervals were determined by the oscillation frequency of each note. They perceived the fundamental beauty of music to be the order created by the relationship between tones, rather than the complex tone of each individual sound. To the ancient Greeks, the ideal body was determined by shape, which in turn was defined by the balance of body proportion.

Balance represented a relationship between two or more elements and did not concern the concrete characteristics of each element, so that if beauty was determined by a well-proportioned figure, then hair style, facial expression, and skin tone or texture became irrelevant. Whether in architecture (the Parthenon), music (as theorized by Pythagoras), or thought (Plato), the almost mathematical order in the forms the ancient Greeks created reflected the structure of the universe and therefore represented ideal beauty.

The Romans continued the tradition of creating and sculpting figures by combining humanization and highly developed mathematical thought, but their nudes were rejected by the Christians of the Middle Ages (476–1450). Christianity regarded the human body in terms of its substance (flesh) rather than its form. The flesh was seen to be in conflict with the spirit and was considered the source of every evil. Therefore, early Christian sculptors created small, thin bodies, covering them with cloth to the greatest possible extent, in no way idealizing the body or the flesh itself.

Greek philosophy eventually reached medieval Christian monasteries through interaction with Islam, and by the twelfth century a comprehensive and rational theological metaphysics encompassing natural theology had been constructed on the basis of Aristotelian logic. From the twelfth century on, Christian theology had embraced the idea that since God created nature, the more humans knew about nature, the more closely they could approach God. In addition, they believed that the human being was created in God's own image. Therefore, there was no reason to distort that image, conceal it, or disfigure it. Consequently, many of the figures adorning churches became more descriptive of the human form in their increasingly well-balanced and beautifully sculpted proportions.

Early Gothic (1100–1600) sculpture treated the human body in a more abstract manner. Facial expressions were terse (e.g., those of the statues at Chartres Cathedral). In the middle of the Gothic period, the treatment of bodies became even more descriptive. Flesh could be seen through clothing, and the subtle, visible expressions of individuality (as seen in the sculptures in place at Reims Cathedral) show the advance of Hellenism, although there had not yet been a full-fledged revival of the ancient Grecian ideals in sculpture.

The Hellenistic revival, which idealized

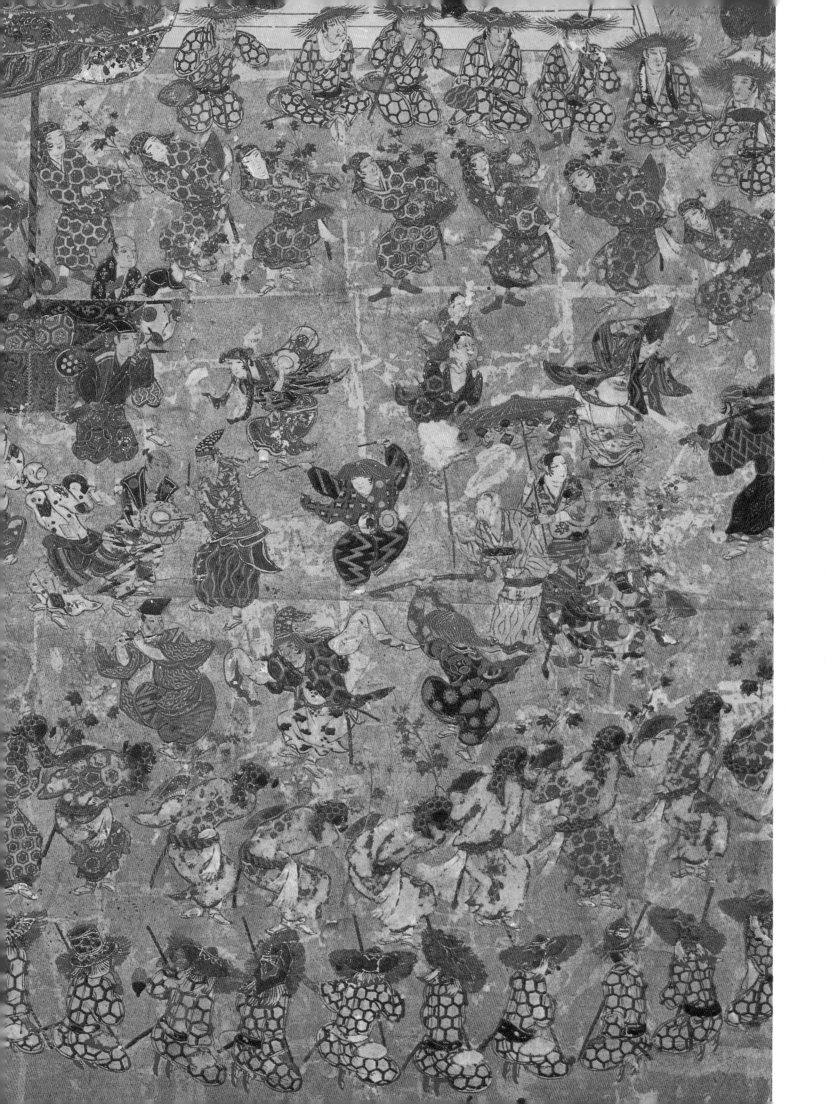

the nude body, occurred in Italy during the Renaissance (1400–1600) with Michelangelo being its most typical proponent in sculpture, Titian in painting. Figures from the Old Testament (e.g., David) or ancient pagan gods (e.g., Venus) emerged in human form. As the painting *Sacred and Profane Love* by Titian well reveals, the idealized nude was in some way divine, transcending history and society and rising above the everyday world. On the other hand, the clothed figure is profane, belonging to the everyday world and history.

The origin of Indian nudes is vastly different from that of Western nudes. Until the twelfth and thirteenth centuries, before Is-

and an anklet. Otherwise, she is nude; her head is tilted and her hips are twisted; her breasts, lower abdomen, and thighs are exposed. Her entire body expresses coquetry, in contrast to those of the Greek goddesses, whose bodies were idealized with an almost abstract balance. The statue of Yaksa exaggerates the sexual vitality of the body, so that if the Greek statues can be described as reflecting the geometric order of the universe, the Indian statues can be described as symbols of the universal strength of sexual power.

Graphic expressions of sexual power might have originated in the representations of fertility gods generally found in agricultural

ABOVE: Okawabata Yusuzumi *by Kitagawa Utamaro (1753–1806). A large* nishiki-e *triptych of courtesans and geisha out for a stroll on a summer evening. The Sumida River and Ryogoku Bridge are in the background. Those in the center and right-hand panel are enjoying the cool breeze, while the panel on the left shows geisha being led by a girl holding a lantern.*

lam reached the subcontinent, emphasis was placed on ample, protruding breasts, and full hips and thighs. Artistically sophisticated examples can be seen as early as the first and second century in Muttra, India. The statue decorating three pillars on the border of a stupa depicting the goddess Yaksa trodding on an evil spirit (excavated in Muttra, now at the Calcutta Museum) shows the goddess wearing a chest ornament, bracelet, sashes,

societies. An example of this expression can be found in polytheistic Hinduism, which had the male and female gods Shiva and Parvati. Shiva, the god of destruction, was married to Parvati, the benevolent mother goddess. The two figures also represent noumenon and phenomenon, respectively, a concept of two elements that are extremely difficult to differentiate. The German philosopher Immanuel Kant (1724–1804) pos-

LEFT: Odalisque *by François Boucher (1752). Louvre Museum, Paris.*

ABOVE: *Bronze statue of Apollo (ca 525 B.C.).*

LEFT (DETAIL): Amayo no Miya Mode *(Visiting a shrine on a rainy night) by Suzuki Harunobu, eighteenth century.*

163

ited that noumenon was the "thing in itself," something that could only be the object of an intellectual intuition devoid of sensuousness. In simpler terms, it is the thing being perceived. Phenomenon, on the other hand, is the thing as it is constructed by the human mind, the thing as it appears. While the distinction between the two halves of the concept is extremely subtle, they share a common origin. Their unity is expressed by sexual union, as seen in the marriage of Shiva and Parvati. In Hinduism, sexual power is seen as the center of the universe, and the sexual union between male and female symbolizes oneness with the universe. Here, that which

veloped. Islamic artists did paint portraits, not as icons intended for religious worship but rather as graphic indications of social status; thus, the figures are clothed.

The civilization of ancient China, particularly in the Confucian world, concentrated on society rather than on nature. It focused on political power rather than on sexual energy, and on history rather than on mathematics. Therefore, motivation toward idealization of the human nude independent of a social role did not exist. There was likewise no reason to regard the flesh and its impulses as sinful, except as influenced by a foreign religion, namely, Buddhism. What

ABOVE (DETAIL): Sacred and Profane Love *(1515–16) by Titian (Tiziano Vecellio). In modern European art, the nude essentially represented the sacred. Borghese Museum, Rome.*

is sacred is not a beautifully balanced body but the sexual union itself, as seen further in Hindu sculptures found at the temples of Khajuraho and Konarak in India.

Islam is relentlessly monotheistic, and since God cannot be seen, idols are forbidden. All forms of idol worship were rejected by the tenets of this religion, and an artistic tradition of creating nude figures never de-

was said and recorded in China scarcely touches upon the human body. The ancient Chinese did not try to depict nude images apart from those seen in Buddhist statues since there was no influence from Indian figurative expression, and they had no strong motivation of their own to do so.

However, the worldly female figures often called *bijin-zo* in Japan (figures of beauty) also existed in China, and probably represented what was considered the ideal beauty of the Tang dynasty (618–907). Characteristic features such as a full body; round face; full cheeks; thick eyebrows; long, narrow eyes; and small, scarlet lips can be found in the females depicted in a number of works: the Tang-dynasty female figurines buried along with the dead (excavated in Central Asia); the *Torige Ritsujo Byobu* (Standing female with bird feather) screen given in the eighth century to the Todai-ji temple in Japan (Shoso-in); and the *Kisshoten-zo* (eighth century) at the Yakushi-ji temple in Nara. Thus, we can surmise that the Chinese ideal

the *Tale of Genji* hand-painted scroll are covered in *junihitoe* ceremonial robes consisting of twelve layers of kimono. The face, hands, and long black hair of the women are barely exposed. The faces are done in a stereotypical *hikime kagibana* style, with narrow eyes and a straight nose drawn in simple lines. Of course, such simple lines can sometimes reflect individual emotions and represent subtle expressions, but these are not personalized faces revealing individual characteristics. It would not be an exaggeration to say that the women of the Heian court depicted in such scrolls are women without faces, simple beings reduced

of feminine beauty was imported to Japan and accepted as standard. Thick clothing covers the aforementioned figures from head to toe, concealing the clear lines of the body. During the Heian period (794–1185), more works began to appear in which the body of the subject was completely covered with clothing.

The women of the Heian court depicted in

to nothing more than long black hair and clothing.

Chinese poets sang of the exquisite facial features and perfectly smooth skin of their legendary beauties, while Western artists painted their detailed faces and figures. That Japanese poets and painters were satisfied with the simple facial portrait of Ono no Komachi, alleged to be the representative

ABOVE: The Birth of Venus *by Sandro Botticelli. This Venus is an exotic beauty who projects a subtle combination of religious and sensual aspects. Uffizi Gallery, Florence.*

beauty of the Heian period, is surprising and actually quite amazing. Judging from this fact, the people of the Heian period seem to have been more interested in clothing than in portrayal of the individual, and it was this element of Heian-period taste that was passed on to subsequent periods. Perhaps there was some form of inherent prohibition at work in determination of style and taste?

It is hard to imagine that Buddhism alone served as motivation to suppress the depiction of the human body, as Buddhism itself introduced the notion of beauty in the human body, at least in the area of formative expression. Confucianism certainly contained belief in the religious practice of abstinence, but this belief did not influence early Edo-period samurai society until much later. If religious mortification of the flesh was not the reason for this type of depiction, then the reason must have been the cultural emphasis placed on the social significance of dress.

The facial features of a beautiful woman are a gift of nature, but her clothing is a symbol of her social standing. Since Heian culture developed within a closed and privileged group, any expression of power that the group was incapable of controlling, such as the beauty of a woman who could influence men, was most likely proscribed. Therefore, the *hikime kagibana* and *junihitoe* style served to reduce all women to the stereotypical roles allocated by their positions in Heian-period society.

in the *Matsuura Byobu* screen are shown in what appears to be clothing of only two-dimensions, and although the screen features eighteen women, some standing and some sitting, the main feature of the screen is not the women themselves but their gorgeous clothing. There were a few exceptions

ABOVE: Water carafe with four dancers, from the fourth to fifth century. Tehran Archaeological Museum, Iran.

BELOW: Figure of Yaksa, dating from approximately the first century. India.

Bijin-ga (portraits of beauty) appeared in Japan as early seventeenth-century genre paintings. The women depicted in these paintings were no longer women of the court, but the wives and daughters of merchants, or dancing girls, prostitutes, and Kabuki actors portraying female roles. Even so, the women

to this style that can still be seen. The *Hikone Byobu* (Ii family, Shiga) and the *Kabuyuen* (also called *So-o-ji Byobu*) from the same period portray individual postures and the movement made by human bodies covered with clothing.

Vibrant lines depict the clothing and pos-

LEFT (DETAIL): Torige Ritsujo Byobu (Woman standing in feathered robe), folding screen from the mid-eighth century (artist unknown). Shoso-in, Nara.

167

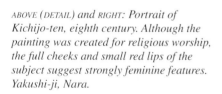
ABOVE (DETAIL) and RIGHT: *Portrait of Kichijo-ten, eighth century. Although the painting was created for religious worship, the full cheeks and small red lips of the subject suggest strongly feminine features. Yakushi-ji, Nara.*

ture simultaneously, even indicating some of the techniques later used in *ukiyo-e* (pictures of the floating world) woodblock prints. An example in that direction, perhaps, would be the *Yuna-zu* (Bathhouse women) (MOA Museum, Atami). The *yuna* was a lower-class prostitute, and in this print, her kimono is nonchalantly tied with a narrow obi, disclosing full thighs and a slightly turned hip line. The facial features of the six women strolling strongly differ from one another. They look coarse but composed, and exhibit almost daring facial expressions. The work is a great accomplishment by an unknown painter who successfully rendered untamed energy expressed entirely through a woman's body. *Ukiyo-e* woodblock prints had, however, not yet arrived.

Artistic depiction of women in the seventeenth century began in Japan with the *Hikone Byobu,* and advanced to the mid-century *Ensaki Bijin* (Beauty on a veranda), (National Museum of Tokyo). By the end of the same century, Hishikawa Moronobu (1618–94), said to be the father of *ukiyo-e,* had created the *Mikaeri Bijin-zu* (Beauty thrice turning back) (National Museum of Tokyo), pioneering a new style in the depiction of Japanese women.

THE ELEMENTS OF *Ukiyo-e*

Ukiyo-e woodblock prints, a product of Edo-period culture, became popular throughout Japan in the latter half of the seventeenth century. There were three basic subjects chosen for *ukiyo-e:* beautiful women; famous Kabuki actors on stage (and later sumo wrestlers); and landscapes, which did not appear until the nineteenth century (landscapes without human figures were originated by Katsushika Hokusai [1760–1849]). A fourth theme was found in the erotic *shunga (*spring pictures).

One of the hallmarks of *ukiyo-e* was the graphic depiction of actors, which represents the main stylistic difference in terms of subject matter between *ukiyo-e* and the earlier *bijin-ga.* While the latter occasionally depicted scenes from the theater or stage, as seen in the screen *Rakuchu Rakugai-zu Byobu* (Scenes in and out of Kyoto), actors in a particular scene or sumo wrestlers never made up the entire composition, but were always just one aspect of it. On the other hand, one of the traditions of *sumi* brush paintings was landscape scenery (see page 94), which *ukiyo-e* did not adopt independently until the end of the eighteenth century, as mentioned above. The portrayal of single actors or sumo wrestlers sharply distinguishes *ukiyo-e* from other contemporary paintings, be they Rimpa (see page 116), Kano-ha (the Kano school of art practicing from the late Muromachi period [1333–1568] to the Edo period [1600–1868]), or *bunjin-ga* literary paintings from the eighteenth and nineteenth centuries. *Shunga* were created by different artists within each separate school from time to time, but it was the Japanese *ukiyo-e* printmakers who first created fine works of art.

While theaters and actors, landscapes, the manners and customs of women, and sexual themes were often depicted in art earlier than the Edo period in Japan and abroad, the phenomenon of all being drawn at the same time in one genre occurred only in Edo-period Japan. How did this school of painting prosper for as long as two hundred years? The worldliness of Edo-period culture, the availability of areas and trends devoted to sensual pleasures (e.g., *kodo,* or the art of incense), the popular red-light districts, and Kabuki theaters all set the stage for the popularity of *ukiyo-e.*

The outstanding characteristics of *ukiyo-e* woodblock prints are composition and perspective, line and color. The framework of the composition was determined by the shape of the paper, but the size and shape of the paper used in *ukiyo-e* vary a great deal. The standard sheet was a slightly long rectangle, in large (approximately 40 x 30 cm) and medium (approximately 30 x 20 cm) sizes. These were occasionally used on a horizontal axis or connected in a triptych to make a large picture. Variations included the use of vertically elongated *tanzaku* (30 x 60 cm strips of paper usually used for calligraphic purposes), or the even more extremely elongated and narrow *hashira-e* (65 x 15 cm, used to hang on pillars) that were sometimes printed horizontally. The paper used to make folding fans was also used to compose a picture within a picture. Another characteristic of the composition of *ukiyo-e* prints was the full use of cropping techniques whereby figures were not included in their entirety. Many such examples of this compositional technique can be seen in the work of Torii Kiyonaga (1752–1815).

Another typical compositional technique can be seen in the large *okubi-e* portraits that employed a technique similar to the close-up said to have been invented by Kitagawa Utamaro (1754–1806). Both Utamaro and Toshusai Sharaku (fl 1794–5) often cropped either the right or left side of the upper torso, or both sides, with the edge of the picture. Both Hokusai and Utagawa Hiroshige (1797–1858) left many examples of similarly cropped landscapes.

The variety of perspective used is another important characteristic of *ukiyo-e,* one particularly apparent in the landscapes. These include a view from above or below, a horizontal perspective, and sometimes even a perspective that changed within a single picture. For example, Hokusai Katsushika's *Shinshu Suwako* found among the *Fugaku Sanjurokkei (Thirty-six Views of Mount Fuji)* features a pine tree in the foreground. The line of the horizon is low in the picture, causing the viewer to look down upon Lake

ABOVE: Statue of Princess Tamayori (1251). Her thick eyebrows, gentle eyes, and white teeth, barely visible between smiling lips, reveal a somewhat mystical beauty. Yoshino, Nara Prefecture.

RIGHT (DETAIL): Bandainagon Ekotoba, *from the late twelfth century. Women's emotions, strongly and violently expressed, are here depicted in great detail. Idemitsu Museum, Tokyo.*

ABOVE (DETAIL): Eshi no Soshi (Good news), *from the late fourteenth century. Imperial Household, Tokyo.*

Suwa, while at the same time Mount Fuji can be seen in the far distance. This traditional technique resembles the depiction of vast space previously seen in *sumi* brush paintings. The same principle is applied in *Yamashita Hakuu,* where the viewer looks down upon the foot of Mount Fuji and the sea of clouds below its peak. Such a high viewpoint obviously did not exist in reality but was often experimented with by *ukiyo-e* printmakers.

The famous *Kanagawa-oki Namiura (Beneath the Wave off Kanagawa)* by Hokusai sets its perspective extremely low. It looks up from the surface of the sea to the crests of high waves. Mount Fuji sits on a horizon lower than the peak of the waves. Likewise, the water in the canal and the warehouses on both sides of *Edo Nihonbashi* are seen horizontally from a perspective just slightly higher than the heads of the crowd. Depth is expressed by a geometric perspective that has a fixed viewpoint and guides the eye along a certain line. The technique was typically employed by Western painters, but in this particular work, the method of cropping used in the lower edge of the picture was unique. Geometric perspective was first introduced into Japanese works of art by Okumura Masanobu (1686–1764) but was used mainly to depict the interior of buildings. Hokusai, and later Hiroshige, applied the method of using a geometric perspective to their landscapes.

Adopting a geometric perspective was characteristic of certain types of *ukiyo-e*. Hokusai's *Fukagawa Mannenbashi-shita* has a fixed viewpoint in terms of perspective, but the eye moves vertically. We look down on the small boats in the river but horizontally across to the faraway Mount Fuji that can be seen under the bridge. Another angle of perspective in the same print has the viewer looking up at the bridge. *Koto Suruga-cho Mitsui Mise Ryaku-zu* depicts a large roof on the right, and a smaller triangular roof on the left with Mount Fuji in the middle. This scene cannot be observed from a fixed viewpoint, no matter which line one follows. The large roof on the right is seen from the left, and the small roof on the left is seen from the right. In other words, the eye of the viewer moves from right to left. As a result, a tight composition is obtained between the three large, medium, and small triangles. The large, inverted triangle is composed of the part of a large roof on the left and the slanted part of the large roof on the right. Cropping techniques and the use of varying perspectives produced many diverse and creative compositions combining close and distant points of view in a dramatic and almost cinematic manner.

Another element of composition often used was the presentation of a large plane of color in a relatively simple shape, mainly as a piece of clothing or as an obi. This two-dimensional plane was often placed in the middle of a three-dimensional picture in a bold and creative combination of a nearly abstract style of drawing that included quite concrete description. One obvious example of the use of the simple shape is seen in the *Gosei Ichikawa Danjuro no Shibaraku* by Katsukawa Shunsho (1726–93), in which a large, geometrically shaped family crest is positioned in and occupies the entire center of the picture.

The majority of *ukiyo-e* woodblock prints generally employed narrow lines. The lines of a kimono flowing from the shoulder of a model are particularly elegant in the work of Kiyonaga and Hosoda Eishi (1756–1829) who further emphasized thinness and height. Utamaro not only controlled the width of such lines, but also used varying shades of *sumi* to express the softness and warmth of female skin in a culmination of the long tradition of Chinese and Japanese line painting. This use of the line can clearly be seen as one of the most outstanding elements of *ukiyo-e* when compared to Western oil painting dating from the seventeenth century on.

In terms of color, the use of tonal shading techniques is absent in *ukiyo-e* prints. Light is emitted from one source and spreads evenly over the entire picture with no sharp contrast between light and dark tones. The color application sequence used on woodblock prints has its origin in the seventeenth century.

First, a red was used, and later yellow, indigo blue, and green were added over the red. A wider variety of color was created through this method of layered printing. In the 1760s, the technique of multiple-layered printing was further developed. Harunobu (ca 1725–70) was the first painter to experience great success with this technique. He had already mastered gray, light purple, and

TOP (DETAIL): Bandainagon Ekotoba. *A woman is here portrayed shouting. Idemitsu Museum, Tokyo.*

BOTTOM: A copy of the Kasuga Gongen Kenki *(Taking a nap) from the first half of the fourteenth century. National Museum of Tokyo.*

matte neutral colors and was skillful at handling black planes. A highly sophisticated harmony of colors ranging from gray to black was seen in Japanese woodblock prints of the eighteenth century, perhaps for the first time in the world.

THE WOMEN OF *UKIYO-E*

In the latter half of the eighteenth century,

BELOW: Modern geisha walking in a traditional Kyoto street.

OPPOSITE PAGE (DETAIL): Rakuchu Rakugai-zu Byobu *(In and out of Kyoto screen), a screen attributed to Kano Suitoku, from the latter half of the sixteenth century. The subtle actions depict the activities of a bustling district. A prostitute is pulling on the sleeve of a passerby, while the monk at the door may be negotiating a price.*

Harunobu, Utamaro, and Kiyonaga took the world by storm with their *ukiyo-e* woodblock representations of the ideal female beauty. Each printmaker's depiction of women had distinct characteristics that can be individually analyzed.

The women in Harunobu's work had relatively small, slightly elongated faces that were outlined with a fine line. The eyes are almost horizontal, so narrow as to appear half-closed, with fine eyebrows raised at both ends. The nose is drawn in one stroke, and the mouth is extremely small, to the extent that any separation between upper and lower lips can barely be distinguished. The eyes cannot be read, and the mouths do not speak. Harunobu appears to have carried on the Yamato-e tradition, but unlike the faces of women in works of the Heian period that were drawn in simple lines showing no emotion, Harunobu's faces reveal a certain virginal quality or innocence, or at least the appearance of naiveté.

The emphasis placed on youth or lack of maturity begins with the face and continues down to the toes. In addition to the extremely small mouth, another radical distortion in the Harunobu style is seen in the small hands that are found, practically without exception, in all his works. Their size is completely unrelated to the overall proportion and balance of the body. For its part, the body is thin and shows no traces of developed breasts, hips, or thighs.

For Harunobu, the ideal young man was basically no different from the ideal young woman. The painter looked at these immature men and women from a certain distance, thereby reducing them to objects of appreciation. The viewer does not feel empathy for them. Transformation is revealed by the technique of drawing a voyeuristic third person peeking at the subject from within the frame of the picture, a technique of manipulation used by Harunobu in many of his works.

Harunobu's works also included dreamlike, sentimental scenes depicting his subjects in their own environment. These figures could be arranged against an almost geometrically ordered space that served to emphasize the curved lines of their figures. This arrangement might consist of several angled lines such as those found on verandas, shoji panels, tatami mats, or the vertical lines of pillars. The background is simplified and the figure's hair or kimono patterns are drawn in detail, almost as if they are themselves miniatures. Nothing dramatic occurs in Harunobu's paintings. No one ar-

gues, fights, or breaks into a run, and as there are no scenes of meeting, there are no scenes of parting.

The color black is often seen, but red is also visible at times, as in the case of the torii and fence illustrated in *Amayo no Miyamode* (A visit to a shrine on a rainy night). The woman's clothing is purple, and as previously mentioned, Harunobu's use of different shades of gray and neutral colors is quite skillful. Therefore, the manipulative measures that Harunobu used in depicting humanity included not only background composition and curved lines, but also the dramatic effect of a wide range of color.

This sensitive painter also often employed the device of literary association called *mitate,* although it was not of his invention. One example of the use of *mitate* is seen in the technique known as *hakkei* (eight views) that originally represented the beautiful landscapes around the southern shore of Lake Dotei in China, which literary artists of the Sung dynasty loved and often used as a theme for ink-brush painting. This technique was imported to Japan and eagerly adopted by Japanese painters of the Muromachi period (1392–1568), although they had never seen the original lake. A replica of Lake Dotei, about one-tenth the size of the original, was created on the southern shore of Lake Biwa, below Mount Fuji. The eight views chosen to be re-created were called the *Omi Hakkei*, and some later Edo-period painters depicted them yet again. Harunobu reduced these scenes even more in his *Furyu Ukiyo Hakkei* and scaled them down even further in his *Zashiki Hakkei* (now at the Chicago Museum).

One of the *Shosho Hakkei*, *Enpo Kihan* (The sailboat returns from the far shore), is a brush painting that depicts a fishing boat adrift on a vast body of water clouded with rain and mist. This scene changed to *Shinagawa Kihan* (The sailboat returns to Shinagawa) in Harunobu's *Furyu Ukiyo Hakkei,* in which a prostitute stands at a

LEFT: Kaka Yuraku-zu Byobu (*People making merry under blossoms*) *by Kano Naganobu, from the early seventeenth century. The facial expressions of the young dancing women are bright and energetic. National Museum of Tokyo.*

RIGHT: Hataori-zu (Weaving), from the first half of the seventeenth century. Weaving traditionally has poetic connotations in China. The healthy beauty of the women is depicted. MOA Museum, Atami.

BELOW: Matsuura Byobu, from the first half of the seventeenth century. Eighteen women are portrayed against a golden background, exhibiting a dazzling array of beautiful kimono. The figures lack individual expression and sensuality since the painter was apparently more interested in clothing than in the female form. Yamato Bunka-kan (Yamato Culture Center), Nara.

RIGHT (DETAIL): Hikone Byobu, from the first half of the seventeenth century. Men and women entertaining themselves at a brothel are arranged against a solid gold background. The people strumming shamisen (Japanese stringed instruments) and playing Japanese games appear somewhat decadent. Ii family collection, Shiga Prefecture.

window gazing at the sea and sailboat outside. Further, in *Zashiki Hakkei*, the scene consists of one woman sitting in a room sewing, while another scoops water from a stone basin placed on the veranda outside. At her side is a towel hanger bedecked with a towel that flaps in the wind, a metaphor for the ship's sail. This print could also be called *The Return of the Towel Hanger*. Having come so far from the original, no one would associate this picture with the original brush-painted landscape. Although the effect is accidental, the emotions of the picture coincide with those contained in the words *hakkei* or *kihan* (returning sailboat) them-

women and feminine male faces, and the use of colors centering on neutral colors were the same. In his works, both men and women rarely take off their kimonos. Sometimes the woman's breasts are exposed for her partner to suckle. The lower torso is also exposed on many occasions, but total nudity is extremely rare. Sexual organs are depicted in some of the works but not in others. When they are clearly shown, male genitals are exceedingly enlarged, following the common tendencies of Edo-period *shunga*. Arms and legs are thin, while hands are particularly small, thereby making the balance appear unreal. In this unrealistic world, the man and the

selves. Such an effect is different in quality from the main characteristics of the picture. The painting, *The Return of the Towel Hanger*, would be somewhat puzzling if the title were not given. This is an echo effect that is tangential to the image. The psychological distance from the picture, created by the device, is a distinctive effect of *mitate-e* (pictures with literary associations).

Harunobu also painted many erotic *shunga*. Their pictorial characteristics are not so different from those described above. In short, he looked at figures placed in a background with medium distance, not too close and not too far. Description of girlish

woman, difficult to differentiate from each other but for their genitals, are innocently and merrily enjoying the act of sexual intercourse. Neither of them appears aggressive or dominant. In short, this is a world of childlike equality between men and women. However, this does not exhaust the characteristics of Harunobu's world. Often a third person observes the behavior of the two from somewhere within the frame. The third person may be a child, a woman with a snowball, or a voyeur. Such eyewitnesses are calm onlookers, revealing not the slightest expression of surprise, accusation, or jealousy. Looking at the scene through the eyes of

such an eyewitness means viewing someone else's sexual act objectively, calmly, and from a distance. This third person whom Harunobu preferred to add to his works was the means by which he was able to creat the psychological distance of the viewer from the ob-

wore kimonos of beautiful color and pattern. His standing figures were the most typical and beautiful, but in his triptychs, the models assumed various postures from among those seen in ordinary daily life. His scenes include, for instance, *Asuka-yama Hanami*

ject. In his world, voyeurism was not sexually exciting. The main interest of his pictures was in the evaluation of aesthetic order.

Torii Kiyonaga was another *ukiyo-e* painter who was popular during the 1780s; his typical beauties were totally different from Harunobu's. Kiyonaga's women had mature faces, tall and almost dignified figures, and

(Flower viewing at Mount Asuka) (British Museum, catalog 75) and *Sumida-gawa Funa-asobi* (Boating on the Sumida River) (ibid, 76). The characters depicted in his paintings usually included a group of women of approximately the same age with some-

individual characteristics, or facial expressions could be detected. Just how much Kiyonaga's tall, female, standing figures suited the taste of the time can be easily inferred by the fact that the artist Hosoda Eishi succeeded Kiyonaga's style and fur-

BELOW, TOP and BOTTOM: Meditating on love and showing love from Kasen Koi-no-bu *(Love songs) by Kitagawa Utamaro.*

times one or two men added. A masterly arrangement of colors can be seen in the black costume of the men or that of some of the women usually placed near the center of the picture. Whether the size of the group was small or large, almost all the women faced straight forward or were turned slightly to the front. In short, little variety in age,

ther emphasized the tall and thin features of his subjects.

Finally, Utamaro emerged. Utamaro is argueably the painter who loved women the most and who, among all Japanese artists, best depicted the finest subtleties of feminine expression and form. His first decisive success in works of *bijin-ga* came with the

ABOVE, LEFT: Sugatami Shichinin Kesho *by Kitagawa Utamaro. A large-size portrait of Naniwaya Okita, who was known as the most beautiful woman of the period. She is depicted from behind; her reflection in the mirror can be seen at the same time. Notice the hairline at the nape of her neck, considered one of the prerequisites for feminine beauty in Japan.*

179

series of busts of beauty, *The Ten Studies of Female Physiognomy,* produced in the early 1790s.

More than any other *ukiyo-e* artist, Utamaro painted many women of differing social classes and roles: prostitutes and geisha, reputable daughters and widows of merchant families, women building fires and wiping dishes, carrying children on their backs in the kitchen, women sewing, dressing, or gathering abalone on a rocky beach. Utamaro depicted women, and only women, in terms of what he saw as feminine traits.

In general, what is feminine was not seen in the subjects' individual characteristics. Most of Utamaro's beauties shared the same

ABOVE (DETAIL): Shikido Juniban (Twelve Erotic Scenes) *by Torii Kiyonaga.*

180

perfect features of full cheeks, straight noses, and small mouths; this was the stereotypical and idealized face of beauty. In that sense, Utamaro was no different from Harunobu and Kiyonaga. Utamaro, however, was gifted with incomparable descriptive capabilities so that he was able to express this femininity through his use of extremely controlled and extremely abbreviated lines.

Utamaro idealized and portrayed more of the physical features of a wider variety of Japanese women than any other Japanese painter of the time. His prints depicting the back of a woman, an angle rarely seen in artwork to begin with, are outstanding in the accurateness of their description, the elegance of their lines, and the harmony of their subtle colors. Utamaro used extremely fine lines, occasionally in flesh-tinted tones, in his descriptions and depictions of the face, neck, and outlines of the body. He occasionally erased the outline, allowing the shape to emerge simply through the dark and light contrast between the object and the background. Of all the *ukiyo-e* printmakers, none but Utamaro attempted to express the softness and smoothness of female skin with a light, flesh-tinted color.

We have already seen how, through the use of high contrast, the figure of a woman could be made to stand out from the background. The composition determined the viewpoint and the position of the figure. Utamaro's viewpoint is often low. For example, the umbrella shared by the couple in his print *Umekawa Chubei* is looked up at from a close and lower viewpoint. The figures are cropped from the knees down, and the top of the umbrella is cut. The area around the portion of the umbrella seen from inside is gray, and the kimonos worn by both the man and woman are close in tone to that color. A bold effect is produced by the black of the woman's hood and by the black used on a part of the man's kimono, and by the red of the woman's under-kimono glimpsed in the collar and edges of her sleeves and in her obi. One print of the series Utamaro himself titled *Utamakura* (1788), combining his name and the Japanese word for "black," is of a woman wearing a black kimono with a large, black plane taking up a portion of the picture. Her lower, left leg looms out in white over the black. A small red tray and saké cup are arranged on the left. The entire picture is genuinely original, a highly abstract two-dimensional composition with an arrangement of planes of color.

In his *shunga*, Utamaro might have been more interested in pictorial adventure than

ABOVE (DETAIL): Sagimusume *by Suzuki Harunobu.*

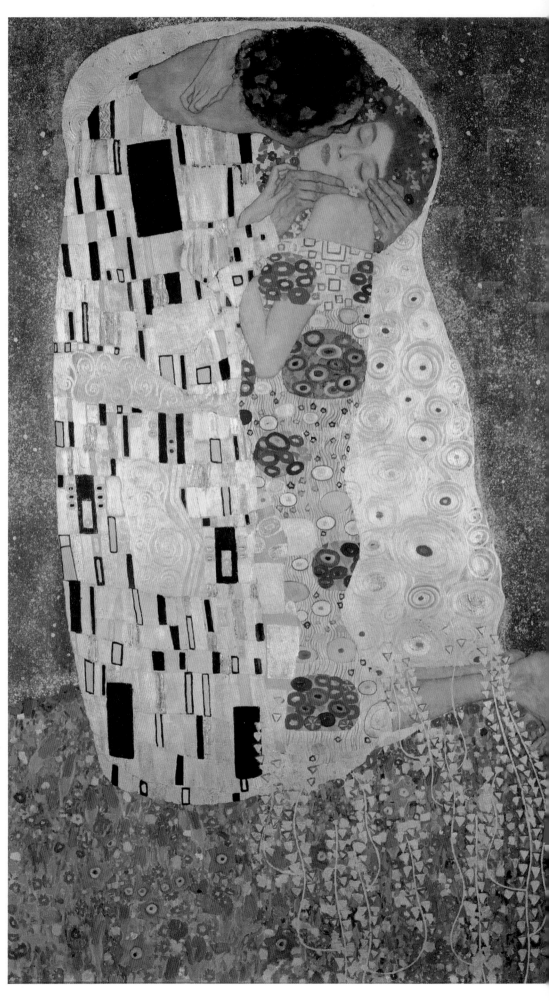

ABOVE: Judith I *(1901) by Gustave Klimt.*
Austrian Gallery, Vienna.

RIGHT: The Kiss *(1907–8) by Gustave Klimt.*
Austrian Gallery, Vienna.

in the description of the sexual organs them-selves. His chief experiment involved the abstract processing of two-dimensional space. The clothing of the couple holding each other takes up most of the picture whereas the background and the bodies or outlines of the figures are hardly shown. The space is mainly composed of varying planes of color intermingling in a complicated and intricate manner.

Utamaro's skillful *shunga* are without vio-lence. None of the women are posed as vic-tims of an aggressive man, and there is no hint of sadism. Moreover, the facial expres-sions of the women, caught for a moment in the ecstasy of sexual intercourse, are beauti-ful, presumably reflecting the artist's tender feelings toward women.

Harunobu realized and objectified the couples in his *shunga* through the distant point of view and through the eyes of a third party. It was the aesthetic of the voyeur, and there was no empathy felt between the par-ties involved. Utamaro, however, drew his viewpoint closer to the couple, at least in some of his representative works. Their ki-monos spread over most of the picture, and parts of their bodies are cropped. The man and the woman as human beings do not exist, or rather, only the act of the man and the woman exists. That is all, and that is the world. If any other expression were used, the surrounding world would disappear, and, in that sense, the loving deed would transcend the entire world and, thus, time itself. It is not a simple pleasure but a transcendental experience that is possible only between lov-ing men and women. Utamaro attempts to bring others into the experience. He steers the viewer in the direction of empathy and it is totally different from Harunobu's direc-tion of objectifying his subjects.

Utamaro's ultimate goal must have been to express the moment of unification of two subjects situated in a transcendental space. From the point of view of the painter, the issue was not to look at them, but to ap-proach them infinitely more closely. Thus, several pieces of Utamaro's work correspond to certain quatrains compiled in an anthol-ogy by the fifteenth-century Zen monk Ikkyu Sojun, bridging the gap of time. One in paint-ing and the other in literature, they both advocate the transcendence of the sexual act and, in that sense, are philosophical and not emotional. This is a particularly exceptional case set among all the other elements of Japanese culture, one that must have set an unprecedented example in late eighteenth-century Japan.

ABOVE: Kurofune-ya *(ca 1920) by Takehisa Yumeji. Note the emotional depth conveyed by tearful eyes.*

Diversion into Fantasy

ABOVE: *Sketch from* Guilty Conscience *by Victor Hugo (1802–85). Victor Hugo Memorial Museum, Paris.*

OPPOSITE PAGE: *Koreijutsu:* Mishima Yukio no Baai *(The Case of Yukio Mishima) (1986) by the painter and graphic artist Yoko-o Tadanori. The two drawings in the upper half of the painting are Yoko-o's reinterpretations of two images of the* Kaidai Hyakusen-so *series by the* ukiyo-e *painter Tsukioka Yoshitoshi (1839–92).*

As we have seen, the shogunate system was relatively stable during the eighteenth century under the policy of Sakoku (national seclusion). Individuals and feudal clans were prohibited from contacting foreigners and foreign cultures. Contact was limited to China, Korea, and the Netherlands; trade was restricted; and Nagasaki became the sole port of international commerce. In this way, the shogunate was able to monopolize foreign trade and regulate information received from abroad. Although Nagasaki was under the shogunate's strict control, incoming information was gradually disseminated among intellectuals, particularly after 1720

when the Tokugawa shogun Yoshimune finally abolished the policy of *igaku no kin* (prohibition of foreign scholarship).

The Edo shogunate (later Tokyo) promulgated a neo-Confucianist ideology, particularly through the Shoheiko academy for Confucian scholars and shogunal retainers governed by the shogunate. However, not all economic and cultural activities were centered in Edo. During the eighteenth century, Osaka and Kyoto played considerable roles. The Kano family of painters and the Hayashi family of scholars were both patronized by the shogunate, consequently contributing to the formation of Edo-period thought.

Apart from the artists making *ukiyo-e* woodblock prints, which developed in Edo merchant society, a number of important painters working in other genres came from around Kyoto, among them Buson (1716–84) and Ike no Taiga (1723–76), who painted *bunjin-ga* (paintings in the literary style); Maruyama Okyo (1733–95) and his two disciples Matsumura Goshun (1752–1811) and Rosetsu (1754–99), who added new dimensions to sketching; and Ito Jakuchu (1716–1800), who illustrated ordinary objects in great detail in his extraordinary paintings.

Ching-dynasty (1644–1911) *bunjin-ga* and sketchbooks arrived in Nagasaki on ships, and Chinese painters such as Shen Nanpin (ca mid-eighteenth century) visited Japan. Nanpin used fine brushes in his employment of both dark inks and ornamental coloring effects. It is not clear to what extent Dutch oil paintings or copperplate printing, including the technique of illustrating books, were utilized in Japan, but both of them imparted the use of geometric perspectives and shading to Japanese creative techniques. In the field of printmaking, an alliance between Kyoto and Nagasaki existed that promoted a tendency toward attempts at realism possibly in reaction against the copying and reproduction techniques of the Kano school.

It was Maruyama Okyo who created giant ornamental landscapes by sketching only orthodox, traditional themes, mainly birds and flowers. In his last painting done on a folding screen, *Hozugawa-zu Byobu* (Hozu River screen) (1795), Okyo did not directly employ geometric perspectives or shading as did Shiba Kokan (1747–1818), but he did pay attention to depth of field and managed to create a three-dimensional effect through the innovative use of different shades of ink. In this way Okyo was able to add a descriptive element to traditional painting that heretofore had mainly consisted of line drawing. He skillfully combined new techniques of detailed description of objects with depth and three-dimensional expression within an unaltered framework as earlier dictated by the conventions of the Kano school ornamental picture. (It should be remembered that the latter was itself a merging of the Yamato-e and *sumi* brush-painting styles.)

Okyo's adoption and adaptation of the old and the new, and his incorporation of sophisticated new techniques, indicated that he was effectively able to separate subject from means or, taken in broader terms, world view from technology. He painted the same flowers and birds, pine trees and rocks, as his benefactors in the Kano school, but he did so in a different manner. His spirit of innovation was a direct result of contact with the international port of Nagasaki and the world of outside influences that had suddenly opened. It must not be said that it was done in imitation of what he had learned, because his new style required a great deal of thought and creativity. Okyo and his group were also successful commercially, and due to this success they could restrict their innovations to those of technique while keeping the existing framework unaltered.

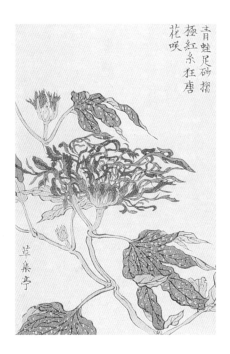

ABOVE (DETAIL): Asagao (Morning glory) (1854) from the Santo Itcho by Ko Ryosuke.

The stability of the basic framework was more than a reflection of the taste and values of the painters' benefactors. The shogunate was virtually unmovable during the eighteenth century, and although Confucianists and Japanese classical scholars often criticized its policies, they never criticized the system itself. *Sekimon shingaku* (practical ethics) supported the merchants' position within society while at the same time emphasizing and defining the notion that one should "stay within one's own share." Ando Shoeki (ca 1702–62), a physician who was also an advocate of egalitarianism, was the sole critic of the shogunate, proclaiming the necessity of revolutionary change. His writings were not widely read, however, and had little impact at the time.

Given that the system was unmovable, people were forced to look for change within the given framework. Thus, they became interested in the individuals in power rather than in the structure of power; in the policies to increase production rather than in the structure of production; and in the particular prod-

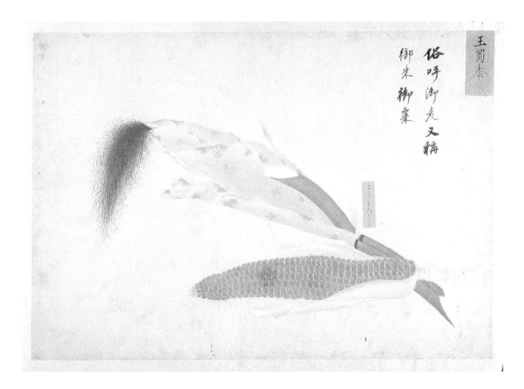

ABOVE: An excerpt from Shuho gafu, a sketchbook by Matsudaira Yoritaka (1711–71). Plants were illustrated and images were created by layering multiple pieces of Japanese paper.

ucts of a region rather than in its general topography. The focus eventually headed toward a separation of object from environment, giving birth to a kind of natural history, which in turn gave birth to the technique known as *monozukushi* (lists of things found in the natural world).

Botany, which was originally devoted to the collection and description of medicinal herbs, was at the root of this trend toward a new perspective on natural history. The educator and natural historian Kaibara Ekiken (1630-1714) compiled the *Yamato Honzo* (1709) late in life when his interest was already extending beyond medicinal herbs and was heading toward natural history. Plants, insects, fish, shellfish, and birds were illustrated with detailed accuracy, and generally without a background. Although realistic depiction may have been demanded by the subjects since these books must have originally been intended to describe their benefits both medicinal and otherwise, the painter's attention was focused on one aspect of a particular object, perhaps due to his intense psychological interest in depiction of that one aspect. It was this psychological inclination that complemented the descriptiveness of Nanpin and Okyo, not the reverse.

Artists are by nature imaginative, and therefore can describe objects that exist in reality as well as those taken from the imagination. Ito Jakuchu, who preferred to draw roosters, also painted phoenixes (e.g., *Oimatsu Hakuho-zu* [Old pine and white phoenix] in the *Doshoku Saie* [Colored series of illustrations of animals and plants][Imperial Household Agency]). Rosetsu, who until that time had mainly painted descriptive portraits, began to draw eccentric depictions of *Yama-uba-Zu* (Mountain witches) (Itsukushima Shrine) and Yurei-zu (Ghosts) (currently at the National Museum of Nara). These supernatural themes were not typical of eighteenth-century paintings. Not until the nineteenth century did the advent of Hokusai's *manga* (comic strip), exhaustively exploring every human posture and fleeting expression, ultimately lead to paintings of traditional and newly created monsters and ghosts. There was an almost logical flow of development from normal depiction of human bodies to the imaginative possibilities achieved through distortion of their shapes.

Such a development did not occur in the peculiar paintings of Soga Shohaku (1730–81), whose landscapes and portraits jump directly into an imaginary world and make no attempt at descriptiveness. His *Shozan Shiko-zu Byobu* (Boston Museum) imparts an Expressionistic effect through its thick, energetic lines of dark ink. Faces contorted in laughter come alive, particularly in the eyes and mouths of *Kanzan Juttoku-zu* (Kosei-ji, Kyoto) and *Kokei Sansho-zu Byobu* (Boston Museum). In his time, Shohaku was

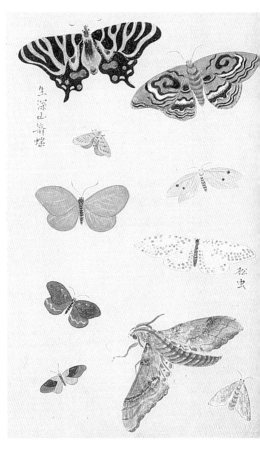

187

virtually isolated from his peers and exerted his individuality in a sphere totally opposite that of the prevailing trends of natural history. His paintings are extremely exaggerated and bizarre, exhibiting an almost destructive intensity.

Ito Jakuchu extended the theme of historic sketching of natural objects even further. He spent ten years completing the Doshoku Sai-e (Imperial Household Agency), a set of thirty paintings, of which *Kaiko-zu* and *Chihen Gunchu-zu* respectively describe various shellfish and insects (as well as snakes and frogs). They are painted in a

sketched, and each possesses distinct color and shape. Each part consists of detailed description, but the whole painting gives a fantastical impression. What sets each shell apart from reality is its positional relationship to the plane. The background of *Chihen Gunchu-zu* is slightly more descriptive, but its principles of composition are the same as those of the *Kaiko-zu*. Both pictures employ the same method used in twentieth-century Western Surrealism. How did Jakuchu arrive at Surrealism at such an early date?

Jakuchu was the eldest son of a vegetable merchant in Kyoto. In his early twenties,

ABOVE and RIGHT (DETAILS): Gunzen-zu Byobu (1764) by Soga Hyohaku. Traditional Chinese themes were treated with strong strokes and vivid, contrasting color in paintings that were almost avant-garde in style.

single uniform manner, not as individual works with separate labels or names. The background of *Kaiko-zu* is a highly formalized deep blue sea, with seaweed painted on silk and a space representing the beach at low tide. The space is not simply a description of a sandy beach, but an abstract two-dimensional space completely filled with shells. Each shell is clearly and vividly

following his father's death, he took over the family business and managed it until his retirement at around forty, at which time he gave the business to his younger brother. He dedicated the second half of his life, approximately another forty years, to painting, became a follower of Zen, and was given the Zen Buddhist name of Jakuchu. It is thought that his placement of various shells within the frame of a single picture must have been influenced by Shen Nanpin's ornamental sketching. Like Nanpin, Jakuchu was averse to leaving any open space in his paintings. He also had a taste for natural history, an inclination toward collecting, and a psychological proclivity toward inclusiveness. For Jakuchu, the imaginary world may have been a more solid and indispensable reality than the everyday, ordinary environment, which is the reason his pictures do not appear merely ornamental.

Jakuchu's experience as a vegetable merchant, combined with his tenure as a Zen world, might have been promoted by his study and belief in Zen philosophy. This denial drew the relationship between the radish and the other vegetables closer to that of the Buddha and his disciples in nirvana. In this painting, Jakuchu proclaimed the universality of such a relationship and emphasized an order that was independent from the individual characteristics of its constituents. Such an interpretation contains elements of a pictorial joke or humor, but to understand Jakuchu's world is to see a conversion of a certain surrealism of order, while each individual object is depicted as realistically as

monk at Shokoku-ji temple in Kyoto, inspired the painting *Yasai Nehan-zu* (Vegetable nirvana) (National Museum of Kyoto). In the center of the *sumi* painting is a daikon (Japanese radish), surrounded by various vegetables. If the Buddhist spirit exists in everything, as Jakuchu believed, then his denial of the order of the vegetable dealer, which is essentially the order of the common possible. One method Jakuchu did not employ was the exaggeration of the size of the objects. It was Rosetsu, a student of Okyo, who made use of that freedom and succeeded in creating imaginative, oversized creatures and objects in his pictures.

Rosetsu's elephant seen in the *Kokubyaku-zu Byobu* (Black and white screen) (Price Collection) is so oversized that it extends

beyond the screen. The body of the elephant, with two birds perched on its back, takes up most of the picture, leaving scarcely any room for anything else. In his illustrations of an ox from the same collection, space remains around the body of the animal with some parts extending to both the top and bottom of the picture plane. A small white dog has been included to further amplify the unrealistically immense dimensions of the ox. Since the elephant takes up the entire picture, it appears to assume aspects of a landscape or a globe, while the cow might resemble a mountain, or a Gulliver surrounded by Lilliputians. It should be noted that, at the time, no one in Japan had seen an elephant. Painting one must have required a serious leap of the imagination, but the familiar body of the ox is drawn in fully realistic lines and blurred details, although it is of enormous size. Certainly, this is a far cry from Okyo, the innovative traditionalist, who naturally denounced Rosetsu. Why did Rosetsu feel the need to exaggerate such an ordinary animal as the ox?

He might have embraced the existentialist concept of "a thing by itself," observing an object as distinct from its environment, thus turning the ordinary into the extraordinary through enlargement. Okyo was an innovator in technique, but he stayed within the boundaries of the traditional and ordinary world. Jakuchu and Rosetsu went further and discovered the extraordinary world beyond the traditional, beginning with *monozukushi* and ending with explorations of the imaginary world; Jakuchu worked with the ordinary subject of shellfish and chickens, while Rosetsu worked with the extraordinary: elephants and fish heads. In the nineteenth century, this sensuality was to become a search for a stimulus, making it inevitable that Japanese culture would excavate and foster a national consciousness rather than completely and quietly adopting foreign influences wholesale.

Nineteenth-century Japan

In the West, the nineteenth century was the era of the nation-state, marking the birth of industrial capitalism and individual determinism that began with Napoleon's army and ended with the political unification of major nations. It was also the age of expansionism promoted by Great Britain and France and their epidemic belief in widespread colonial imperialism.

Western imperialism arrived in the Far East after large portions of the African and Asian continents had been colonized. To eighteenth-century Japanese, the West had been represented by nothing more than a few artifacts and technologies imported through Nagasaki. It was not until the nineteenth century that the Japanese began to become aware of the West as something that actually existed and, more specifically, now posed a threat. The ruling samurai class was aware of China's total defeat in the Opium Wars, and at least some of its members must have been aware of their own military inadequacy, not having fought for two centuries. When the Tokugawa shogunate gave in to the pressure of the American fleet without engaging in battle, the military weakness of the shogunate was confirmed. Its surrender

resulted in the opening of Japan's ports. Clearly, one of the decisive conditions of nineteenth-century Japan was the imminent threat of Western imperialism. The Japanese response was to counter the threat by learning from the West so as not to be defeated by it. Thus, the Japanese learned not only military technology from the West after the ports were opened, but also gained industrial power and a social system that could support this new technology.

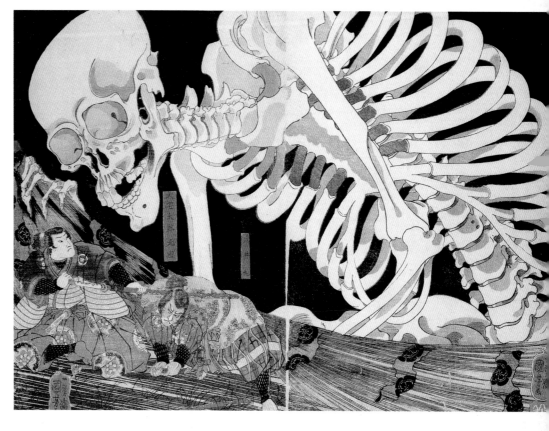

OPPOSITE PAGE (DETAIL): The great Ansei earthquake of 1855 that destroyed much of the Yoshiwara red-light district occurred at about 10:00 p.m.

ABOVE (DETAIL): The skeleton of Soma no Kodairi *by Utagawa Kuniyoshi is illustrated with anatomical accuracy, a result of Kuniyoshi's studies of a Western anatomy book. From a large* nishiki-e *triptych.*

Nineteenth-century Japan was defined solely by its response to Western imperialism, however. The political structure of the shogunate was about to collapse from within, since the Tokugawa regime had weakened both economically and militarily. The Satsuma clan monopolized the Okinawan trade route, the Choshu clan had trained its own civilian soldiers, and the shogunate remained unable to stop the revolutionary activity of its subjects. In addition, the administrative functions of the shogunate and local clans were becoming increasingly inefficient and lacked efficient distribution systems to meet

began to involve commoners and townspeople, escalating to *uchikowashi* riots, destruction that occurred on a larger and more frequent scale as time went on.

The samurai class tried to suppress this grass-roots movement and prohibited artistic or verbal description of such scenes. Some of the more courageous painters, such as Utagawa Kuniyoshi (1797–1861), depicted the destruction that occurred in the Tempo era (1831–45) following the particularly bad harvest of 1833–36. In his *Tempo no uchikowashi* he depicted a crowd withdrawing from a wealthy household after ransack-

ABOVE: Ryugu Tamatorihime no zu, *a large* nishiki-e *triptych, by Utagawa Kuniyoshi. This piece appears in Edouard Manet's painting* Berthe Morisot *(1870).*

the high capacity of demand. Thus, many young samurai, frustrated by the ineptitude of the high-ranking officials, left their clans, thereby precipitating a crisis within the ruling class itself.

Outside of samurai society, calls for social reform were frequent. Peasants were rioting because of such economic factors as bad crops, famine, and an increase in the price of rice due to monopolization. The peasants' demands included reduction of taxes, guaranteed provision of money and rice, a moratorium on debts, and a reorganization of the bureaucracy. The riots soon

ing it. They are shown emerging from the house carrying *fusuma* (sliding doors), folding screens, and boxes and bags. They are swinging rods and throwing lanterns and sticks into the air. This scene was also used as the background of an erotic painting known as *Hanagoyomi* (1835). The subjects of the painting, a man and a woman, are posed in the foreground wearing cloth headbands similar to those of the people in the crowd. The man is eating a boxed lunch he must have brought along to the event, and the woman is saying in effect "I'd rather do it *before* eating." If Kuniyoshi intended to record the destruction, then such an illustration was a useful means by which to do so. Prior approval was not required for such paintings since sexual scenes were not censored. Moreover, the pairing of the destruction with the sexual act clearly indicates two points of great concern to the everyday people of the time. These were the two areas, social and private, where people could respond against the forced order and official value system instituted by those in power. Eight years later, Kuniyoshi painted *Minamoto Yorimitsu-ko no yakata ni tsuchigumo yokai-o tsukuru no zu* (A spider producing monsters at Minamoto Yorimitsu's mansion) satirizing Tempo reforms.

The urge for social reform did not always express itself in destruction. The *Namazu-e (Catfish Portrait)* that became popular after the great Ansei earthquake of 1855 not only used the catfish as a symbol of the destructive power of the earthquake, but also made the fish representative of the positive values of social reform and the symbolic incarnation of a great god of reform. Toward the end of the Edo period, before the Meiji Restoration (1868), mass hysteria, wild dancing, and rioting called *Eejanaika* (Why not, it's okay!) broke out in the Tokai area, extended to Kyoto and Osaka, and eventually reached the far island of Shikoku. Several million people took to the streets, dancing wildly and chanting for social reform.

The people believed that sacred amulets from the great imperial shrine at Ise would fall from the sky, and Ochiai Yoshiiku (1833–1904), a disciple of Kuniyoshi, painted the *Honen Okagemairi no zu* depicting a scene of a myriad of amulets inscribed with the words "Amaterasu Shrine" falling from the sky. Hundreds of men and women were shown attempting to catch them, holding their hands up in the air. It is not known who made and scattered the charms, but this scene vividly depicts the self-intoxication of the masses blindly following one another in pursuit of the wish for social reform through an appeal to the mercy of the gods. Arguably, these phenomena probably did not pose a direct threat to those in power.

The common people's desire for social reform reflected their perception that the present world was evil, although the future was uncertain. The Meiji Restoration of January 3, 1868, in which the emperor was restored to power, reduced the authority of the shogunate. It did not occur along the lines of the grass-roots movement for social reform, but rather, it symbolized the victory of the

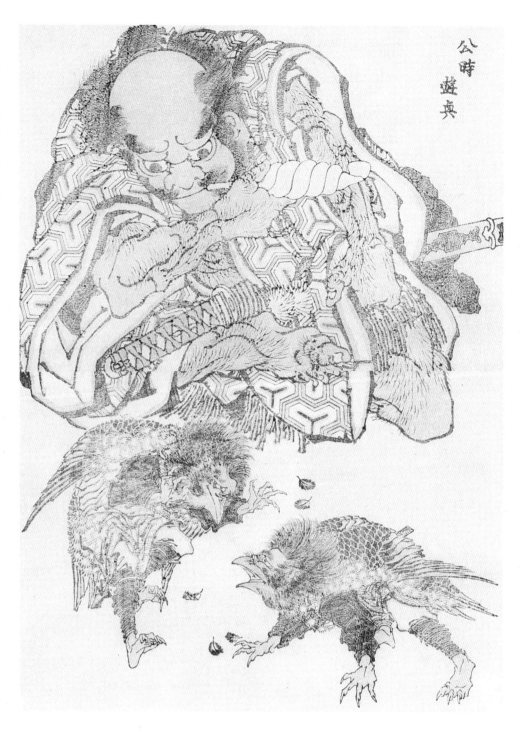

Satsuma-Chochu alliance against the Tokugawa shogunate, the progress of planned institutional reform instituted by intellectuals from the lower samurai classes, and the success of the British-Asian policy over the French in the Far East.

The Frenchman Georges Ferdinand Bigot (1860–1927), who resided in Japan from 1882 to 1899 and taught French at Nakae Chomin's French school, inherited the role of Kuniyoshi after the Meiji Restoration. He was said to have studied Japonisme, but he must also have been familiar with Honoré Daumier's (1808–79) satirical cartoons. His

ABOVE (DETAIL): From a manga *(comic strip) by Katsushika Hokusai, the painter who reportedly began to draw this series when he was fifty-five years old. It includes hills and water, flowers and birds, figures, implements, and patterns that are believed to have had an influence on the Impressionists.*

193

ABOVE and BELOW: Toshiyori no yona wakai hito da *(A young woman who looks old) and* Hito o baka ni shita hito da *(A man making a fool out of others) by Utagawa Kuniyoshi.*

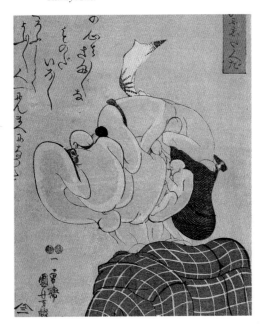

work includes sketches, copperplate etchings, and lithographs. His use of line is outstanding, sharply observant, and simply arranged. He affectionately depicted Japanese customs such as mixed bathing in the *sento* (public baths), rickshaws, fishing villages, and rice fields, while also incisively and brutally satirizing the suppression of newspaper reporters by the police, the corruption of high officials, and the decadent sprees at the Rokumeikan social club in Tokyo. However, when foreign privileges were abolished in the treaty revision of 1899, one of the first things the Japanese government did was to expel foreigners such as Bigot, who dearly loved Japanese culture and people, but who would not suppress his criticism of authority.

Ukiyo-e woodblock prints developed during the latter half of the eighteenth century. They used Edo's Yoshiwara red-light district and the Kabuki theater as subject matter and spawned the spectacular landscapes of Hiroshige (1797–1858), Hokusai (1760–1849), and Kuniyoshi who were working in the first half of the nineteenth century, when subject matter suddenly extended beyond the vicinity of Edo to such things as the Tokaido highway and Kiso-ji temple.

Many of Hiroshige's landscapes were of notable places, an idea taken from the a tradition of ancient Yamato-e and *sumi* brush painting. However, his *Tokaido Gojusantsugi (Fifty-three Stages of the Tokaido)* (1833) do not necessarily depict notable sites. Rather, the painter was interested in the diversity of the landscapes observed by travelers rather than in the literary resonance of famous views. He depicted such typical Japanese landscapes such as waterfronts, mountainous areas, and inns along the highway as seen at midday, at dusk, in the snow, in the spring rain, and in summer evening showers. Roofs, bridges, trees, and the sails of ships on water can be seen in most of the landscapes. Hiroshige painted nature permeated by culture, or culture as seen through the

shower. Each individual can recall his or her "lost time" in the landscapes; one can be reminded of the cold air in a town buried in snow, or the rocking sensation experienced while riding a familiar ferryboat. What more could one hope for in viewing such scenes? Hiroshige's landscapes were thoroughly Japanese in that what they depicted existed only in nineteenth-century Japan. Because of that fact (and not in spite of it) they had mass appeal in the same manner that Impressionist paintings were consummately French and, at the same time, extraordinarily universal.

Nineteenth-century Japanese painters pro-

natural environment. The discovery of such landscapes was also the discovery of a form of cultural nationalism.

Among Hiroshige's later works, *Meisho Edo Hyakkei (One Hundred Views of Edo)* include masterpieces of composition. For example, each composition of *Kameido Umeyashiki, Ohashi Atake no Yudachi, Atago-shita Yabukoji*, and *Yoroi no Watashi Koami-cho* represent a calm atmosphere, dramatic movement, the liveliness of everyday life, and strong ambience. Whether these places are famous or not, each picture invokes notable sensory aspects, the scent of plum blossoms, or the sound of the wooden shoes of a figure taking cover in a sudden evening

duced more than Hokusai's *Manga* or *Meisho Edo Hyakkei*. The Japanese painters of the time exhibited their imaginative capacities by painting numerous ghosts and monsters, going beyond mere realism. They used strong colors in their depiction of brutal and stimulating scenes. Further, some studied in the West, particularly in France, where they learned oil-painting techniques.

Why did such phenomena occur in Japan? Ghosts and monsters emerge from the depths of human consciousness, but they are usually kept in check by social order. When order is lost, collective hysteria surfaces (*Eejanaika*) and visions of ghosts and individual imaginings are allowed to emerge in

ABOVE (DETAIL): Oshu Adachigahara Hitotsuya no zu *(1885) by Tsukioka Yoshitoshi. This painting is an illustration of the legend of the witch of Adachigahara who lived in Oshu. In the legend an old cannibal witch caught and killed pregnant women and consumed their fetuses.*

ABOVE LEFT (DETAIL): Shirai Gonpachi *by Tsukioka Yoshitoshi. Shirai Gonpachi was a convict who escaped from prison to see his girlfriend and was caught and executed shortly thereafter by the police.*

works of art. Hokusai, more than any other painter, preferred to paint monsters. The Hokusai who painted realistic portraits of humans can be described as the Hokusai of the direct method. In other words, he did not display an obvious affection for women (as did Utamaro), nor was he particularly taken with certain Japanese customs (as was Bigot). Instead, he used his intellectual curiosity and incomparable descriptive skills to radically depart from the norm. After Hokusai had exhausted all the formal postures possible in depicting a woman's body, he broached the question as to what that woman's body would be like if the neck were elongated. And if the lower body of a figure were erased, making it float in the air, what kind of facial expression would be suitable? Monsters and ghosts represent Hokusai's transition from a direct method to a subjective one that allowed him to explore the possibilities and potential embodied in the natural, historical world of Jakuchu and Rosetsu.

Sara Yashiki (Plate Mansion), one in a set of five prints from the *Hyaku Monogatari (One Hundred Tales)* (1830), depicts the ghost of a maid emerging from the well into which she jumped after being mistakenly blamed for breaking a plate. Her body from the neck down consists of overlapping plates arranged like the scales of a snake. Her pale face, with its tangled strands of hair floating in a dark blue space, is shown spitting a thin trail of smoke from the mouth. She has a lonely profile; her one visible eye is filled with spite, possibly reflecting feelings hidden in the subconscious mind of every maid.

Kohada Koheiji depicts the skull and skeletal fingers of the traveling actor Koheiji, whose wife was abducted as he was murdered. He is shown at the bedside of his sleeping murderer, preparing to pull the mosquito net away and kill him. The picture does not show the murderer or Koheiji's wife who might conceivably be accompanying him. The composition is adept in its clear portrayal of action motivated by ill feelings and the intention of revenge.

In 1824, Hokusai created his famous portrait of a woman with octopuses as an entry in his illustrated book series titled *Kinoe no Komatsu (The Young Pines).* In the print, known as *The Dream of the Fisherman's Wife,* the subject, a woman, is bending backward, her legs wide apart, washed by a wave. A large octopus is sucking her genital area, and a small one is sucking her mouth. The tendrils coil around her body, caressing her.

The woman's face bears an ecstatic expression. The octopus has been said to be the personification of the artist Hokusai, and is symbolic of repressed sexual desire. The suppressing agent, in Hokusai's case, was the culture and society of the time. Because of the uprisings and the inevitable changes that would follow, the suppressor was about to lose its function as a psychological inhibitor.

However, Hokusai's painting is not truly representative of the sadism that became more evident in the Nanboku Kabuki theater, whose gory scenes were designed to stimulate the senses of the audience. Influenced by this form of theater, *ukiyo-e* be-

ABOVE (DETAIL): Altar painting at Issenheim, central portion of the first panel, by Matthias Grunewald.

came dominated by strong primary colors used to emphasize brutal scenes, particularly in the work of Utagawa Kunisada (1786–1865) and Kuniyoshi, and further in the work of Tsukioka Yoshitoshi (1839–92). Of course, ghosts and monsters often appeared. Among Kunisada's monsters, the most unique were the giants depicted in the land of the giants of the print known as *Sento Shinwa*. The female giant's genitals are so large that the man visiting the land of the giants can enter them on foot. The male giant's penis stands twice as tall as the woman depicted beside it. Kuniyoshi's painted skeleton (*Soma no Kodairi*) is also

enormous, shown soaring over a man holding a long sword. The skull by itself is probably larger than the entire body of the man. The skeleton is white, partially shaded, and distinctly stands out from the dark background. The enormous genitals and skeleton can be seen as symbols of life and death.

Oshu Adachigahara Hitotsuya no zu (An isolated house in Oshu Adachigahara) (1885) by Yoshitoshi is one of the most outstanding examples of the pictorial style that graphically depicted cruelties. A witch is sharpening a knife she obviously intends to use to slash open a pregnant woman's belly in order to eat the fetus, a theme that came from

the Kabuki play *Oshu Adachigahara,* which was itself based on a puppet play of the same name by Chikamatsu Hanji (1725–83) first performed in 1762. Yoshitoshi's painting is vertically longer than was usual. The witch sharpens a knife in the foreground of the lower half of the painting. The pregnant woman is hanging upside down from a dark ceiling over the witch. Her ankles are tied with a rough rope, and a scarlet undergarment barely covers her from her legs to her hips, while her large, white abdomen and breasts are exposed. The terrified woman's head is tilted at an angle above the witch's face. After completion of the com-

position, Yoshitoshi himself went insane and died.

While Japanese *ukiyo-e* woodblock painters reached the height of their powers at this time, Japanese artists suddenly attained a high level of professionalism in the fields and schools of oil painting. This movement was led by Asai Chu (1856–1907) who studied under the Italian professor Antonio Fontanesi at the Technical Fine Arts School in Tokyo for two years from 1876. Before Asai, the only person working in oil was Takahashi Yuichi (1828–94), who was self-taught. Harada Naojiro (1863–99), who studied in Munich, and Kuroda Seiki

(1866–1924), who studied in Paris, followed Asai. The one common element of their work was that they absorbed not only the techniques but also the themes of contemporary Western academism. They painted everyday landscapes and portraits, almost completely discarding fantasy, ghosts, and monsters. Eliminating fantasy is akin to disregarding the imagination, however, and suppression of illustration of monsters and ghosts effectively served to conceal the subconscious world. In late nineteenth-century Japan, artists learned the techniques of modern Western painting and applied them to a superficial consciousness in much the same manner that their native land digested industrial technology. What became of the subconscious world? Whatever its denouement, it was in that world that traditional culture continued to live.

MONSTERS: SYMBOLS OF THE END OF A CULTURE

The first appearance of monsters and ghosts in Japanese art was not during the Edo period. Heian-period literature, such as the *Ise Monogatari* and *Konjaku Monogatari,* contained tales of people eaten by ogres, while other tales told of people being haunted or killed by live or dead spirits. The oral tale of a hundred monsters marching at night, the *Hyakki-yagyo,* was also popular along with such others such as *Okagami.* Illustrations or paintings of these tales were rare, and monsters were not widely depicted until after the Kamakura period (1185–1333).

The *Hyakki-yagyo Emaki* (Daitoku-ji temple) shows a plethora of monsters, including ogres who are apparently *oni* (Japanese demons). *Oni* with human forms, horns, and frightening faces are depicted, as are monsters in the form of birds, animals, musical instruments, or even pots and pans. The latter monsters are utensils over a hundred years old that consume souls and trick people. These illustrations are vividly colored, often detailed in fine brushwork. No background has been added and no human beings appear. The whole picture scroll is basically a phalanx of monsters either chasing or threatening one another or running away, not fighting or brutally killing one another. We see an autonomous world, and although it appears that the monsters struggle among themselves, their struggles are separate from those of the human world.

It is interesting to note that the monsters in the *Tsukumo-gami Emaki* (White hair of an old woman scroll) (Shotoku-ji temple,

Gifu Prefecture) appear to have more aggressive feelings for human beings. In this work, old, abandoned implements and utensils mysteriously transform themselves into monsters who exact revenge upon mankind. According to the written explanations added to the picture, they kill and steal food from humans, cattle, and horses, although actual scenes of killing and pillage are not depicted. The monsters are eventually conquered by attendant deities of Buddhism and converted to the Shingon sect. The former aspect probably reflects the far-off world of animism, while the latter represents the separation between the world of man and the

world of monstrosities, and shows that this picture scroll was, at one time, used to promote the Shingon sect.

Monsters began to be depicted more often, and it is possible that two events that had occurred during this period helped prompt their frequent appearance. The first was the tendency toward the decentralization of power that, having begun in the Kamakura period, was accelerated as civil wars, famine, riots, and epidemics ran rampant. The second event was seen in the spread of culture toward local areas and the lower classes. This phenomenon must have signaled the collapse of Heian culture (794–1185), which was based on a centralized power system difficult to separate from the cultural hege-

OPPOSITE PAGE: Giant *(ca 1808–12) by Francisco de Goya (1746–1828). The theme of this painting remains an enigma. Prado Museum, Madrid.*

ABOVE: Depiction of a huge mushroom by Victor Hugo. If one stares at the image, the illusion of a human face emerges from the cap of the mushroom. Victor Hugo Memorial Museum, Paris.

mony of the aristocratic class. The Ashikaga shogunate (1338–1598) attempted to supplant Heian culture but failed. In short, the confusion of social order (symbolized by the expression *gekokujo,* "the lower dominating the upper") and the end of one form of culture overlapped.

The monsters and ghosts of Hokusai and Kuniyoshi appeared during the first half of the nineteenth century, when the shogunate had not yet become unstable and the Edo townspeople had not yet begun to sense that their social order was on the verge of collapse. This stage can be viewed as a terminal one in the Japanese culture of the time. No new philosophy appeared, as one had toward the end of the eighteenth century, and the culture as a whole leaned toward the pursuit of more potent sensual stimulation. The Edo red-light district was becoming increasingly sophisticated, and Kabuki plays were becoming more exciting and stimulating. At

this terminal stage of the culture of the common people, monsters were created by artists as entertainment, although images of ghosts and skeletons were seen more often than monsters on theatrical stages.

Edo-period artistic representations of ghosts had regular patterns of form and appearance. Their hair was generally disheveled, the color of their kimono pale as death, and they often appeared without legs. Nameless women (rather than high-ranking officials or historically important people) were often depicted as ghosts who bore a grudge or were intent on avenging a wrong. This type of portrayal signified the individualization of death.

The same can be said of skeletons, which were not symbols of death in general (as in the paintings or passion plays of the Middle Ages) but were rather visualizations of a particular individual's death. The fear of death accompanied the Edo epicureanism,

and visualizations of that fear provided strong stimulation and an inverted sense of pleasure.

If early nineteenth-century Edo can be characterized as the terminal stage of a culture devoid of societal confusion, then the late Ming (1368–1644) and early Ching (1644–1911) dynasties of China can offer a contrasting case. The culture of these dynasties remained stable despite extreme social changes occurring within. Badashanren (1626–1705) and Sekito were painters who came from the imperial household of Ming and painted in the *bunjin-ga* style in the early Ching period. They never drew ghosts, skeletons, or monsters. In their paintings and sketches, they painted and drew only what they could actually observe: birds, fish, lotus flowers, faraway mountains, trees, streams, landscapes, and distant figures seated on rocks. In doing so, they were able to retain the traditional framework of Chi-

nese paintings that had prevailed since the Sung and Yuan dynasties.

Badashanren was an outstanding painter who took the tonsure and isolated himself in a hermitage, where he reportedly went mad. The sketch called *Ketsugyozu* taken from his sketchbook entitled *Anbansatsu* (1694, Izumiya Hakko-kan, Kyoto) depicts a fish with its eyes wide open. Its mouth hangs slightly open, exposing one tooth as if it might take a bite out of something. No background image has been supplied and because of its fantastic nature, one must wonder if the fish is not a fish at all but a monster. The same sketchbook includes the drawing *Hasu-zu* (Lotus flower). In this drawing, two stalks of a lotus plant are arranged to the left. The triangular space between the upper left and right corners is filled with lotus leaves. The leaves are drawn without outlines and extend out of the frame. The picture seems to be approaching Abstract Expressionism although it is based on an attempt at realism. One cannot call this a monster of a lotus plant, but it obviously displays an element that a true lotus plant could never contain, an element inspired by the shape of the object. In this piece of Edo-period artwork, the artist Badashanren was able to transfer his inspirations or thoughts about a simple common object to the absolutely highest level of imagination.

In the West, the fifteenth century was characterized by the overlapping events of societal confusion and the collapse of a culture. The work of Hieronymus Bosch (ca 1450–1516) revealed an apocalyptic and eschato-

Two centuries earlier in the same area of Flanders, painters such as Jan van Eyck (1390–1441) and others had been painting descriptive and quiet pictures in a traditional style. Bosch was obviously an exception, radically different from his predecessors and contemporaries. It is difficult to try to explain Bosch in relation to the work of other artists of his time. It should, however, be noted that Bosch's monsters appeared at the end of the Middle Ages in a period that was beset by raging famine, epidemics, and war. As the Dutch historian Johan Huizinga (1872–1945) has stated, the late Gothic style of Northern France, the Netherlands, and

ABOVE: Gensanmi Yorimasa Nue-taiji *(ca 1819–25) by Utagawa Kuniyoshi. The terrifying nature of the monster is symbolized by the scrolling black clouds.*

logical view encompassing a wide variety of monsters, ghosts, and spirits. Unlike the Japanese *Hyakki-yagyo*, which depicted monsters that took familiar forms, his works included an assortment of insects, reptiles, amphibians, and fish, as well as animals, birds, and implements of labor that had been transformed into monsters. Bosch's backgrounds contained buildings, mountains, and bodies of water and were often accompanied by scenes of natural disasters. Human males and females are shown being threatened or eaten or dismembered by the monsters. Bosch's apocalyptic visions opened the way for the painter Pieter Brueghel (1525–69).

Germany, popular from the end of the fourteenth century to the fifteenth century, exhibited the tendency to "self-analyze all sorts of shapes and existences and give an infinite amount of workmanship to each part." He also notes that the "unnecessary prosperity of shapes and phenomena" was dominated by a "fear of space," all of which might be seen as "one of the signs that a culture was approaching its end." Through analysis of this observation, it becomes quite easy to understand the reason for and the importance of the prophetic appearance of monsters in the work created by the artists of the late Edo period.

BELOW: The Cyclops *(ca 1895–1900) by Odilon Redon (1840–1916).*

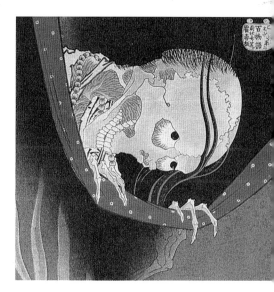

ABOVE: Sarayashiki *from the series* Hyaku Monogatari *issued in 1830 by Katsushika Hokusai. The maid Okiku threw herself into a well after being accused of breaking a treasured plate owned by her employer. The ghost's body is comprised of overlapping plates.*

RIGHT: Kohada Koheiji *from the* Hyaku Monogatari *series (1804) by Katsushika Hokusai.*

Tokyo: A City of Transition

ABOVE: A nishiki-e *(woodblock print) triptych by Utagawa Hiroshige II depicting Tokyo's Ginza area, rebuilt in stone and brick in 1874. Kanagawa Prefectural Museum.*

OPPOSITE PAGE: An aerial view of Shinjuku ward, Tokyo. The Tokyo Metropolitan Government Offices, designed by Tange Kenzo and completed in 1991, now stand in the open area in the left center.

Tokyo was the cultural center of Japan for almost three centuries during the Edo period (1603–1868), and to this day, many traditional forms of Japanese culture can be found thriving in the capital. Kabuki, Noh drama, and sumo wrestling still enjoy immense popularity and attract many visitors, including foreign tourists.

Until 1868, Tokyo was called Edo, and it was the base for the Tokugawa shogunate for 265 years. The shogunate was toppled in the Meiji Restoration of 1868, when the power of the shogun was replaced by that of the emperor. The capital was moved from Kyoto to Edo, which was renamed Tokyo, "eastern capital." The name was given to differentiate it from Kyoto, earlier known as Saikyo, or "western capital."

In Kyoto, where the imperial family had held administrative power during the Heian period (794–1185), cultural achievements flourished, as we have seen. Tokyo, conversely, was mostly countryside and was sparsely inhabited. There were areas that contained aristocratic manors, but most of what we now know as Tokyo was then vast, uninhabited land.

When the government by aristocracy began to disintegrate, local samurai clans gained power. One of those clans, the Taira, eventually seized control of the government. In the early twelfth century, an affiliate of a powerful family from Chichibu (a mountainous region north of present-day Tokyo) built a small castle in the plateau where the imperial palace now stands. The leader of the affiliate named himself after the area, Edo, and the region became controlled by the power emanating from the castle.

The Minamoto clan took power in 1185, seizing it from the Taira clan. The castle of Edo continued to exercise power as the local authority, and in 1457 a high-ranking figure called Ota Dokan, who was a member of the Kamakura government, built a full-scale castle in the area. This was the beginning of Tokyo as we know it today.

It is a well-known fact that the city of Tokyo comprises the largest urban population in the world (just under 12 million) and that this same population is crowded into a relatively small land mass of 2,166.26 square kilometers. It stretches within a narrow range of 80 kilometers from east to west and contains 23 wards (*ku*), 26 cities, and 14 towns and villages. Two of the towns and 7 of the villages are located on the Seven Isles of Izu and include the Ogasawara Islands. The 23 wards cover a total area of 599.73 square kilometers. The 26 cities are all concentrated in the western portion, and are bedroom communities for Tokyo commuters. Of course, there are other cities in the world that are just as densely populated. Mexico City, New York, and Los Angeles are comparable to Tokyo in terms of population, with India's Bombay and Calcutta and China's Beijing and Shanghai close behind. Tokyo is foremost among international cities in Asia, and has diplomatic envoys of most nations, as well as more foreign businesses than any other city in Japan. There are 217,295 foreign residents of Tokyo according to 1990 statistics, and many more if all unregistered residents are also taken into account. There are many foreign visitors to Tokyo, nearly 3 million in 1989, and the city is regularly the site of international conferences and symposia. Yet the overwhelming majority of those who live in Tokyo are Japanese, have uniformly dark hair and a similar manner of dress, distinctive particularities that help emphasize the extreme density of population. This phenomenon, which can be termed the first defining characteristic of modern-day Tokyo, is virtually unheard of in any major Western city.

The second defining characteristic is seen in the immense territory the city itself covers. As we have noted above, as a locus for political, economical, and cultural activities, Tokyo extends far beyond the boundaries of the administrative jurisdiction of the Tokyo metropolitan area; it stretches over the Tamagawa river into Kanagawa Prefecture to the west, crosses the Edogawa river into Chiba Prefecture to the east, and cuts deeply into the Kanto Plain to the north. When referring to the Tokyo metropolitan area, the outlying areas must be included because of their proximity.

The third defining characteristic of Tokyo is the nearly complete lack of city planning. Partial attempts at city planning were recently made in the Marunouchi and Shinjuku municipal districts, but Tokyo extends outward, almost as if it were the result of spon-

taneous generation rather than the product of an ordered system. Concrete high-rises are built on chaotic city blocks with major highways erected between them, while elsewhere one can find wooden bungalows crowded into narrow alleys. The contrast is particularly visible within certain areas of the city, although Tokyo is not the only major metropolis where these two elements co-exist. There is, however, a positive aspect to the latter element; if all modern cities consisted of concrete high-rises on wide streets arranged in square or radiating patterns, their atmosphere would be decidedly cold. They might be suitable for automotive traffic, but not for strolling on foot. It is in the narrow alleyways that people walk, stopping to meet someone or to discover something new. The back streets of Tokyo are imbued with human warmth and the scent of life, a decisively important element.

The fourth defining characteristic of Tokyo is safety and cleanliness. Of all the major cities in the world, none is as safe as Tokyo. Physical threats from strangers and robberies seldom occur. When a wallet is left in a parked car, chances are that it will remain secure. Women can walk safely at night. This is a rather exceptional situation. The metropolitan sanitation system is also comparably efficient and systematic. It could easily be argued that Tokyo ranks as one of the cleanest urban areas in the world.

However, cleanliness and beauty are two different matters, and this brings us to the fifth defining characteristic. In an aesthetic evaluation of world cities, Tokyo is unattractive. In terms of its architecture and the aesthetic appeal of its streets, it is far inferior to Paris, cannot match Rome, and is surpassed by London and New York. Historically, however, Japanese architecture was quite aesthetically sophisticated; the Japanese teahouse and the Katsura Rikyu detached palace are prime examples of an exquisitely refined aesthetic. Why, then, is Tokyo so unattractive?

ABOVE, LEFT: *Daiei Fudosan building in Nihonbashi, Tokyo. Designed by the Meiji-period architect Tatsuno Kingo, it was completed in 1915. Unfortunately, a freeway was built directly in front of the building, destroying its waterfront view. The building was demolished in 1987.*

LEFT: *The residence of Shibusawa Eiichiro in Kabuto-cho, Tokyo. In 1888, Shibusawa commissioned construction of the building by Tatsuno Kingo, then an up-and-coming architect.*

A city cannot remain beautiful unless there is a conscious effort made to maintain its beauty. In Japan, aesthetic sophistication and continuity of tradition are more readily apparent in the details of daily life and in private spaces than in the public domain. When a move is made toward more public space, attention to detail is lost. Unless the extension of aesthetic values moves from private space into the public sphere and becomes an accepted custom, cities remain aesthetically unpleasant places. Certainly, some of the structures built by Japanese architects today are beautiful, but the beauty of an individual structure usually cannot exert an influence on the entire street or on the city as a whole. On a practical level, buildings have to be designed to conform to area planning and construction laws, as well as to earthquake and fire regulations. Unfortunately, few, if any, regulations take into consideration the maintenance or development of the city's intrinsic or potential beauty.

The sixth defining characteristic of Tokyo is the rapidity with which it changes. Drastic changes can be felt and seen yearly. Such a rapid rate of change is connected to the city's

ABOVE: Daiichi National Bank was located beside the Kaiun-kyo bridge in Tokyo. This structure is an example of the compromises made between Western and Japanese styles typical of the time. Completed in 1872, the building was often depicted in woodblock prints as a symbol of the Meiji era.

BELOW: Kaiun-kyo Bridge (1876), a large woodblock print by Kobayashi Kiyochika showing the Daiichi National Bank building surrounded by snow. Kobayashi produced a series of woodblock prints of famous spots in Tokyo. Many of the buildings depicted represented a mixture of Western and Japanese elements that was often seen during the rapid advancement and enlightenment of the Meiji era.

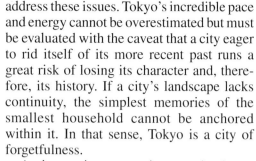

ABOVE: *Babasakimon Street was modeled after First Street in London and was called Itcho (first town). The Mitsubishi Ichigo-kan building on the right was preserved until after the redevelopment of the downtown Marunouchi area during the postwar period, but has since been demolished.*

BELOW: *Mitsubishi Ichigo-kan (1894) in the Queen Anne style designed by Conder to mark the conversion of the Marunouchi area into a business district modeled after Lombard Street in London.*

economic dynamism. There is also a notable lack of regulations requiring consideration of aesthetic harmony with the surrounding area during the earliest planning stages of architectural design. Urban renewal in Tokyo is carried out with virtually no deference to the past. It is generally believed that the old must be destroyed in order to create space for the new or else the city will not progress. Naturally, issues such as air and water pollution, waste and sewage disposal, and housing and transportation have to be dealt with; new plans are developed and facilities are constructed to service and to

address these issues. Tokyo's incredible pace and energy cannot be overestimated but must be evaluated with the caveat that a city eager to rid itself of its more recent past runs a great risk of losing its character and, therefore, its history. If a city's landscape lacks continuity, the simplest memories of the smallest household cannot be anchored within it. In that sense, Tokyo is a city of forgetfulness.

An interesting comparison can be drawn with the main section of the city of Warsaw, which was destroyed in the war to the same extent or to an extent greater than that of Tokyo, but reconstructed to match the original. It should be noted that construction of a more efficient and modern Warsaw would have been possible at a fraction of the cost of reconstruction, but despite this fact the citizens of the city consciously chose to resurrect the city's individuality and history. By comparing these two opposing attitudes toward reconstruction, Tokyo and Warsaw can be seen as prime examples of their citizens' attitudes toward continuity of culture.

During World War II, Vienna was also heavily bombed; the National Opera House was destroyed. After the war, the citizens of Vienna constructed an exact reproduction of the old opera house, despite the lack of basic personal necessities such as food, clothing, and coal. Opera continued to be performed, uninterrupted, at another location throughout construction. The exterior of the opera house was completely restored, while the interior was designed to remain faithful to the original. Much more time and money were required to complete the restoration of the opera house than would have been required had a totally new building been erected on the site.

The music of Wolfgang Amadeus Mozart cannot be separated from the architecture of Vienna's opera house, which itself cannot be separated from St. Stephen's Cathedral and the central streets of the city. The affection the people of the city feel toward Vienna and its architecture is the same affection they feel toward the waters of the Danube. The emotion is rooted in the concept of cultural continuity. If it exceeds a certain level, the velocity with which a city changes deeply affects the psychology of its inhabitants and the characteristics of its culture, even if the change is presumed to be for the better. In such an environment, cultural shallowness and an increase in cases of mental instability would not be seen as surprising. This is an overt danger in a culture that only knows how to proceed but remains ignorant of how

to reflect on its past. Thus, Tokyo's aesthetic sensitivity as a city reflects an economic dynamism while indicating the superficiality and shortsightedness of its consumer-based society.

MODERN ARCHITECTURE: HISTORIC STAGES OF DEVELOPMENT

During the Edo period, Sakoku prohibited contact with foreign countries save through a small window left open at the man-made island of Dejima in Nagasaki Harbor. This effectively excluded technological innovation in architecture, as well as in many other fields. As a result, few new tools, technologies, or construction materi-

RIGHT: Weekly concerts are held in the north dome of Tokyo Station.

TOP: Tokyo Station is shown at about the time of its inauguration (1914) in Marunouchi, Tokyo. Designed by Tatsuno Kingo to serve as a gateway to the city, the structure was enlarged and elongated in keeping with the original plan for its use as a commemorative memorial for Japan's victory in the Russo-Japanese War. The fully ornamental style was in sharp contrast to the simpler and more functional buildings found in the rest of the city. The general populace entered under the dome on the right; the exit was under the dome on the left, while the central gate was for the exclusive use of the imperial family.

CENTER: Tokyo Station today. The original roofs and interior were destroyed in the firebombings of World War II. Initially a three-story structure, it was lowered to two stories featuring simplified roof ornamentation. As the largest existing red-brick structure in Japan, it stands majestically as a gateway to Tokyo, although it has lost some of the buoyancy of the Tatsuno style.

211

als were introduced to Japan, and those already in existence became extremely conservative, making the emergence of a new style of architecture a remote possibility at best. The only direction to take was a return to traditional techniques that consequently became increasingly sophisticated.

Like the cities of modern Japan, the cities of the Edo period were characterized by the absence of urban planning, although they were neither chaotic nor ugly, as many scenes depicted in woodblock prints of the time will certainly attest. If we accept the impression given by *ukiyo-e*, particularly those of Hiroshige, it seems that Edo-period towns were comprised of orderly streets full of the hustle and bustle of everyday life. Neighborhood shops and dwellings had aesthetically pleasing, tiled roofs and whitewashed walls, the moats had ample water, and the rivers were studded with boats and crossed by bridges. The architecture remained simple and unchanging for hundreds of years, undeviating both in terms of material and in style, as reflected in the form of the structures, their height, and their color. The fact that Edo-period architecture and streets were beautiful and orderly can easily be surmised

ABOVE: Nikolai Cathedral (Nikorai-do) (1891), designed by Josiah Conder in Chiyoda-ku, Tokyo, was the first Byzantine-style church in Japan bearing a cross-shaped structure crowned by a dome. It was destroyed by fire in the earthquake of 1923, but was rebuilt by Okano Shinichiro, who employed a somewhat different design in its domes and towers.

LEFT: Nikolai Cathedral under construction.

ABOVE RIGHT: The headquarters of the Bank of Japan (1896), designed by Tatsuno Kingo, Chuo-ku, Tokyo. This was the first central government building designed by a Japanese architect. It was the first stone structure in Japan and was modeled after the National Bank of Belgium in Brussels.

from a stroll along the city streets that still retain the original flavor of the Edo time, such as those found in the city of Takayama in Gifu Prefecture and in parts of Tokyo and Kyoto.

However, the beauty of Edo-period streets was not the result of conscious effort on the part of the citizens, nor was it due to mandates from the shogunate. Essentially the result of technological limitations that forced the architects of the time to turn inward and to develop existing skills, the beauty of the streets clearly resulted from the limitations imposed by the policy of Sakoku. History, after all, has demonstrated the artistic and economical limitations that resulted when the policy of Sakoku was lifted.

Since Japan opened its doors to the West in 1868, it has pursued a steady course of Westernization. The history of city planning in Tokyo from the Meiji era (1868–1912) to the present day can roughly be separated into five phases. The first phase occurred when the early Meiji-era carpenters built quasi-Western structures; the second phase occurred during the Taisho (1912-26) era, when Western architecture was being imitated wholesale; the third phase occurred in the period between the two World Wars, when Japanese-style architecture was pursued against a background of nationalism through an eclectic combination of Eastern-style architectural elements grafted onto Western-style structures; the fourth phase occurred during the postwar period when architectural design was further inspired by international influences; and the fifth phase began with the advent of Postmodernism in the 1970s.

There are examples in Tokyo of each phase except for the first, as structures of this type no longer exist. The first phase came about as a result of the Meiji government's unrelenting pursuit of Westernization that led to an increased interest in Western architecture and Western-style city planning. The proclivity toward Western design was first seen in the red-brick streets that were laid in the Ginza district after a fire demolished the area in 1873. Further, Inoue Kaoru, who was elected to the post of minister of foreign affairs in 1879, invited the German architects Hermann Ende (1829-1907) and Wilhelm Bockmann (1832-1902) to help facilitate the great conversion of Tokyo to a political capital modeled after those in Europe. The architect Josiah Conder (1852-1920) was invited from Great Britain to undertake the conversion of the Marunouchi area into a London-style business district. While in Japan, he designed the Rokumeikan (1883), Nikolai Cathedral (Nikorai-do, 1891), and the Navy Ministry Building (1895). He also lectured at the Kobu Daigakko to Japanese architects on the architectural styles of England. Due to international influences such as these, several proposals were produced that would transform Tokyo into a European-style city.

What were the basic conditions required for adoption of Western-style architecture, and what capacity and skills did Japanese architects of the time possess? As we have noted, the creation of wooden structures had

become increasingly advanced during Japan's period of national seclusion and had reached the pinnacle of sophistication by the end of the Edo period. By that time, master carpenters had begun to receive orders for construction of residences by foreigners and were being shown Western-style structures and asked to build similarly styled buildings. Working in the new style enabled them to take full advantage of the traditional techniques they had mastered. One architect who did so to remarkable effect was Shimizu Kisuke (1815-81), the father of Western-style architecture in Japan. His buildings

ABOVE: The elegant interior of the Mitsui Club (1913), designed by Josiah Conder.

213

included the Suruga-cho Kawase Bank Mitsui-gumi (1874) and the first large-scale hotel ever constructed in Japan, the Tsukiji Hotel-kan (1868). There were quite a few other master builders who took on the challenge of creating Western-style architecture using traditional skills. They built schools, public offices, and city halls not only in Tokyo but throughout the countryside. The flexibility these craftsmen exhibited in incorporating Western elements into their designs only served to reinforce the strength and variety of their skills in this first phase of the adoption of Western architectural styles by Japanese architects.

The second phase saw the construction of genuinely Western-style architecture, including the Hyokei-kan in Ueno (completed in 1908). Western-style buildings constructed during the first phase were a far cry from typical Western architecture with their compromised styles, materials, and techniques based on traditional Japanese methods. It was only a matter of time before more accurate reproductions of Western models eventually began to appear. First, foreign architects such as Conder designed the Nikolai Cathedral and the residence of Iwasaki Hisaya (completed in 1896, currently the Supreme Court Training School). Following this, Japanese architects who had studied under Conder came into prominence, including Tatsuno Kingo (1854-1919), who designed Tokyo Station and the headquarters of the Bank of Japan, Sone Tatsuzo (1852-1937), who designed the Keio University Library, and Katayama Tokuma (1854-1917), whose works include the Akasaka Detached Palace and the aforementioned Hyokei-kan. Their works were completed in imitation of Western styles and attained a nearly perfect level of construction. Many of their buildings remained intact through the

Kaikan, 1936), whose design was also solicited publicly with the requirement that it must express grandeur and spaciousness, characteristics that were thought to reflect national honor and dignity. Another example from a slightly earlier time is the Kabuki-za theater (1924, rebuilt in 1951). Taking Japa-

Great Kanto earthquake that leveled much of the city of Tokyo in 1923.

The third phase sought to unify Eastern and Western cultures against a background of growing nationalism. The representative example of this phase was the main building of the Tokyo National Museum (1937). The design was publicly solicited with the specification that "the style of the architecture is to be in harmony with what is inside the building, thus oriental style based on Japanese taste is preferred." The building, still standing today, is a peculiar structure of steel and concrete designed in a style that blends Indonesian architecture with a Japanese-style roof. A similar example of this type of mixing can be found in the former Gunjin Kaikan meeting hall (now the Kudan

nese forms that were created for structures completely different in size and intent which were made of completely different materials, and imposing them onto concrete, Western structures in an attempt to make those structures appear traditional or Japanese, is akin to grafting bamboo onto an oak tree. If, in fact, the resulting structure may be peculiarly Japanese, it in no way constitutes Japanese architecture. These types of combinations of Eastern and Western elements are essentially compromises, not unions. Grafting of shapes from traditional wooden structures (e.g., roofs and pillars) of Japanese design onto newly designed structures does not then make those structures Japanese architecture. Likewise, such architectural compromises between Eastern and

ABOVE: The Hyokei-kan, designed by the imperial architect Katayama Tokuma, who had studied under Josiah Conder. It was dedicated by the citizens of Tokyo in commemoration of the marriage of the Taisho emperor.

Western cultures does not create true unity. The penchant of many Japanese architects of the 1930s to graft traditional elements (such as sloping roofs) onto concrete buildings resulted in many unsightly buildings. The ancient Egyptians placed bird heads on top of human bodies in their art, essentially ignoring the structure of the body and its proportions. For that matter, the ancient

(b 1913) Olympic pools at Yoyogi (1964), Tokyo Cathedral (1964), and the Sogetsu Kaikan (Sogetsu School of Flower-arrangement Hall, 1977). These structures differ from buildings constructed in the third phase in terms of sheer quality. Frank Lloyd Wright (1867-1959) expressed himself in an international architectural language in his creation of the Imperial Hotel (1922) in Tokyo,

ABOVE: An onigawara (guardian demon tile) decorates a corner of the roof by the front entrance of the Tokyo National Museum.

BELOW: An ornamental design found on both ends of the outer wall.

Greeks placed human torsos onto the bodies of horses, also disregarding overall structure and form. The results were monsters. And while many of the buildings of 1930s Tokyo were similarly unsightly, they also bore witness to the architects' technical capacity. This capacity and skill enabled Japan to completely assimilate the techniques of building concrete structures in the period between World War I and II.

During the fourth phase, an international language in architecture began to surface in the work of Japanese architects. The representative examples are Tange Kenzo's

and after the end of World War II, first-rate Japanese architects followed his example in the development and employment of an "international language." This was not the result of the development of prewar eclecticism, but rather of rejection of the eclecticism that had characterized the previous period.

Japanese architects became creative after the end of the war for a variety of reasons, the first of which was that those who had been studying Western-style architecture since their first contact with it in the beginning of the Meiji era had completely acquired Western technologies. Furthermore,

Conder's Japanese disciples had learned how to construct stone and brick structures and in the postwar period diversified their use of materials to include concrete, glass, plastics, and metals, all of which enabled a variety of new, molded shapes to be reproduced that were closer to the pillar-supported Japanese structures than to their wall-supported Western counterparts. The steel suspended roof-

of the mainstream. The architects of the Bauhaus emphasized the idea that rational and functional buildings could also be beautiful, and that the beauty of a structure could be achieved without elaborate ornamentation. Further, a building's shape did not have to be determined by materials such as stone and brick that had been used previously to define the Western architectural tradition. As this

ABOVE: The simple yet ornate balcony on the third floor.

LEFT: The main building of the Tokyo National Museum (1937). The architect was the winner of the open competition for a design in an "oriental style based on Japanese taste." Taito-ku, Tokyo.

BELOW: Elegant glass windows are set into the ceiling over the front entrance.

ing of the Yoyogi National Stadium designed by Tange Kenzo is closer in design to the former. This new use of molded shapes was one of the elements that facilitated the work of Japanese architects of the period.

This shift in styles can be attributed to the fact that Western architecture itself had split away from styles that initially had been closely connected to the nationalistic culture of the nineteenth century in Europe. The functionalism of the Bauhaus architectural and design school established in Weimar in 1919 by Walter Gropius, initially deemed revolutionary, was eventually to become part

philosophy was entirely rational and therefore universal, the tenets of the Bauhaus gained international acceptance and ultimately were adopted into mainstream practices, eventually influencing many Japanese architects.

According to Gropius, the Bauhaus attempted to create new architectural space in addition to a new functionalism. Yet the architect's vision, his creative imagination, fueled his designs. Nevertheless, modern architecture is a result of structural needs. A building must perform a certain function, after all. If it is an assembly hall, it must

217

accommodate people. If it is an art museum, it must hold art and allow space for viewers to perceive that art. Literature and fine arts are ends in and of themselves, but architecture must fulfill an end that transcends itself. Many beautiful buildings were built by members of that generation in Japan in a style that could not necessarily be labeled Japanese architecture.

The fifth phase of modern Japanese architecture began with the era of Postmodernism that occurred in the 1970s. The fundamental philosophy of Postmodern architecture is different from that of the Bauhaus school, which essentially supported purist architecture and eliminated anything not architectural from the category. However, Postmodern thought presumes architecture to be a comprehensive paradigm of expression and, as such, incor-

porates pictorial and sculptural elements. The functionalism of the Bauhaus school, under a single philosophy, described an architectural work as a unified whole and demanded beauty in the structure as an entirety, whereas the tenets of Postmodernism emphasized individual components; the harmony of the whole was not as highly esteemed as the accumulation of its complex parts. This idea is to some extent the impetus for the philosophy behind traditional Japanese architecture embodied in the concept of starting with a portion or detail and working outward into the whole. Postmodernism allowed the incorporation of Gothic walls, Romanesque windows, and Japanese paving stones in a single building; the resultant variety of perspectives would possess a certain rhythm as they harmonized to make the whole.

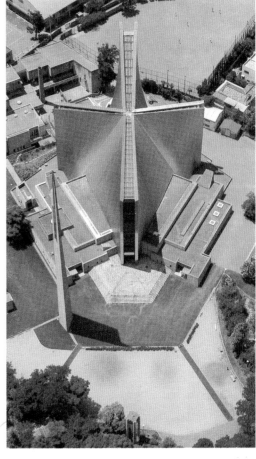

ABOVE LEFT: *Saint Mary's Cathedral (1964), designed by Tange Kenzo. Natural light streams through the interior. Bunkyo-ku, Tokyo.*

ABOVE RIGHT: *An aerial view of Saint Mary's Cathedral.*

LEFT: *An aerial view of Yoyogi National Indoor Stadium (1964), designed by Tange Kenzo and constructed for the Tokyo Olympics.*

One of the representative structures of Postmodernism in Japan is the Tsukuba Center Building (1983) located in Ibaragi Prefecture and designed by Arata Isozaki (b 1931). One of the ideas behind Postmodernism is to open art and architecture to randomness or accident, to expand the "frame" and let more human, uncontrolled, and even chaotic elements influence the work at hand. This attitude can be seen reflected in the words of Arata Isozaki, who described some of his ideas behind the construction of the Tsukuba Center as follows: "I decided to let the details speak clearly . . . and to generate new meanings by drawing them into conflict with each other. I decided to create a style . . . in which continuity is lacking and confusion is allowed to exist." In the Tsukuba Center, pillars surfaced with shiny metal are placed next to neoclassical stone pillars inspired by those created by the French architect Claude-Nicholas Ledoux and by the pillars seen in the temples of ancient Greece. An abundant range of sources can be seen in the pillars alone, yet they are not true imitations. Rather, they are distinct and alternate views that help construct a complex and diverse world.

PROBLEMS OF FREEDOM, ISOLATION, AND TRADITION

Tokyo is a city of disorder, but several pockets of order can be found within its borders. The urban center of Shinjuku is one such area, with its recently constructed Tokyo Metropolitan Government complex (1991) and its large concentration of skyscrapers. From the Nijubashi bridge of the Imperial Palace, one can see a far more orderly area in which a skyline is evenly composed of buildings of nearly equal height.

Typically, it is the architect's prerogative to create a building of a specific height, shape, and color in a given space developed from his personal aesthetic point of view. Since the city of Tokyo lacks much aesthetic harmony to begin with, an architect need not consider how to make his buildings blend in with those surrounding them. In fact, the obvious disharmony of the Tokyo cityscape may actually lend architects a certain freedom with which to be more adventurous—always remembering, of course, the

LEFT: *The future Japanese cityscape may take the form of a Postmodern mix of innovative and adventurous architecture. Shown here is the Tsukuba Center Building (1983) designed by Isozaki Arata. Tsukuba City, Ibaraki Prefecture.*

221

limitations set by financial considerations. One of the benefits of a cityscape that is composed of no planned or established design is that it can act as an experimental ground, spawning innovative architectural design. One of the detractions is that it also creates a whole new set of problems that its architects must negotiate and overcome.

An architect with a certain amount of design freedom faced with a limited space generally cannot influence the atmosphere of the neighborhood. He can create spectacular designs for his structures, but he cannot eliminate an unattractive billboard hung on the building next door. Therefore, architectural freedom in Japan essentially means architectural isolation, and given environmental limitations, the architect can accept

overwhelms its surrounding area. In his design, Shirai combined a square tower that has rounded or shaved corners with an adjacent cylindrical edifice. Windows placed into a dark brick outer wall lend the large and heavy structure an overwhelming presence and create an impression somewhat similar to that made by the medieval towers of San Gimignano, Italy. While the cluster of medieval towers grouped together at San Gimignano respond to each other, the tower of the Noa Building stands in isolation. The longer one stares at the tower, the sooner unsightly surroundings disappear. It stands like a desert ruin, transcending time. When an architect ignores the never-ending alterations that occur in any Tokyo neighborhood, an attempt is made to transcend history

OPPOSITE PAGE: The National Noh Theater (1983), designed by Oe Hiroshi. Shibuya-ku, Tokyo.

one or two challenges that are also choices. The first choice is to emphasize the building's isolation in the early stages of design and completely disregard the surrounding environment. The other is to create a miniature self-contained cityscape.

The first approach can typically be seen in the work of Shirai Seiichi (1905-83), whose structures virtually ignore their surroundings and insist on their own individuality, disregarding any potential relationship to their environment. The Noa Building (1974) located in Iikura-cho, Tokyo, for instance,

and to confront the viewer with the force of the architectural vision.

It is important to remember that a space that is apparently impenetrable from the exterior can be expansive and open on the interior. Subtle and sophisticated handling of interior details comprises and creates a world of its own. Kohaku-an (1970), Shirai Seiichi's private residence, has a white wall with but one opening facing the street, an opening that is a small entryway that might be just as well-suited to a casbah as to a residential structure in the middle of Tokyo.

ABOVE LEFT: The courtyard of Kohaku-an (1970), residence of the architect Shirai Seiichi, of his own design. Nakano-ku, Tokyo.

ABOVE RIGHT: The extremely innovative buildings of the Tsukuba Center. These stone steps located on the corner of the plaza exhibit an arrangement of natural stone and concrete.

However, once inside, one sees a perfect harmony in the dark rooms and in the bright white sand shining in the inner courtyard. The current season and weather are enjoyed in the view of a single flowering tree visible from the inner, surrounding rooms. The visual effect of each of the details represents the architect's craftsmanship, which is closer to that of a master sculptor, carpenter, stonemason, or cabinet maker, all of whom utilize the defining characteristics of certain carefully selected materials fully intending not only to create maximum visual effect but to permeate the senses.

Shirai Seiichi's goal was the emplacement of an isolated piece of architecture among the chaos of the city, almost as if the building were itself a large sculpture. Shirai's

dynamic structures are a combination of curved and flat surfaces that possess a characteristically solid and heavy external appearance. The internal spaces consist of an intellectual order comprising ever-changing perceptual details. The main office of the Shinwa Bank in Sasebo is a perfect example of Shirai's architecture, both as a representative artistic work and as a vision of the architect's self-expression. Are these buildings "Japanese"? If we take this question to mean "Did he employ traditional elements of Japanese architecture?" the answer must be no. Nevertheless, taken in broader terms, Shirai's work is undoubtedly imbued with the principles of traditional Japanese architecture: the preference for simple and explicit structures, the affection for natural materials, and the integral and deferential interest in details. Consequently, his manipulation of all these elements suggest that his works could be viewed as being quintessentially Japanese.

The second approach taken by Japanese architects was the establishment of a miniature city. Several buildings are positioned within a given space by architects who felt they had no choice but to create isolated works. This is an attitude of persistence, an attitude that seeks resolution of some sort, however partial, in the relationship between the architecture and the surrounding environment. One Japanese architect who consistently conveyed this attitude of persistence was Maekawa Kunio (1905-86). Being a functionalist and at one time a student of Le Corbusier, his primary approach was to position his structures in a relatively orderly location, if such a place could be found. Thus, many of Maekawa's buildings, particularly public buildings such as concert halls and museums, were constructed in parks. For instance, the Ueno Bunka Kaikan (Ueno Culture Center, 1961) located within Tokyo's Ueno Park sits amid a grove of trees and is thus set apart from neighboring buildings—at least by Tokyo standards. One must walk through the grove to approach the entrance. Upon entering the building, one discovers a spacious, split-level area. Before entering the concert hall itself, one must continue to stroll through the lobby area. The development of an interior that incorporates the initial approach to the building with a large entrance hall of various levels that eventually lead up to a concert hall is quite different from the generally seen continuum of crowded street, narrow hallway, concert hall. The surrounding neighborhood of Tokyo's Ueno Park is not the stately Kärtnerstrasse of Vienna, but the somewhat seedy quarters of after-hours amusement.

Secondly, Maekawa usually attempted to build a high-rise in a third of the available space, leaving the rest to passers-by. For instance, the Kaijo Kasai building (1974) in Otemachi, Tokyo, stands amid many high-rises, set apart from the rest by the dark red ceramic tiles on its surface and by the fact that it stands slightly back from the street. A small plaza is set in front of it. The building was originally planned to be thirty stories high, but was lowered to twenty-five stories because looking down upon the imperial palace is considered an impropriety. (The imperial system is apparently still able to exert an influence on architectural practices.)

Thirdly, Maekawa often created an open space in the form of either a courtyard or well that functioned in the same way the plaza does in an Italian city; people rest and relax, meet others, or stop for a chat. The sides of the building can be seen from the courtyard, while the courtyard can be seen from the inside of the building. In short, this type of structure creates a peaceful city on a reduced scale. The Tokyo Metropolitan Museum (1975) in Ueno Park has a courtyard featuring staggered levels between the upper and lower buildings that provide changes in scenery for pedestrians.

Maekawa's three strategies, those of utilizing the optimal conditions of a location, creating a plaza within a site, and developing a courtyard or well within the building, were brilliantly employed in the Kyoto

ABOVE: The National Opera House in Dresden was restored to its original state in 1985.

Kaikan (1960), located near Heian Shrine in Kyoto where more optimal conditions were available than in Tokyo. A courtyard surrounded by corridors is accessible from the street, and the borrowed scenery of the Higashiyama hills can be seen from inside. A pool of water reflects the giant wall facing west, emphasizing the main building's horizontal parallel lines as well as its architectural accents. This building represents an extremely successful culmination of postwar modern Japanese architecture.

Japanese architects faced more than having to consider a building's relationship to the environment when creating their designs. Another central issue concerned resolution of the relationship between the aesthetics of Japanese architecture that developed in an agricultural society during the Edo period with the materials, construction methods, and styles of modern architecture. This is a problem that has not been completely re-

日本橋

小網町

227

solved in postwar Japan in a general sense, but has been left up to each architect to resolve on an individual basis. This problem is not limited to Japanese architects but is also shared by Japanese artists, musicians, and writers. The problems facing the Japanese architect Isozaki Arata and the modern composer Takemitsu Toru (b 1930) are essentially one and the same.

Naturally, each artist has his own way of resolving these issues. Tange Kenzo departed from the tradition of Japanese architecture as far as he could, while Shirai Seiichi maintained its underlying philosophical principles, as mentioned. Maekawa Kunio might have been continuing the tradition of positioning Japanese houses low to the ground in emphasizing horizontal parallel lines such as those used in his Kyoto Kaikan. His works have never been vertical structures that extended straight up to the sky, and even the

Kaijo Kasai building was designed to be covered in a warm color that serves to soften the sharpness of its vertical lines. The approach to his Saitama Prefectural Museum (1971) arouses a sensation similar to what one experiences while strolling the pathway of a teahouse garden. He did not borrow from the teahouse directly but substituted some of its elements for his own perception of order.

Another example of an extremely intimate creative relationship with tradition is seen in the national Noh theater (1983) designed by Oe Hiroshi (1913–89). Oe designed several Noh stages, including some that were situated in large buildings. Here, however, he designed not only the hall that contains the Noh stage and seats, but also the concrete one-story building housing the hall. Upon entering through an unobtrusive gate, the visitor is greeted by an open space covered with white pebbles that extends out-ward. The structure is closed to the outside but opens up to a grove of trees located in the courtyard. Inside, one passes through a hall that appears to be constructed of thin wooden pillars. One passes through yet another hall-way before finally arriving at the door to the theater itself. Such an arrangement contains the promise of the *hashigakari* (a bridgelike passageway that connects the stage to the greenroom) and carefully ushers the visitor into the world of the theater. Perhaps this effect could be described as a functional order overlapping the aesthetic order of the Noh drama itself with its *johakyu* (introduc-tion-development-conclusion) in which one experiences fast and slow movement as well as unexpected turns and twists. The clear lines of the wooden pillars and handrails and the warm texture of the wood are coupled with the soft lighting and the trees seen in the courtyard, together offering a closeness to and familiarity with nature. In this, we find traces of the traditional aesthetics still alive today. Such individual masterpieces are scattered like unexpected oases through-out the architectural desert of modern Japan because the architects have long been del-egated the extremely difficult task of seek-ing and finding diverse solutions to the problem of how to unify Japanese tradition with modern architectural concepts.

 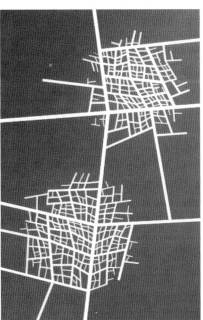 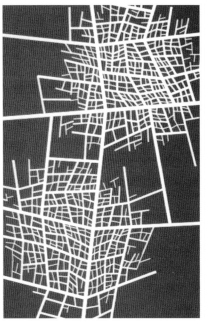 

ABOVE: Fractal images created by computer graphics based on the image of Tokyo as a random space.

RIGHT: Fractal imagery can also be seen in a street map of Tokyo that reveals the complex arrangement of an ever-expanding sphere.

ABOVE: The multitude of cracks in the glaze of a ceramic bowl can also be seen in terms of the fractal theory developed by Benoit Mandelbrot (b 1924). Fractal theory is one of the nonlinear systems of mathematics under the rubric of Chaos Theory. Fractals are natural shapes that multiply and infinitely recur.

229

Throughout Japan's history, several waves of culture arrived from the Chinese continent. The first was during the transitional stage that occurred between the Jomon (10,000–300 B.C.) and Yayoi (300 B.C.–A.D. 300) periods, and lasted until about the beginning of the Kofun period (300–710). The cultural influences that arrived from the continent at that time were basic technology such as that required for rice growing, the introduction of metalware, and the utilization of animals for development and industry. Although many aspects of the continental influence are not yet fully understood, it is believed that a tribe equipped with more sophisticated tech-

Modern Japan and Beyond

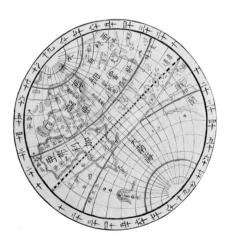

ABOVE: *This map,* Sairan Igen, *gives us a sense of how people in the Edo period imagined and understood the world.*

OPPOSITE PAGE: *Optic fibers that have the capacity to transmit information at a speed several tens of thousands times greater than that of coaxial cables have raised great expectations about the future of our technologically advanced society.*

nology arrived from the continent at some point and very possibly conquered the indigenous people of Japan. However, several possibilities regarding what actually happened are still under debate, possibilities that range from the theory that a continental tribe eventually flourished and completely replaced the indigenous Japanese, to the theory that half of the indigenous population was eventually replaced by people of mixed blood whose descendants later became what we now know as the Japanese. Regardless of which theory ultimately proves true, it remains clear that the first wave of continental culture had a decisive and irrevocable influence on Japan and its culture.

The second wave of continental culture was imported with Buddhism from the fifth century to the sixth century. During this influx, many scholars and technicians came to Japan, mainly from the Korean Peninsula. They introduced a writing system, the production of documents, architectural technologies, and various arts and crafts. Their descendants built grand temples such as Hoko-ji and Horyu-ji, created arts and crafts such as *tamamushi zushi* (iridescent miniature shrines), and constructed Buddhist statues. They also introduced the calligraphic inscription of religious sutras. The second

wave differed from the first in that no use of force was applied in conquering and converting the indigenous people. National unification centering on the Yamato *chotei* (Yamato court), located in the area that was later renamed Nara, occurred at the same time that Buddhism was becoming widely accepted as a national religion in Japan. Thus, throughout the Asuka (593–710) and Nara (710–794) periods, a new form of culture strongly influenced by the continent spread across Japan.

The third wave of the spread of continental culture was instituted by Taira no Kiyomori (1118–81) and was represented by increased trade with the merchants of the Sung dynasty (960–1279) in China. This economic and cultural connection began in the period of the northern and southern dynasties and continued into the Kamakura period (1185–1333), maintained by Zen monks. The nature of the connection can be explained in terms of China's shift from the Sung to the Yuan dynasty (1279–1368) in the thirteenth century, a shift that was marked by changes in religious beliefs. Sung China initially emphasized Confucianism as well as Buddhism, but Buddhism came under oppression during the Yuan dynasty. This led many Chinese Buddhist monks to seek asylum in Japan. At the same time the most distinguished Zen temples of Kyoto and Kamakura were sending their monks to China to study, together with delegations from the shogunate. Later, during the Ming dynasty (1368–1644), the Muromachi shogunate further deepened exchange with the Chinese continent through trade. Despite all of this, the continental influence of the third wave was rather weak when compared to that of the first and second waves. The window of cultural exchange was limited to Zen temples and trade with Ming, and thus only a few areas of culture were recast under influences from China. Nevertheless, influences from the continent continued uninterrupted through the Edo period (1603–1868), and many of them had important implications for Japanese culture. Some examples of important influences could be seen in the acquired customs of drinking tea and eating foods such as tofu, and in the adoption of new architectural styles, brush-painting techniques, and the development of the technology necessary to perfect ceramic ware. The subsequent arrival of vast amounts of Chinese literature was another important phenomenon, one that greatly influenced Japanese intellectuals.

In the latter half of the sixteenth century, Japan experienced the influx of a culture totally different from that of the continent: the encounter with Christianity and its European cultural sphere. There are two aspects behind the stimulating influence that led to its arrival. First, it was the age of exploration, an age symbolized not only by the technological advancement of shipbuilding and the opening of ocean passageways, but also by the expansionist philosophy prevalent in Europe at the time. During the sixteenth century, through exploration,

the field of theology and concerning the boundaries of church activities created agitation on both sides. The Catholic side not only assumed a defensive attitude against the rise of Protestantism, but also promoted aggressive and expansive missionary work in an attempt to convert non-Christians to the faith. The most significant example was seen in the Society of Jesus (Jesuits) formed by Ignatius Loyola in 1543. After the initial and successful exploits of Loyola, the age of exploration was connected to the missionary activities of the Jesuits. European expan-

BELOW: Shotoku Taishi E-den (*Illustrated story of Prince Shotoku, 1323). Prince Shotoku is shown lecturing on a Buddhist sutra. He had a deep understanding of and sympathy with Buddhism. Jogu-ji, Ibaraki Prefecture.*

Europeans "discovered" America and Africa. In the process of discovering Asia, Europe discovered Japan.

The second aspect can be attributed to the internal situation of sixteenth-century Christianity. It was during the sixteenth century that Protestantism arose, while Catholicism simultaneously reacted against the Reformation in various ways. Serious debates in

sionism in religious, political, economic, and military aspects was the predominant motivation behind the arrival of Francis Xavier (1506–52) in 1549, an event that ultimately brought about tremendous changes in the expanding relationship between East and West.

The Japanese reaction to Xavier's visit can be characterized by three major responses. First, the Japanese were greatly interested in things to which they had never before been exposed such as binoculars, etchings, parrots, Western dogs, and the enormous ships entering their harbors. They were eager to learn about any imported technology that appeared to be useful.

Second, they approached European customs and manners as a source of amusement and enjoyment. Western manners, taste, and design became popular and soon began to be known as the Nanban (Southern Barbarian or Early European) style. The strong interest

time. These screens were clearly made to be looked at and enjoyed, rather than for practical purposes. Such attitudes did not constitute or substantially represent diplomatic interest toward the countries of the West, however. To most Japanese, the West was never recognized as a real place, and Westerners were seen as rare birds that had arrived for a visit. There was certainly a high level of cultural interest, but this did not lead to a closer diplomatic relationship.

It should also be noted that the Japanese did not look upon Westerners with any sense

BELOW: Nanban Byobu *(Southern Barbarian Screen), dating from the first half of the seventeenth century. This screen depicts Jesuit missionaries greeting the arrival of Western ships. Japan's trade with Spain and Portugal brought massive amounts of wealth and aroused interest in creating a new culture through the revitalization of the economy. Suntory Museum, Tokyo.*

in Western manners can be seen in the many *nanban byobu (southern barbarian screens)* depicting the arrival and unloading of Western ships in port, the parade of Westerners and curious Japanese observing them (on screens created mainly by the Kano-ha school of artists), and copies of imported Western paintings such as the *Taisei Oko Kiba-zu* (Western kings on horseback) or the *Yojin Sogaku-zu* (Westerners playing music). Such works were popular from the end of the sixteenth century until the end of Sakoku (national seclusion).

Third, the Japanese were immensely curious about the world outside the Chinese continent and about what was happening there. The fact that maps were often produced around this time serves as evidence of their intellectual curiosity. Maps of the world made up as *byobu* were also popular at that

of inferiority. Certainly, Westerners had unusual and wonderful things, but Japan was also in a phase of social and cultural development and advancement. The relationship was seen to be an equal one, at least on the part of the Japanese, who initially did not fear or feel threatened by Western influence or Westerners.

When Christianity first came to the shores of Japan, the daimyo accepted it with equanimity, and some even converted to Christianity. Ouchi Yoshitaka (1507–51) of Yamaguchi gave permission to Francis Xavier to pursue his missionary work in 1550, and in 1563 the daimyo Omura Sumitada (1533–87) of Kyushu was baptized. It is not clear how serious those daimyo were about their conversion to Christianity. It was their interest in Western technology and customs, particularly in trade and scien-

BELOW: Tiles excavated at Musashi Kokubunji. Temples such as those found at Kokubunji were established in every municipality to promote Buddhism during the Nara and Heian periods. This site in Tokyo appears to have contained shrines for ujigami (clan deities) as well. Kokubunji Municipal Cultural Museum, Tokyo.

233

RIGHT, ABOVE and BELOW: *Western-style game board, 53 cm in height, sixteenth to seventeenth century. The exterior of this backgammon set depicts the Kiyomizu-dera and Sumiyoshi shrine in Kyoto and was done in the Yamato-e style in mother-of-pearl inlaid mosaic. The interior is of mother-of-pearl inlaid mosaic and red lacquer.*

ABOVE: *Gunpowder flask with picture of Westerners, 36 cm. Gunpowder was stored in this bottle which was carried slung over the shoulder. National Museum of Tokyo.*

ABOVE: *A pyx (container for sacramental bread), 9 cm in height, sixteenth to seventeenth century. This case was used for storing the Eucharistic host and was possibly created for export. Tokei-ji, Kanagawa Prefecture.*

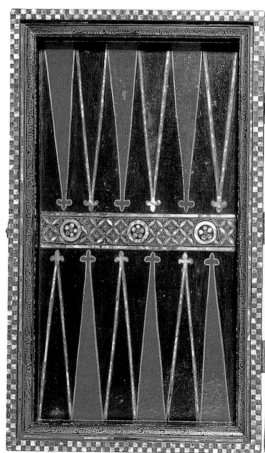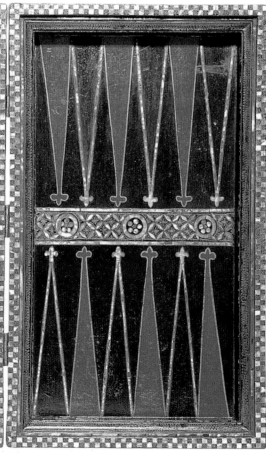

tific technology, that seems to have played the most important role in their conversions. Once a daimyo converted, his men followed suit, converting to Christianity en masse. Although this practice went against the Christian doctrine of faith as strictly an individual matter, Japanese social customs were obviously much stronger than the doctrines of foreign religions.

How did the nation's ruling power respond to the growing spread of Christianity? Initially, it viewed the new Christian daimyo with suspicion, and then became increasingly cautious of Christianity, eventually considering it outright dangerous. From the purge of Jesuit missionaries ordered by Toyotomi Hideyoshi in 1588 to the total ban of Christianity instituted by the Tokugawa shogunate in 1612, the suppression of Christianity escalated drastically. There were two reasons Christianity was considered dangerous. First, it denied the coexistence of other religions or value systems, and was a monotheism that demanded faith in one absolute God. The Tokugawa shogunate had taken the Confucianist parent-child relationship and adopted that ethic to extend to ruler and ruled. This was done in an attempt to main-

the apex of the Japanese ethical order, began to regard Christianity as dangerous.

Second, any physical threat to the nation would have been reason enough to react. There were many Westerners in Japan at the time besides the Jesuits, and confrontations began to occur among the factions of missionary priests. The largest was one that took place between Dutch Protestants and Spanish and Portuguese Catholics.

From the rule of Toyotomi Hideyoshi (1582–98) to the early years of the Tokugawa shogunate, Japan had skillfully taken advantage of its windows on two worlds created and sustained by contact with Protestant and Catholic countries. These windows were useful in collecting information from abroad and in comparing and analyzing the two spheres. The Dutch must have provided critical information about the Spanish and the Portuguese, including the true nature of the concept of European expansionism (colonization) that had accompanied missionary activities. Thus, the major reason behind the ban on Christianity was Japan's fear of being colonized and the potential threat of Christianity to the Japanese ethical order.

Purging the country of Christianity sig-

ABOVE: Rojin Dokusho (*Old man reading*), attributed to Nobukata, sixteenth to seventeenth century. Nobukata was said to have learned Western-style painting at one of the seminaries. However, this piece is neither ornamental nor religious, and is rather different from the other Western-style paintings of the period.

tain the order of samurai society with the shogun as ruler. But with the advent of Christianity, Japan's ruling class was told that the highest authority was neither parent nor ruler, but God himself. Naturally, the Tokugawa shoguns, nearly deified in their position at

naled the loss of this source of vital information. It also meant that Japan had to give up most of the income it had acquired through trade. In order to lessen the damaging economic impact, the shogunate, despite its policy of suppression of Christianity, de-

ABOVE: Taisei Oko Kiba-zu Byobu (*Western kings on horseback*), sixteenth to seventeenth century. This Western-style screen painting depicts a battle between Western knights and pagans. It was produced at a Jesuit school and was based on a Western etching. Kobe Municipal Museum, Hyogo Prefecture.

cided to allow foreign ships into Nagasaki Harbor. The only trading partners allowed in were from Korea, China, and Protestant Holland by command of the shogunate. The Dutch were able to successfully remain Japan's sole Western partner in trade through their tactic of separating trade from religion.

Another method used to further ban and suppress Christianity was that of the temple registration system, in which Buddhist temples that were already established and scattered throughout Japan required registration of all citizens at a temple; this would prove that they were not Christians. On the island of Kyushu, people were forced to trample on a *fumi-e* (copper tablet engraved with a crucifix) to prove that, if once converted, they had foresworn the Christian faith.

The second tactic the shogunate used was to dispatch armed troops that could forcefully quell any Christian uprisings. The Shimabara Uprising (1637–38) was one such instance of this use of force. At first, the shogunate did not consider the incident to be a major threat and sent a relatively small army to combat several thousand peasants (including several foreign missionaries) who were protesting the dismal conditions in which they lived, only to have the army suffer a disastrous and humiliating defeat. The shogunate was not able to quell the rioters until extensive forces of tens of thousands were employed, backed up by the military assistance of the Dutch. By the end of the struggle, 37,000 citizens had died.

The temple registration system, coupled with forceful suppression, eradicated most Christian influence in Japan, but a small number of people became Kakure Kirishitan (Christians in hiding) and remained faithful believers. They surreptitiously prayed to the Virgin Mary who was given the disguise of Kannon, the Buddhist Goddess of Mercy, and continued to keep their Christian faith under the guise of Buddhist practices. As generations passed, the distinction between the Virgin Mary and Kannon was lost. Consequently, the tenets of Christianity became integrated with a facet of Buddhism, thereby creating an eclectic religious phenomenon. The conditions of extreme oppression contributed to the phenomenon, but it had become evident that any foreign religion imported to Japan would have to assume some kind of eclecticism in order to gain popular support among commoners. Buddhism openly assumed an eclectic form, and was thus able to reach a large range of people. Christianity was not openly eclectic, and therefore did not easily spread among com-

moners. However, if a foreign religion was to somehow manage to reach the common people even through surreptitious practices, a certain eclecticism must necessarily be created.

THE WEST WITHIN AN ISOLATED JAPAN

Since its adaptation of the first edict of the

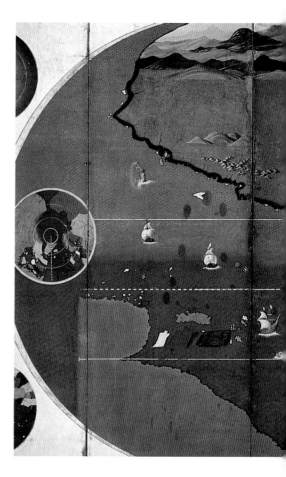

policy of Sakoku (national seclusion) in 1633, the shogunate under Tokugawa Iemitsu (r 1623–51) strictly controlled information and goods entering Japan. Later, Tokugawa Yoshimune (r 1716–45) encouraged scholarship during the Kyoho era (1716–36) and relaxed the ban on books. Books, except for those on Christianity, could be imported through Nagasaki, and with that the monopoly on access to information ended.

Most of the books imported to Japan during the seventeenth century were Dutch academic treatises, but in the eighteenth century Chinese versions of Western science texts began to be brought into Japan as well. As Edo-period intellectuals could easily read Chinese since written Japanese is derived from Chinese, these books began to have a great impact in many areas.

ABOVE: Portrait of Francis Xavier, sixteenth to seventeenth century. Xavier arrived in Japan in 1549 as a member of the Society of Jesus (Jesuits). The names of both the saint and the painter are written on the bottom portion of the painting. Kobe Municipal Museum, Hyogo Prefecture.

Three reactions typify the Japanese response to increasing knowledge about the West. First, the Japanese were very much interested in new technology. The shogunate itself encouraged imports of Western scientific books (in Chinese translation), fostered *rangaku-sha* (scholars who pursued Western science by means of the Dutch language), and was particularly interested in the study of medicine.

Chinese herbal medicine was in use in Japan at the time, but as the effectiveness of Western medicine became apparent, the number of doctors using Dutch medicinal practices increased. The scholar Yamawaki Toyo (1705–62) recorded his observations of a dissection of a human body in a work entitled *Zoshi.* In the dissection, he discovered that the *Gozo Roppu* (Five viscera and six entrails) theory, long believed as scientifi-

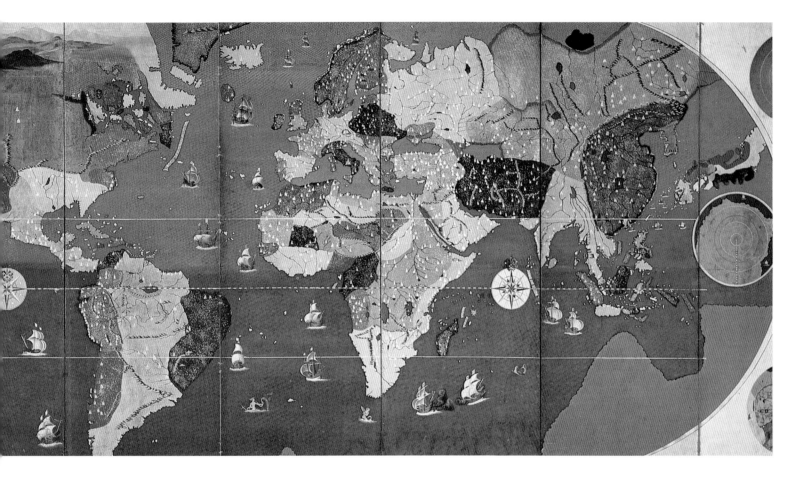

cally correct by the Japanese, was incorrect and that the Dutch anatomy books were more accurate. A 1771 dissection performed in Edo prompted Sugita Genpaku (1733–1817) and Maeno Ryotaku (1723–1803) to translate into Japanese the Dutch version of an anatomy book entitled *Anatomische Tabellen* by the German Johan Adam Kulmus. *Kaitai Shinsho (New Anatomy)* was subsequently published in 1774.

Japanese interest in Western science and technology focused on medical technology, particularly surgery, followed by the fields of astronomy and calendar making. New knowledge of astronomical observation was in great demand by seafarers, and Western astronomy books were studied and translated in hopes of revising the Japanese calendar.

ABOVE: Byobu *dating from the sixteenth to seventeenth century. This work was done by a Japanese painter who was a member of a Jesuit art school. Detailed illustrations represent Christian buildings around the world. Kobe Municipal Museum, Hyogo Prefecture.*

LEFT: Cover of a sacred chest. Tokugawa Museum, Ibaraki Prefecture.

ABOVE: Grieving Mary, *probably Italian, sixteenth to seventeenth century. This oil painting on canvas was discovered at a historic residence in Fukui Prefecture in the mid-Taisho era and is thought to have been done by a painter during the late Renaissance period. Nanban Bunka-kan, Osaka.*

BELOW: The site of the former Shimabara execution grounds in Nagasaki Prefecture. The monument to commemorate Christian martyrs is inscribed with the words Namu Amida Butsu *(I take my refuge in the Amida Buddha).*

The second typical reaction to knowledge from the West was the adoption of Western culture as amusement. In the middle of the Edo period, lifestyles became more affluent, and many new forms of entertainment or pastimes were invented. Watching fireworks, boating on the rivers, flower viewing, and attending the theater became popular activities, as did the creation of *haikai renga* (linked verse). *Ukiyo-e* woodblock prints also contained an element of entertainment, and parties for exchanging *egoyomi* (picture calendars) were regularly held. These forms of amusement were also reflected in literature and resulted in the creation of *kyoka* (comic tanka), *kyoshi* (comic poems), or *senryu* (satirical verses). All aspects of Western culture deeply stimulated the curiosity of the people of the Edo period, and items such as mechanical clocks and binoculars were chosen and regarded as articles of amusement. People of the Edo period never used clocks as an accurate measure of time, and there is even less evidence that clocks were used to ensure smooth administrative functions or to increase productivity. Clocks became popular simply because people thought they were amusing. Since the artist Suzuki Harunobu (ca 1725–70) painted the *mitate* (literary association used in artwork) painting entitled *Tokei no Bansho* (Chime of the evening clock) and since his woodblock prints were quite popular at the time among commoners, we can surmise that clocks were extremely popular as well.

Some oil paintings and a vast amount of etchings were imported through Nagasaki. When Japanese painters and intellectuals first looked at Western etchings, they undoubtedly noticed that the most outstanding difference between them and traditional Japanese paintings was the use of the techniques of geometric perspective and shading incorporated within, effective methods with which the artist was able to create the illusion of three dimensionality. Originally, techniques creating depth in painting were related to the artist's perception of and attitude about spatial existence. The use of planned and constructed geometric perspective began in the Renaissance in the West, when the technique was also an expression of the desire to describe the world.

The Japanese who first encountered Dutch etchings did not analyze the difference in attitudes toward spatial orientation between Japanese and Westerners. Rather, they simply evaluated the unusual idea and its interesting aspects. When technology departs from its purpose, it becomes amusement. A

typical example was the *uki-e* (floating pictures which employed the use of perspective) technique used by *ukiyo-e* painters. Okumura Masanobu (1686–1764) used geometric perspectives in his *Ryogoku-bashi Yusuzumi Uki-e* (Floating picture of people at Ryogoku Bridge) as early as the Kyoho era, but the technique was used only for interior views. Exterior views were painted in the traditional bird's-eye perspective. This was done because the effect of the geometric perspective is more pronounced when used in the depiction of streets and the interior of theaters. *Uki-e* took advantage of the peculiarity of that effect, and the same painter usually made traditional pictures as well as pictures using *uki-e*. In fact, more often than not, traditional paintings were their principal trade. Here, the technique of creating perspective was used as pure entertainment.

The third reaction to Western learning was a rather limited one found among certain intellectuals who perceived Western art and knowledge as a distinct challenge to Japanese and Chinese traditional world views and value systems. For them, Western technology was not seen as a means of contributing to a more stable traditional structure, but rather as a means of reevaluating the soundness of the tradition itself. In painting, the deep interest in Western Realism was one expression of such an attitude.

One reason why Japanese painters of the eighteenth century were interested in Real-

ABOVE: Young women praying at Christmas mass at Xavier Church in Kagoshima.

ABOVE: Nagasaki Daijunkyo-zu (*Nagasaki martyrdom*), *first half of the seventeenth century. This work depicts the Christian martyrs of Nagasaki during the purge of 1622. Church of Christ Jesus, Rome.*

ism was due to the influence of Shen Nanpin (fl mid-eighteenth century). Nanpin was a painter of the Ching dynasty (1644–1911) who came to Japan in 1731 to teach Japanese painters how to use Chinese techniques of realism. Although he stayed only two years, he had considerable influence. A second reason was founded in the interest in natural history that gradually had increased from the late seventeenth century to the eighteenth century sparked by the import of Chinese botanical studies and firmly grounded by the publication of Kaibara Ekiken's (1630–1714) *Yamato Honzo* (Yamato plants) in 1709. Soon, knowledge of Western natural history was added to this base by some of the imported European texts that had a great impact on increased understanding of botany and zoology.

Interest in natural history also contained an element of entertainment, while involving scientific interest as well. In order to exhibit different species of plants and birds,

accurate description was required. The descriptive ability of painters became the decisive factor in the popularity of their works. Due to the demand for accurate description, the superior realism of Western etchings garnered attention and increased the popularity of the style. However, depiction of realism as the main function of paintings indicated a shift in aesthetic values, at least from the viewpoint of the tradition of *sumi* brush painting. This shift was augmented and promoted by increasing contact with Western artwork.

Japanese painters looked at the adoption of Western techniques of attempting realism as both a means of entertainment and as a symbol of the confrontation of two cultures. Maruyama Okyo (1733–95) incorporated techniques of Western Realism into the traditional framework of Yamato-e, paintings of the Kano-ha school, and *bunjin-ga* (paintings in the literary style). However, Shiba Kokan (ca 1747–1818) consistently devoted himself to the pursuit of realism and was a

ABOVE: Kanbun Nagasaki Byobu, *1782. The fan-shaped island on the right side of the image is Dejima, through which European civilization continued to be imported despite the policy of national seclusion in effect at the time. Although trade was reduced in scale, it eventually had a great influence on Japanese culture. Nagasaki Municipal Museum, Nagasaki Prefecture.*

complete convert to the Western style of realism. He created the first Japanese etching, learned oil-painting techniques, and actively introduced theories of Western natural science. His works were not necessarily artistically creative, yet he demonstrated that the purpose and technique of a painting did not necessarily have to be one and the same. He also proved that there were multiple systems from which one could choose, and that it was possible to shift one's personal values.

These issues typify the concerns of eighteenth-century Japanese artists and intellectuals in regard to adoption and manipulation of Western techniques and technologies.

In the nineteenth century, however, there was an advent of Japanese painters who had learned to completely assimilate the techniques of perspective and shading and who were able to develop and to create their own unique vision. Katsushika Hokusai (1760–1849) and Utagawa Hiroshige (1797–1858)

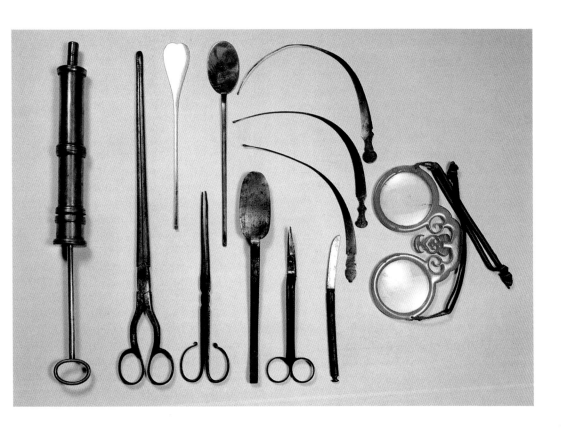

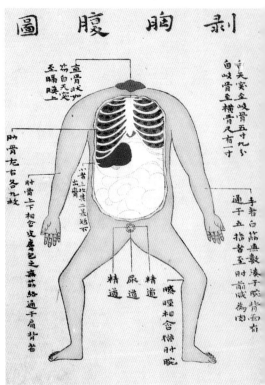

ABOVE LEFT: Hanaoka Seishu's (1760–1835) surgical instruments and glasses. Hanaoka Seishu was born in Kii (present-day Wakayama) and learned traditional medicine and Dutch medicine in Kyoto. After a long period of study on his own, he successfully operated on a woman with breast cancer, the first time such an operation had been performed in the world. His wife also contributed to furthering the state of Japanese medical research by allowing him to test his anaesthesia on her. Wakayama Prefectural University of Medicine.

ABOVE RIGHT: Zoshi (1759) by Yamawaki Toyo (1705–62). Yamawaki, skeptical of ancient Chinese anatomical theory, obtained the shogun's permission to dissect the body of an executed prisoner in 1754, the first time such an action was performed in Japan. Zoshi was the record of this dissection and served as a catalyst in encouraging examination of the human metabolism.

BELOW: Kaitai Shinsho (New anatomy) (1774 edition, Kitasato Memorial Medical Library) and the Dutch translation of Anatomische Tabellen (Tokyo University Library) are shown. Sugita Genpaku and Maeno Ryotaku translated this work into Japanese from the Dutch in an attempt to promote accurate scientific knowledge in Japan.

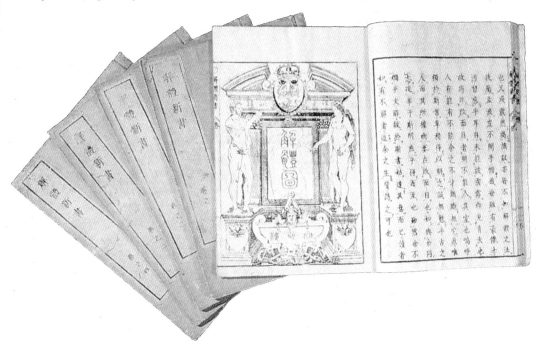

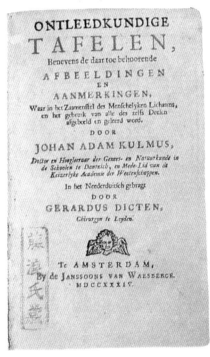

ABOVE: *Semicircular compass, mid-Edo period. Ino Tadataka (1745–1818) produced the first scientific map of Japan using such an instrument, accurately measuring the location of mountains and islands. Ino Kinen-kan, Chiba Prefecture.*

ABOVE: Butsurui Hinshitsu *(1763) by Hiraga Gennai (1728–79), who learned Western natural science through his study of the Dutch language, held five exhibits, and compiled this volume describing each product of the regional areas of Japan. The book is open to an explanation of how to refine sugar.*

both employed revolutionary techniques such as dynamic cropping and different angles.

Another nineteenth-century Japanese artist who assimilated Western techniques into his own particular vision was Watanabe Kazan (1793–1841), who utilized the technique of tonal shading to produce realistic portraits such as the *Takami Senseki-zo* (Portrait of Takami Senseki). Here, the portrait is interesting not only because of its three-dimensionality, but also because it reflects a keen interest in using the art of painting as a means of mirroring and capturing reality.

THE GENIUS OF MODERN PAINTERS

The Meiji-era (1868–1912) government's adoption of the policy of copying Western models in an effort to modernize and industrialize Japan can be seen as similar to Prince Shotoku's adoption of Buddhism as a means through which to introduce Chinese continental technologies. The goal of the Meiji political leaders was to establish a centralized nation, as well as to catch up with other more advanced nations. In the process, overwhelming foreign influences came to the fore in the fields of fine art, music, and literature. Looking at the field of fine art, the Meiji era saw the emergence of oil painters and other artists who discovered ways to employ new materials and techniques in order to deal with fairly new subjects. Particularly noteworthy was the work of Takahashi Yuichi (1828–94).

In the midst of the social uprisings that occurred toward the final days of shogunate rule and in the beginning of the Meiji Restoration, Takahashi stood alone in his pursuit of oil-painting techniques. Although it is not entirely clear how he learned to paint with oils, he apparently collected every bit of available information on the subject and spent time studying with the illustrator Charles Wrigman (1832–91) who was in Tokyo employed as a correspondent for the *Illustrated London News*. Takahashi's primary goal was to create epoch-making realistic paintings that would be a radical departure from the Eastern-style paintings generally seen up until that time. His strong drive to pursue the limits of realism in painting objects can be seen in his still-life paintings *Salmon* (1877, Art Reference Museum, Tokyo National University of Fine Arts and Music), *Tofu and Abura-age (Tofu and Deep-Fried Tofu)* (1876–77, Konpira-gu Museum, Kanagawa), and *Namaribushi (Dried Bonito)* (1877, Konpira-gu Museum, Kanagawa). The dense depiction of a solitary object makes *Salmon* much closer to seventeenth-century Dutch still-life paintings than to the Eastern art that had been created earlier.

In the new government's policies of modernization, the emphasis on the importance of education was a stroke of genius on the part of the Meiji leadership. It helped prompt the introduction of a compulsory education system wherein teachers were invited from more advanced countries in order to contribute to higher education in Japan. Those invited to Japan included not only specialists in the areas of industrial technology, medicine and agriculture, but also masters in music, fine arts, and philosophy.

The Italian Antonio Fontanesi (1818–82), who taught the technique of drawing from a plaster cast and who imparted basic techniques of oil painting using typically European academic methods, was among the foreign instructors invited to the first public art school in Japan, the Kobu Bijutsu Gakko. His students included Koyama Shotaro (1857–1916), Matsuoka Hisashi (1862–1944), and Asai Chu (1856–1907), the first generation of Japanese painters to study the techniques and to learn oil painting directly from a skilled European painter.

Asai Chu proved to be Fontanesi's most exceptional student. Although Fontanesi emphasized basic techniques, he also taught the philosophy that regards the art of painting as a fine art and imparted the notion that merely sketching an object in a realistic manner did not necessarily constitute successful artistic expression. He taught, rather, that the depiction of an object should reveal an

aesthetic world. Thus, Asai attempted to realize a beautiful world through accurate description based on European aesthetics as taught by Fontanesi. With the work of Asai, the encounter between Japanese and oil painting suddenly attained new heights.

Another important policy carried out by the Meiji government was the dispatch of Japanese students to Western educational institutions. This policy was promoted for scholars in a variety of studies. Medical doctors and musicians went to Germany, industrial engineers went to the United States and Germany, naval officers went to Great Britain, and most army officers went to Germany. Some fields saw groups of its scholars always concentrated in certain countries, but in the early days painters were sent to a variety of places. Harada Naojiro (1863–99) went to Germany, Matsuoka Hisashi (1862–1944) went to Italy, and Kuroda Seiki (1866–1924) went to France.

The most influential painter of the three was Kuroda Seiki. When he returned from Paris and began to exhibit his work in Japan, Japanese painters suddenly became intensely interested in going to Paris. However, the sudden popularity of Paris as a destination was not the result of Kuroda's influence alone, and was not a phenomenon limited to Japan. It seems that from the latter half of the nineteenth century, from around the time that Impressionism began, Paris became known as the center of European fine arts just as Italy once had been regarded in the same way and was the primary destination

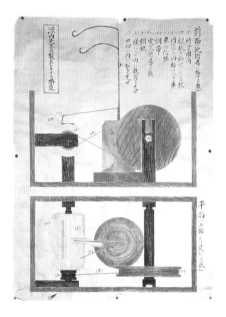

TOP, LEFT and RIGHT: Painting of a looking glass (1783) by Shiba Kokan and a looking glass through which the painting was supposed to be viewed. The picture is reflected on a mirror and enlarged.

ABOVE: Illustrated diagram of Hiraga Gennai's Erekiteru *(An Electric Generator, 1776). Gennai, a genius scientist of the Edo period, also produced a magnetic compass and a thermometer.*

LEFT: Ryogoku-zu *by Aodo Denzen, late Edo period. The owner of an inn is shown seeing off two sumo wrestlers who are embarking on a boating party. The red of the carpet the girl carries and the red in the geisha's kimono sparkle amidst the overall dark tones. Note the use of perspective.*

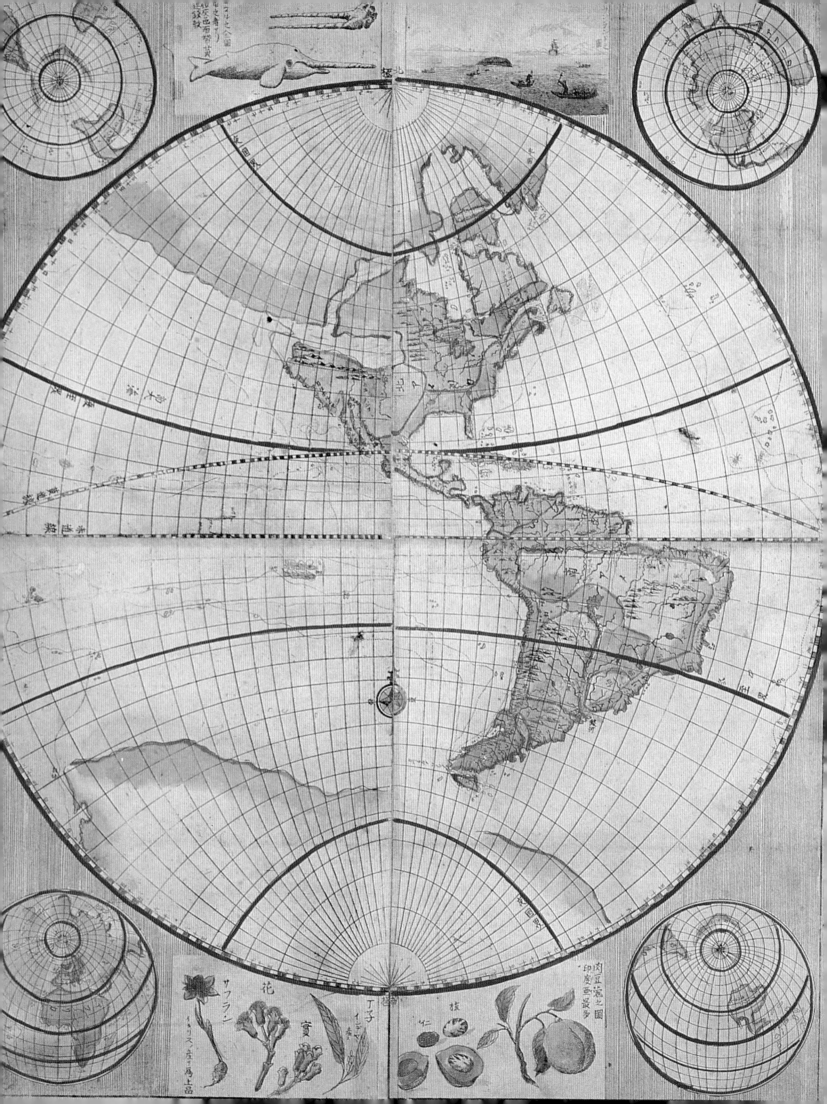

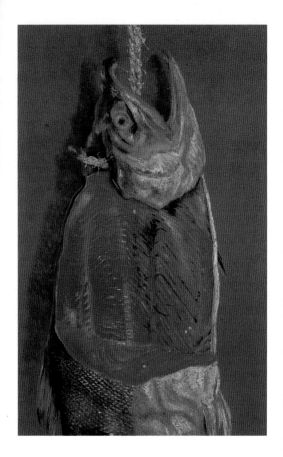

for fine artists. In Japan, the movement was augmented by the cultural tendency toward group activity.

However, Japanese painters living in Paris constituted a different phenomenon than that of the British, American, German, or Russian artists who resided there. Choosing what to draw (subject) and how to draw it (style) has a close relationship to an aesthetic consciousness that is consequently conditioned by lifestyle. Generally, a painter cannot totally separate his studio from the society that surrounds it, nor can a painter living abroad exist and successfully work in isolation. How were such problems handled by the Japanese painters in Paris?

To answer the question simply, the Japanese painters then in Paris dealt with the problem by looking at the art of painting as technology. Thus they were able to separate art from life by putting aside the question of subject matter. Instead, they turned their interest and attention to the question of how to paint. By concentrating exclusively on tech-

nique, they ostensibly replaced the question of what to paint by painting what was popular in Paris at the moment. It was in this way that the general and overwhelming trend that leaned toward adoption of revolutionary techniques and styles was born.

The social and artistic background in Paris at that time was one of conflict between academism on the one hand and Impressionism on the other. A mass conversion to oil-painting techniques was in progress and interest in other new techniques must have been greatly encouraged. In this atmosphere, Japanese painters went to Paris to acquire new painting techniques, just as if they were scientists intent on acquiring new technology in natural science.

The question "What is Western painting?" had been completely abandoned by Kuroda Seiki since he seemed to be solely concerned with what was then popular in Paris. Therefore, modern Western-style paintings done by Japanese artists at the time were quite similar to the works of certain Western paint-

ABOVE (DETAIL): Salmon *by Takahashi Yuichi, 1877. The fine details mark the culmination of Yuichi's realism. Tokyo National University of Fine Arts and Music.*

PRECEDING PAGES: A map (1793) by Shiba Kokan. This work was based on an illustration of the globe that came from Amsterdam at the time of the Russian visit to Nemuro, Hokkaido. The original illustration was appropriated by the shogunate.

ers. This phenomenon continued until the advent of Surrealism. As mentioned, Asai Chu, however, was an exception.

The most prominent of the Japanese painters who took their inspiration from Western styles was Saeki Yuzo (1898–1928), who was able to skillfully imitate the teachers at the École de Paris. He masterfully depicted the streets of Paris in a refined style close to that of Maurice Utrillo (1883–1955) and Maurice de Vlaminck (1876–1958). However, his mastery of the technique was limited to the work he produced during his stay in Paris. Works completed after his return to Japan can be said to lack vividness. While Saeki could have been an honored student during the time he spent in Paris, he ultimately failed to create his own unique world. In order to produce something new, one has to learn from what has gone before and eventually transcend it. Unfortunately, the Japanese artists who went to Europe did not have the opportunity to transcend existing traditions, since one cannot transcend or reject an established, foreign tradition while simultaneously learning from it.

This problem is not limited to painting; every modern Japanese who studied in the West faced the same situation, to a certain degree. Even in the field of philosophy, popular trends in Europe at the time were imported and eventually became popular in Japan. This tendency lasted for a long time until the development of Existentialism and Structuralism, which occurred during the postwar period. In this sense, the history of Western-style painting in Japan brilliantly encapsulates the problems of modern Japanese culture and its artists and their technical relationship to the West.

There were, of course, some exceptions. Some Japanese painters did not adopt new techniques simply because they were popular in Paris, but rather pursued what they wished to express, proceeding with their work by searching for appropriate techniques with which to realize their goals. For instance, Aoki Shigeru (1882–1911) was one such

ABOVE (DETAIL): Shukaku (Harvest, 1890) by Asai Chu. This major work established a realism based on Japanese sensitivity. Tokyo National University of Fine Arts and Music.

LEFT: Miyagi Kencho Monzen-zu (The gate of Miyagi Prefectural Hall, 1881) by Takahashi Yuichi. An X-ray taken of this work revealed that the carriage was added after the background had been completed. Yuichi apparently followed the rule of oil painting of that time. where landscapes were to be painted starting from the farthest point and ending at the nearest. Miyagi Prefectural Museum.

artist, and his *Yomotsu Hirasaka* (1903, History Museum, Tokyo National University of Fine Arts and Music) and *Umi no Sachi* (Products from the sea) (1904, Bridgestone Museum, Tokyo) took their themes from ancient Japanese mythology. This struggle to capture personal visions within a painting can clearly be seen in the work of Aoki, who certainly appears to have had something to say.

Another example was Kishida Ryusei (1891–1929). Kishida learned from the Pre-Raphaelites and from the works of the Northern Renaissance artists, but he did not imitate their styles. His portraits of his daughter Reiko are the result of his attempt to pursue methods he felt allowed him to best capture her true nature. In effect, this struggle illustrated the tension between the concepts of "how to express" and "what to express." Another Kishida masterpiece is *Kiritoshi no Shasei* (Sketch of a path cutting through a hill) (1915, Tokyo National Museum of Modern Art) that, in addition to being an excellent oil painting, reveals his skill at creating what can be termed "proto-scenery." This path through a hill was not a scene the artist happened to stumble upon, but is something universal in that it very possibly depicts scenes found throughout the entire world.

There were some Japanese painters who left Japan and never returned. The most representative of these were Fujita Tsuguharu (1886–1968), also known as Fujita Tsuguji

LEFT: Dojo Mai Sugata (*A young girl dancing, 1924*) *by Kishida Ryusei. Ryusei moved to Kyoto after the Great Kanto Earthquake (1923) and devoted himself to hand-drawn* ukiyo-e *and paintings done in the style of the Sung and Yuan dynasties. He ultimately created his own style that incorporated various expressions in a unique personal vision.*

ABOVE: Reiko (*1921*) *by Kishida Ryusei. Kishida started a series of portraits of his daughter Reiko which began when she was five years old. His style became more Japanese as the series progressed. Tokyo National Museum.*

BELOW: Sori Ketsubetsu *(1901) by Hishida Shunso (1874-1911). A Japanese-style painter often criticized for being a fanatic for things Western, Hishida attempted to overcome the barriers between Western and Japanese painting.*

ABOVE RIGHT: Kiritoshi no Shasei *(Sketch of a path cutting through a hill, 1915) by Kishida Ryusei. Tokyo National Museum of Modern Art.*

RIGHT: Terasu no Kokoku *(Advertisement at a street café, 1927) by Saeki Yuzo. Saeki studied in Paris under Maurice de Vlaminck and was greatly influenced by the lyrical style of Maurice Utrillo.*

and Léonard Foujita, who spent most of his life in France and eventually became a naturalized French citizen, and Kuniyoshi Yasuo (1867–1943) who stayed in the United States. Fujita joined the École de Paris group during the 1920s, and was particularly influenced by the Fauvist painters and by their primitive, vivid styles. He did not attempt to squarely challenge the métier of oil painting, but used oil paint in a manner similar to that used in employment of the lighter colors of Japanese paintings. Fujita ultimately created a miniaturist style using subtle lines that were uniquely his own. He was also a superb sketch artist. For this reason, he was able to fully utilize the elegant lines that Japanese painters had been employing in their works since the invention of *ukiyo-e* woodblock prints. In short, he attained success in Paris by consciously taking advantage of Japanese artistic techniques

Kuniyoshi did not take advantage of traditional Japanese brush techniques, yet the sensitivity of Japan, the country he lived in until the age of seventeen, seems to have contributed to his style. This includes a certain static quality that can be found in his depiction of cattle, children, and scenery; his use of the semi-bird's-eye view; his em-

phasis on a frontal view; his strong distortion of shapes; and his use of subdued dark colors. He was particularly skilled in his description of subtle facial expressions. By the time he reached his forties, the influence of his years in Europe had become more evident; the shade of Japan had disappeared.

Japanese-style painters were drawing on silk and paper using *sumi* ink and traditional paints during the same period. As discussed, Japanese painting has a very long history, and any discussion of its style must also include a discussion of traditional society, contemporary lifestyles, and the people of the Edo period's aesthetic worldview. All of the elements of Japanese painting—fixed technique, choice of subject, precise depiction of atmosphere—were firmly blended into Edo-period culture, although lifestyles and value systems abruptly changed with the Meiji Restoration. The culture that supported traditional Japanese painting suddenly no longer existed. Many Japanese-style painters actually tried to revive traditional painting styles by introducing new techniques into their work, but there was no obvious or consistent means of expression that could connect a style tied so closely to Edo-period culture with painters who did not live within that culture.

The painter Tomioka Tessai (1863–1924)

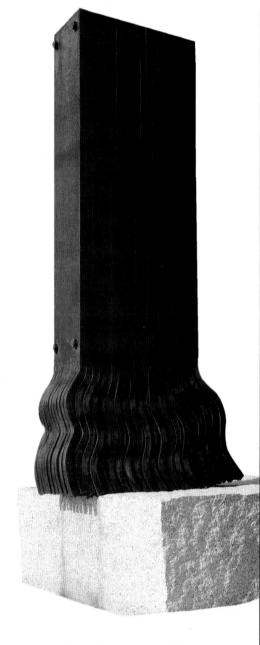

ABOVE: Aruku Tetsu (*Walking iron, 1981*) by *Tsuchitani Takeshi. Iwaki Municipal Museum, Fukushima Prefecture.*

LEFT: Kyoshikyoku (*Rhapsody, 1962*) by *Nambata Tatsuoki. Iwaki Municipal Museum, Fukushima Prefecture.*

251

OPPOSITE PAGE, FAR RIGHT: *Detail from a mural by José Clemente Orozco (1883–1949) drawn on an administrative building in Guadalajara (1937).*

OPPOSITE PAGE, BELOW (DETAIL): *From the mural* Diaz and the Women Surrounding Him *depicting the dictatorship of Diaz and the Mexican Revolution, painted by David Alfaro Siqueiros (1896–1974). Subsequent scenes in the mural unfold in the same manner as a Japanese picture scroll. Museum of Chapultepec.*

BELOW (DETAIL): History of Mexico *(1929) by Diego Rivera (1886–1957). Detail from a mural on the stairwell of the Mexican National Palace. The mural covers a total surface area of 275 square meters, depicting the history of Mexico from the era before colonization until after the Mexican Revolution.*

was most clearly notable among the artists of the Meiji Restoration. Tessai directly succeeded the line of *bunjin-ga* artists that had included Ike no Taiga (1723–76), Yosa no Buson (1716–84), and Tanomura Chikuden (1777–1835), both in his education, lifestyle, and perhaps in his perceptions of everyday life as well. His works are arguably the most creative and original produced by the modern Japanese painters. For instance, he completely filled in the entire canvas of his landscapes, giving them a dynamic power closer to modern Western paintings than to the Abstract Expressionism that is approached in *sumi* brush painting. However, an exception such as Tessai does not alter the overwhelming general tendency of a lack of potent self-expression among Japanese painters of the 1920s.

It is interesting to note that around the same time, on the opposite shore of the Pacific Ocean, the revolutionary painters of Mexico were discovering a unique and powerful style of self-expression. Diego Rivera (1886–1957) and Alfaro Siqueiros (1896–1974) returned from Europe to Mexico in 1921, bringing modernity with them from Paris, including the techniques of Cubism and Expressionism. What they found on their return to Mexico was the blazing sun and the power of nature, the life of peasants and commoners (touched by poverty and incited to rebellion), and a culture that contained violence, death, and the energy of life. The "culture of the people" had already found expression in the prints of José Guadalupe Posada (1852–1913), while José Clemente Orozco (1883–1949) was also active as a revolutionary painter and can be said to have been a direct successor to Posada. The creativity of their art eventually led to the art of the mural that essentially illustrates a powerful combination of modernity and the "culture of the people." Their murals were innovative within the framework of pictorial expression, but also led to the utilization of

new materials, particularly since paint had to be durable to survive the weather conditions suffered by stuccoed and plastered exterior walls. In addition to their aesthetic power, the murals attempted to provide a pictorial explanation of the history of oppression and were an excellent illustration of revolution, done for the sake of the masses. The epic style of the subject was resolute, necessitating the use of bold colors and new angles of perspective. A close relationship between theme, framework, technique, and style can be seen in the murals of Mexico. Why did such a marriage occur in Mexico and not in modern Japan when artists from both countries had experienced contact with European paintings centered on the artistic culture of Paris?

The Mexican Revolution enabled the common people to reject the culture and the promises of the ruling class and, in turn, led to common perceptions shared by Mexican artists and the Mexican people. In contrast, Japan did not experience such a revolution or any similar rejection of cultural hegemony. Therefore, the "culture of the people" could not have emerged as a strong force in the face of overpowering cultural traditions long promoted by the ruling class. This fact remains evident even today, when Japanese artists remain largely confined to artistic expressions of their own individual visions, always keeping an eye open toward international appeal. Throughout the ages, Japanese culture has received enormous artistic and technological benefits by looking to the world at large.

Twentieth-century Japanese artists, particularly architects, composers, designers, and dancers have been tremendously productive in their worldwide search for means by which to express international culture. They would now do well to turn back to the world at their doorstep, to the "culture of the people" of their own country, for future artistic inspiration.

Chronology

	JAPAN *History*	JAPAN *Civilization*
10,000–300 B.C.	**Jomon Culture**	Neolithic, straw-rope pottery, creation of female clay figures and tools, shamanistic and animistic practices
300 B.C.–A.D. 300	**Yayoi Culture**	First bronze tools; *dotaku* in the form of bells; bronze mirrors and coins imported from China; expansion from Kyushu towards Honshu
300–710	**Kofun Period** Formation of the first kingdoms Conquest of Korea	Large funerary tumulus *(kofun)* between Nara and Osaka; funerary statues created from clay *(haniwa)* as mentioned in Chinese literature and writings
3–710	**Asuka Period** *593–622* Prince Shotoku becomes regent. *645* Taika Reform	*552–558* Buddhism introduced from Korea *594* Buddhism becomes the state religion *607* Construction of Horyu-ji temple in Nara *623* Bronze sculpture of Shaka Trinity, Horyu-ji; influence of China (Tang Dynasty) on Buddhist bronze and clay sculpture
672–86	**Hakuho Period** *702* Taiho Ritsuryo (the code of the Taiho era) established.	Art begins to exhibit characteristics of Chinese Buddhist art
710–94	**Nara Period** *710* Transfer of the capital to Nara *740* Transfer of the capital to Kyoto *781–806* Reign of the emperor Kammu	*752* Consecration of the Great Buddha at Todai-ji temple *756* Treasures of Shoso-in Construction of the largest Shinto shrines *780 Man'yoshu,* first anthology of Japanese poetry
794–1185	**Heian Period** *838* Last legation to China *866–1160* Fujiwara period, rise of the Fujiwara clan *895* Rupture of diplomatic relations with China *1180–85* War between the Taira and Minamoto clans	*805–806* Introduction of the Tendai and Shingon sects of Esoteric Buddhism; sixteenth-century development of the Japanese syllabary *(hiragana* and *katakana);* flourishing of the art of the Heian court (Kyoto) *905 Kokin Waka-shu,* imperial poetry anthology *1000* Creation of the world's first novel, *The Tale of Genji* *1053* Construction of the Byodo-in temple of Uji *1175* Foundation of the Jodo Buddhist sect by Honen; lacquer and precious metal objects
1185–1333	**Kamakura Period** Kamakura military government established *1192* Minamoto no Yoritomo becomes shogun *1274* First invasion by Mongolia repulsed *1281* Second invasion by Mongolia repulsed	The appearance of a new aesthetic along with the rise of the samurai class; introduction of Zen Buddhist monasteries in Kyoto and Kamakura *1205* Collection of poetry in the *Shin Kokin-shu* *1260* The Great Buddha at Kamakura; important schools of celebrated masters of printing; realism in sculpture; pictures scrolls *(emaki)* inspired by stories or legends; ancient ceramics from Seto used in the tea ceremony

CHINA
History and Civilization

EUROPE
History and Civilization

6000–2000 B.C.	Continuation of Neolithic culture	Neolithic from 2600 B.C.; Copper Age until 1900 B.C.; Bronze Age until 1800 B.C.; castles of Tyr and Mycenea;
2100–1600 B.C.	Legendary **dynasty of Xian**	first period of the Iron Age
		750–500 Hallstatt civilization
ca 1600–1100 B.C.	**Shang Dynasty,** writings from 1200 Bronze rituals	*480* Battle of Salamis
		387 Plato's Academy
		356–23 Reign of Alexander the Great
1030–222 B.C.	**Zhou Dynasty**	
221–206 B.C.	**Qin Dynasty** Foundation of the empire; the Great Wall	
206 B.C.–A.D. 220	**Han Dynasty** Expansion in central Asia and in the south	*44 B.C.* Assassination of Julius Caesar
		A.D. 64 Persecution of the Christians by Nero
		325–37 Constantine the Great
		326 Church of Saint Peter established in Rome
220–280	**Three Empires** Progression of Buddhism	*451* Battle of Catalonia
		475 Decline of the Roman Empire Kingdom of the Visigoths
222–589	**Six Dynasties** Civilization of north China, expansion of southern civilization	
581–618	**Sui Dynasty** Reunification of the empire, construction of the Grand Imperial Canal	
618–907	**Tang Dynasty** Empire, expansion towards the west, the south, and the northeast; contact with Western regions of Asia *671–95* Xuan Zang's pilgrimage to India	*711* Arabs in Spain *714–41* Charles Martel
	Flourishing of Buddhist art Flourishing of poetry and prose *701–62* Li Po *768–824* Han Yu *755–63* Rebellion of An Lu Shan *806* Paper currency *845* Persecution of Buddhists	*768–814* Charlemagne *843* Treaty of Verdun
907–960	**The Five Dynasties** Collapse of the empire; appearance of landscape painting	*919–36* Henry the First *936–73* Otto the First
960–1279	**Sung Dynasty** Height of poetry and painting Non-Chinese northern dynasties *1101–26* Reign of the Emperor Hui Zong, patron of the arts	*962* Holy Roman Empire *1066* The Battle of Hastings *1096–99* First Crusades *1211–1300* Reims Cathedral

Chronology

	JAPAN *History*	JAPAN *Civilization*
1338–1598	**Ashikaga Period and Muromachi Period** Shogunate of the Ashikaga clan in Kyoto *1467–77* Onin Wars	*1397* Temple of the Golden Pavilion (Kinkaku-ji), Kyoto *1489* Temple of the Silver Pavilion (Ginkaku-ji), Kyoto Height of ink painting by Sesshu *1420–1506* Height of lacquer ware *1542* Arrival of the Portuguese at Tanegashima, introduction of Western firearms *1549* Francis Xavier arrives in Japan
1586–1600	**Momoyama Period** Leadership by the regents *1592–98* Invasion of Korea by the Japanese Army *1600* Battle of Sekigahara	*1586* Construction of Osaka castle; murals and paintings of gold leaf; decorative arts; austere ceramics created for the tea ceremony *1614* Ban on Christianity
1600–1868	**Edo-Tokugawa Period** Edo (Tokyo) becomes capital *1639* Closing of the country *1688–1703* Genroku Period *1853* Arrival of Commodore Perry demanding opening of Japan's ports *1858* Trade and commerce with the United States	*1622–23* Suppression and persecution of Christians *1690–92* Engelbert Kaempfer in Japan, flourishing of bourgeois culture *1720* Study of Western sciences and literature is authorized; development of Kabuki theater and *ukiyo-e* woodblock prints *1823–30* Philipp Franz von Siebold in Japan; Western art influences Japan opens its doors to the West
1868–1912	**Meiji Era** Proclamation of the Meiji constitution *1894–95* War with China *1904–15* Russo-Japanese War *1914* Japan enters World War I	*Post-1873* economic reforms and reforms to the fiscal system; reforms in the legal system and military *Post-1877* industrialization of the country; Japanese artists in Europe; European artists and city planners come to Japan
1912–26	**Taisho Era**	
1926–89	**Showa Era** *1937* Sino-Japanese War *1941* Japanese attack on Pearl Harbor; Japan enters World War II *1945* Atomic bombings of Hiroshima and Nagasaki; Japan's surrender.	Industrialization and the influence of Western civilization evident in all areas Rise of Japan as an economic power. *1964* Olympic Games in Tokyo
Since 1989	**Heisei Era**	

CHINA
History and Civilization

EUROPE
History and Civilization

1280–1368

Yuan (Mongol) Dynasty; first appearance of the Mongolian empire; Lamaism becomes state religion
1216–94 Kublai Khan

1291 Swiss Confederation

1339 Beginning of the One Hundred Years' War
1348–52 Plagues in Europe

1368–1644

Ming Dynasty
Nationalist Renaissance
1408 Yongle Dadian, encyclopedia in 11,000 volumes
Manufacture of important porcelains in Jingdezhen
Schools of painters in the provinces established

1356 Gold Standard

1419–36 War of the Hussites
1450 First moving press created by Gutenberg

1452–1519 Leonardo da Vinci
1475–1564 Michelangelo Buonnaroti
1493–1519 Maximilian the First
1562–98 War of the Huguenots
1587 Execution of Mary, Queen of Scots
1588–92 Construction of the Rialto Bridge, Venice

1583–1610 Matteo Ricci in China

1606–26 Construction of Saint Peter's Cathedral, Rome

1577–1640 Peter Paul Rubens
1618–48 Thirty-year War
1683–99 Turkish War

1644–1912

Ching Dynasty
Manchu emperors:
1662–1722 Kang Xi
1736–95 Qian Long

1720–80 Rococco art
1789 French Revolution
1837–1901 Reign of Queen Victoria of England
1839–1906 Paul Cezanne

1839–42 First Opium War
1850–64 Revolt of Tai Ping

1900 Boxer Rebellion

1853–90 Vincent van Gogh
1840–1926 Claude Monet
1881–1973 Pablo Picasso
1872–1944 Piet Mondrian

1912–49

Beginning of Republic

Since 1949

People's Republic

Bibliography

Amino, Yoshihiko. *Nihon no Rekishi o Yominaosu* (A rereading of Japanese history). Tokyo: Chikuma Shobo, 1991.

Castille, Rand. *The Way of Tea.* New York and Tokyo: Weatherhill, 1971.

Egami, Namio. *The Beginnings of Japanese Art.* New York and Tokyo: Weatherhill, 1973.

Forrer, Matthi. *Hokusai.* Munich: Prestel-Verlag, 1991.

Grilli, Elise. *The Art of the Japanese Screen.* New York and Tokyo: Weatherhill, 1970.

Grousset, René. *Chinese Art and Culture.* New York: Orion Press, 1959.

Ienaga, Saburo. *Painting in the Yamato Style.* Volume 10: Survey of Japanese Art. New York and Tokyo: Heibonsha/Weatherhill, 1973.

Index of Japanese Painters. Compiled by the Society of Friends of Eastern Art. Tokyo and Rutland, Vermont: Charles E. Tuttle Company, 1959.

Japan: An Illustrated Encyclopedia. Tokyo: Kodansha Ltd., 1993.

Japan: The New Official Guide. Tokyo: Japan Travel Bureau, Inc., 1991.

Japanese Ink Paintings. Edited by Yoshiaki Shimizu and Carolyn Wheelwright. Princeton, N.J.: Princeton University Press, 1976.

Joly, Henri L. *Legend in Japanese Art.* London: Kegan Paul, Trench, Trubner and Company, date not available.

Kato, Shuichi. *Form, Style, Tradition.* Translated by John Bester. Tokyo: Kodansha International, 1981.

Keene, Donald. *The Pleasures of Japanese Literature.* New York: Columbia University Press, 1988.

Konishi, Shiro. *Nihon no Rekishi,* vol. 19 (Japanese history). Tokyo: Chuokoronsha, 1974.

Masterworks of Japanese Art. Compiled and edited by Charles S. Terry. Tokyo and Rutland, Vermont: Charles E. Tuttle Company, 1959.

Michener, James L. *Japanese Prints: From the Early Masters to the Modern.* Tokyo and Rutland, Vermont: Charles E. Tuttle Company, 1962.

Miller, Roy Andrew. *Japanese Ceramics.* Tokyo and Rutland, Vermont: Charles E. Tuttle Company, 1960.

Mizuo, Hiroshi. *Edo Painting: Sotatsu and Korin.* New York and Tokyo: Weatherhill, 1972.

Mori, Hisashi. *Sculpture of the Kamakura Period.* New York and Tokyo: Weatherhill, 1974.

Munsterberg, Hugo. *The Arts of Japan.* Tokyo and Rutland, Vermont: Charles E. Tuttle Company, 1967.

Munsterberg, Hugo. *The Ceramic Art of Japan: A Handbook for Collectors.* Tokyo and Rutland, Vermont: Charles E. Tuttle Company, 1964.

Munsterberg, Hugo. *The Folk Arts of Japan.* Tokyo and Rutland, Vermont: Charles E. Tuttle Company, 1958.

Okakura, Kakuzo. *The Book of Tea.* Tokyo and Rutland, Vermont: Charles E. Tuttle Company, 1956.

Pollack, David. *The Fracture of Meaning: Japan's Synthesis of China from the Eighth Through the Eighteenth Centuries.* Princeton, New Jersey: Princeton University Press, 1986.

Sadler, A. L. *Cha-no-yu: The Japanese Tea Ceremony.* Tokyo and Rutland, Vermont: Charles E. Tuttle Company, 1962.

Smith, Bradley, ed. *Japan: A History in Art.* New York: Simon and Schuster, 1964.

Stanley-Baker, Joan. *Japanese Art.* London: Thames and Hudson, 1984.

Stern, Harold P. *Birds, Beasts, Blossoms, and Bugs: The Nature of Japan.* New York: Harry N. Abrams Inc., 1976.

Ueda, Makoto. *Literary and Art Theories in Japan.* Cleveland: Case Western Reserve University Press, 1967.

Van Briessen, Fritz. The *Way of the Brush.* Tokyo and Rutland, Vermont: Charles E. Tuttle Company, 1964.

Watson, William, ed. *The Great Japan Exhibition: Art of the Edo Period, 1600–1868.* London: Royal Academy of Arts, 1981–82.

Yanagi, Soetsu. *Folks Crafts in Japan.* Tokyo: Kokusai Bunka Shinkokai, 1949.

Photography Credits

Archives Motovun SA, Lucerne: 38, 114 (bottom, left and right), 115 (left), 143
Busch-Reisinger Museum, Cambridge, Massachusetts: 25
Galerie Welz, Salzburg: 138 (right)
Giraudon, Paris: 198
IFA-Bilderteam, Munich: 40–41
National Museum of Archaeology, Athens: 163 (right)
Oesterreichische Galeria, Schloss Belvedere, Vienna: 182 (left and right)
Photola/Gérard Boullay, Paris: 88
Sekai Bunka Photo, Tokyo: 142–143 (center)
Staatliche Kunstsammlungen/Gemaldegalerie Alte Mesiter, Dresden: 14 (bottom)
Vincent van Gogh Foundation/Vincent van Gogh Museum, Amsterdam: 132

JAPANESE SOURCES:

Kiichi Asano: 104–105 (center)
Kazuhiko Fukuda: 15 (right), 180 (left, top and bottom), 181
Shigenobu Hayashi: 142 (top left)
Heibonsha: 23 (right), 24, 33 (bottom right), 36 (right), 37, 42 (center right), 52 (left), 55 (top and center), 72, 73 (right), 79 (right), 90, 91, 92 (left), 95, 112 (right), 117, 124, 125 (top), 127 (bottom), 128 (bottom), 129, 130 (left), 134–136, 137 (left), 139 (left), 140, 144–150, 153 (right, top and bottom), 154 (center), 155 (top), 156 (left top, center, and bottom), 157, 167 (right top), 211 (center bottom), 216, 217, 220–221, 223 (right), 229 (bottom, left and right), 233 (bottom), 234 (left top and bottom), 238 (bottom, left and right), 241, 242, 243 (right, top and bottom)
Yasuo Higa: 54
Hiromichi Inoue: 47, 48, 52 (right), 59, 64 (left top and bottom, right), 141, 151, 152 (right)
Taikichi Irie: 49 (right), 58 (left), 168, 169
Kaoru Kato: 252, 253
Tadao Kodaira: 153 (left)
Harumi Konishi: 65 (left)
Akihisa Masuda: 208 (left), 210 (bottom), 212–214
Kazuo Miyazaki: 7, 207
Shu Murai: 216–217 (center), 222, 223 (left)
Kuniaki Nakagawa: 156 (right)
NHK: 18–19, 33 (top), 42 (left, right top and bottom), 70, 98, 99, 102, 158–159, 197 (right), 224, 225
Kozo Ogawa: 15 (top), 50–51, 62 (center and right), 64 (center left), 71, 74–77, 79 (left)
Tadahiro Ogawa: 26, 27, 28, 29 (right top and bottom), 30, 31, 33 (left), 34, 35 (right top and bottom), 39, 43
Shizeo Okamoto: 17
Jiichi Omichi: 96, 97
Hideyo Sato: 166 (left)
Sekai Bunka Photo: 142 (bottom)
Mikihiro Taeda: 62 (left)
Bin Takahashi: 16 (right), 35 (left), 36 (top left), 55 (bottom), 60, 73 (left), 106 (right), 108–109, 110–111, 118–119 (center and right), 125 (bottom), 173, 176 (bottom), 235 (bottom)
Kozo Takahashi: 56, 57
Haruo Tomiyama: 61, 63 (left)
Urasenke Foundation, Kyoto: 143 (right, top and bottom)
Toshimasa Watanabe: 53
Yoshio Watanabe: 2
Noriyuki Yoshida: 142 (top, left)